What we learned
(the hard way) about

Supervising Volunteers

JARENE FRANCES LEE

WITH JULIA M. CATAGNUS

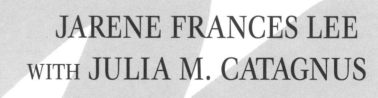

SUSAN J. ELLIS, EDITOR

Library of Congress Cataloging-in-Publication Data

Lee, Jarene Frances.
  What we learned (the hard way) about supervising volunteers : an action
guide for making your job easier / Jarene Frances Lee, with Julia M. Catagnus.
    p. cm. -- (Collective wisdom series)
  Includes bibliographical references and index.
  ISBN 0-940576-20-1 (pbk.)
  1. Voluntarism--Management. 2. Volunteers. 3. Supervision of employees.
I. Catagnus, Julia M.   II. Title.   III. Series.
HN49.V64L44 1998
361.3'7'068--dc21   98-31531
                                                           CIP

Copyright ©1999 by Energize, Inc.
        5450 Wissahickon Avenue
        Philadelphia, PA 19144
        www.energizeinc.com

ISBN: 0-940576-20-1

Collective Wisdom Series ISBN 0-940576-19-8

PRINTED IN THE UNITED STATES OF AMERICA

Table of Contents

Foreword to the Collective Wisdom Series i

Introduction 1

1   What Is Supervision? 5

2   Defining Expectations 15

3   Training and Providing Support 29

4   Communicating Effectively 45

5   Coaching and Encouraging Your Team 57

6   Solving Performance Problems 71

7   Conducting Formal Evaluations 93

8   Adjusting Your Supervisory Style to the Individual or Group . . .107

9   The Role of the Coordinator of Volunteers 127

10 Assessing Your Own Skills 139

Annotated Bibliography and Resources 143

Contributor Credits 147

Index 153

About the Authors 155

Special Thanks

From Jarene:

First and foremost, thanks to the folks at Energize, Inc.: to Susan J. Ellis, for her confidence in me, her wonderfully high standards and skillful editing; to Julia M. Catagnus, ever calm, steady and resourceful, a full partner from the start; and to secretary Ann Brennan, who buoyed me up with her warmth and thoughtfulness every time I called the office.

Thanks to the hundreds of students who have been in my workshops and courses over the years. We have had so much fun learning together. Your imprint is on this book.

My family—my husband, daughters and parents—deserve special acknowledgment for their support and understanding. And thank you, Gina, beloved friend, for your patience.

And finally, thanks, coupled with fond memories, to Mr. Lund and Mr. Wittern, English teachers at Pleasantville (NY) High School, who taught me to write—and to appreciate good writing.

From Julia:

Thanks to those whose unique talents helped bring this guide to life: to Susan J. Ellis for her vision for the series and for offering me the opportunity to be involved, to Jarene Frances Lee for sharing her knowledge of the field and for being a true collaborator, to the many leaders of volunteers who took the time to share their experiences verbally and in writing, to Ann Brennan for skillfully facilitating all our communications and cheering us on, to Diane Miljat Jacobs for providing a genuinely attractive book design, to Susan Magee whose "way with words" helps us make the book appealing to those who need it, to Rachel Markley for taking time from packing books to proofread the manuscript, and to Loretta Igo at Kutztown Publishing for expertly putting it all together.

I am also grateful for the love and support of my husband, Richard Sauls, whose encouragement has sustained me through many a new adventure. My step-daughter, Barbara, has my lasting gratitude for teaching me what love is really about. Thanks also to Albert Mancini, high school guidance counselor, for nudging me to reach beyond my comfort level. And a special thanks to Lois for being there so long ago to light the way for many of us to follow.

Foreword to the Collective Wisdom Series

It is always a leap of faith, and perhaps an overdose of self-confidence, to publish a new book and announce that it launches a "series." So I want to explain why we are so delighted to be starting on this venture.

For the last twenty-one years, Energize, Inc. has tried to produce materials for the volunteerism field that push the envelope of best practices further and further. In the beginning, that meant starting from scratch. It may surprise some to learn that the very first "how-to" book for leaders of volunteers, *Volunteers Today* by Harriet Naylor, was only published in 1974. Two years later Marlene Wilson wrote *The Effective Management of Volunteer Programs*. And two years after that, in 1978, Katie Noyes Campbell and I produced the first edition of *By the People: A History of Americans as Volunteers*. In 1978, those three titles were "it." So every one of the approximately 200 books available today about volunteer management are less than twenty and, in most cases, less than ten years old. We've come a long way, but there are still major gaps in our literature, as well as too little connection between academic theory and actual practice.

Rationale

Given this historical perspective, the rationale for the *Collective Wisdom Series* comes from several observations. First, on a positive note, there are many superb practitioners out there working daily to create and facilitate outstanding volunteer efforts. Together they hold a wealth of information ranging from a few outstanding innovations to countless small tips on how to do things better, faster, and more effectively. We wanted to go mining for the gold.

Second, but on a less positive note, we have a field that simply does not write. Many of you know me as the official "nagger" on this subject! For the last fifteen years, I have been urging, cajoling, and pushing many of you to share your expertise with others in print, either in *The Journal of Volunteer Administration* or elsewhere. There are many reasons why I am only occasionally successful. Some don't like to write or feel they don't know how to craft an article. Others are uncomfortable putting themselves into the role of "expert," feeling that what they do or know cannot possibly be of value to their colleagues. And most folks think they don't have the time!

Now it's probably true that only a small percentage of practitioners have a full book "in them," though I'm convinced many more could write great articles if they tried. But this project accepted the resistance and tried a new approach: asking people for one or two practical suggestions on a single topic. We even offered to interview colleagues who couldn't bring themselves to complete the form in writing! We were determined to prove that there is truly "collective wisdom" among us.

The third observation relates to printed materials. I have been collecting books, journals, articles, workshop handouts, agency guides, and anything else about volunteerism I could get my hands on for more than 25 years. The majority of the more than 8,000 items in the Energize library are not in bound book form. There are many loose-leaf notebooks and files of paper. With few exceptions, most materials are out-of-print and therefore inaccessible today, or were produced originally for some in-house purpose and never received wide dissemination. (Besides, with the notorious turn-over rate in our field, even something that was published five years ago may not be known to newcomers.) Buried within all these papers is more gold. I believe that if something has basic, timeless value, it doesn't matter what the copyright date is. And because our field has so few materials generally available, it's a crime to have so much early thinking gathering dust. So the *Collective Wisdom Series* also attempts to resurrect ideas and suggestions that deserve to be kept current.

Lastly, we felt that too much of what is written about volunteers does not include *their* perspective. Thanks to Jarene's cogent observation on this, we tried to do something about it here. Jarene conducted a number of focus groups with frontline volunteers to gain an understanding of their suggestions about how to supervise. We intend to keep asking volunteers for their point of view on all management subjects—they are, after all, part of the "collective."

Why "Supervision" Is the First Topic

There are three major reasons why we selected "supervision" as the first topic for this series:

1. We all do it. All volunteer activities require some form of supervision. It may be expressed in the vocabulary of the paid work world, with terms such as "supervision" or "coaching." Or it may be labeled "coordination," "leadership," or "mentoring." Volunteers need facilitative support whether they are working in an agency side by side with employees or they are tackling a project in an all-volunteer organization. Not only do we all supervise (not to mention being supervised ourselves), but most of the techniques of good supervision work anywhere. That's because supervision is fundamentally about human productivity.

2. Almost nothing has been written on it, except in chapter form or articles isolating certain issues. Sure, you can find mention of the need for supervision, but how-to-do-it suggestions are rare. So this was a gap in the literature we wanted to fill.

3. It's critical. It's the glue that binds the volunteer program together, linking training, ongoing motivation, evaluation, recognition, employee/volunteer relationships. One reason supervision is hard to talk about is that it is something of an umbrella term that covers so many tasks. In many ways it is an *approach* to working with people.

Which tips presented in the following pages you like or don't like will reflect the tone you want to set and how you want to treat volunteers. While we start from the positive attitude that most volunteers will be excellent team members if they receive the right kind of supervision, we are not Pollyannas. There will be times when you will also need to practice problem and conflict resolution, and enforce discipline and standards. Yes, this is the "tough stuff" that ultimately tests what you believe about volunteer involvement. If you truly value the contributions volunteers make, you will approach possible problems with the expectation of solving them.

It bears saying that we hope people who supervise *paid* workers will read this, too. It's just as relevant. In fact, for years many of us have held the belief that our goal should not be to treat volunteers as if they are employees. A far more useful objective is to treat employees the way we should treat *volunteers*!

Because of this philosophy, we have included "wisdom" about supervision from fields other than volunteer management. You may find yourself surprised, after reading a great suggestion, to discover its source. Maybe the highest compliment to the volunteerism field will be finding this book quoted some day in, say, a business management text. After all, who knows best about motivating workers? The supervisor who thinks money is the only incentive or the supervisor who understands the intrinsic value of meaningful work?

How to Read this Book

Each chapter has running text discussing an element of effective supervision. Interspersed throughout the text is the material contributed from all the sources mentioned above. We've designed four ways to present this material so that you can immediately recognize what each is:

- Columns headed with "From the Field" and showing a "postmark" are suggestions submitted directly for this book by our colleagues. You will sometimes see a computer button icon, since a number of these contributions originated as e-mail or as postings to CyberVPM, our field's wonderful electronic listserv (see the Resources section at the end of the book for more information on CyberVPM).

- Text shown in the shaded "folders" with the tab marked "Archives" is material previously published in another source. Reference credits are shown with each excerpt and again in the Contributor pages in the back of the book.

- The shaded boxes with large quotation marks bracketing italicized text indicate comments made by volunteers in the focus groups we ran.

- At the end of most chapters, you will find a collection of brief "tips" from colleagues. These are short, pithy suggestions meant as last thoughts on that chapter's subject.

The Energize Web Site as Appendix

Quite a number of colleagues took the time to share stories and suggestions that simply did not fit into the final printed text, either because of space considerations or because the situations were too specialized. However, we valued each contribution and debated how to handle this "embarrassment of riches." It was Steve McCurley who used that phrase after reviewing an early version of the manuscript, and it was Steve who suggested the elegant solution: use the Energize Web site. Thank you, Steve!

So, with this book, Energize takes a technological leap forward. The daily number of visitors to our Web site **[http://www.energizeinc.com]** increases each month and will only grow larger. We have therefore decided to inaugurate a virtual appendix to this book.

When you visit our Web site you'll find more and diverse "From the Field" examples of supervision issues and techniques. We are especially pleased to be able to post examples that are very setting-specific or assignment-specific. Even more important, you can increase the *Collective Wisdom* by adding your own examples to share with others (we expect to maintain the site for a long time, so it isn't too late even if you are reading this book after several years). In this way, the Web site will be a dynamic learning center on the important topic of volunteer supervision. Having never done this before, we will all be part of this publishing experiment. Let us know what you think.

Many Thanks

Jarene Frances Lee rose to the occasion and has written a wonderful text, presenting important ideas, framing the concepts, and linking the submissions. Thank you!

Julia Catagnus, Energize's Publications Director, contributed her talents to conducting many telephone interviews of contributors, the literature search, and editing of the submitted material. Thank you, too!

Much gratitude to Linda Graff for her thorough and extremely helpful review of an early manuscript of this book—and for making us take the gloves off!

And, of course, huge rounds of applause to each and every one of you who shared your experiences. Whether or not your submission appears in the following pages, we valued each one. You will always be the pioneers who helped us start this series.

We also appreciate all the copyright holders of previously-published materials who granted permission to include their work in these pages.

Finally, those of us with long memories will remember a book compiled in 1983 by Pat Chapel called *The Best of the Best*. She asked everyone she could think of for one "tip" they would like to share with their colleagues in volunteer management. The resulting potpourri of suggestions made for fun and useful reading. Thanks, Pat! The *Collective Wisdom Series* takes your innovative publication one step forward. That's what will build our field successfully: the synergy that comes from sparking one another's creativity. We must always ask each other why and how—and we must be eager to share the answers.

Susan J. Ellis
Philadelphia
December 1998

Introduction

This book is written for those who supervise volunteers.

In some organizations the supervision of all volunteers is the responsibility of the coordinator of volunteers.[1] In others, the volunteer program has been decentralized; the coordinator of volunteers has overall responsibility for: program planning; interviewing, screening and placing volunteers; agency-wide recognition; program evaluation; and recordkeeping and reporting. Training, supervising and evaluating volunteers is delegated to the employees with whom the volunteers work and perhaps also to other volunteers. In this decentralized model, the coordinator of volunteers supervises only those volunteers who work in the volunteer services department.

I believe that the decentralized volunteer program is the more common mode in today's non-profit and governmental organizations. Therefore, this book is written to the employee or volunteer who is the direct supervisor of one or more volunteers, with references throughout the book to the liaison relationship between the direct supervisor and the coordinator of volunteers. Chapter 9 deals in detail with this relationship and highlights how the coordinator of volunteers can help those who supervise volunteers do so effectively.

Whether you are an employee with many responsibilities including the supervision of volunteers, a volunteer whose responsibilities include supervision, or your agency's coordinator of volunteers, this book will give you not only a comprehensive understanding of what it means to be a supervisor, but also practical tips on how to be an outstanding supervisor of volunteers. While the focus of this book is on supervising individual volunteers, I believe you will find that most of the ideas also apply if you are working with volunteers in groups (such as auxiliaries) and if you supervise employees, too.

Five Principles

Our approach to the subject of supervision rests on five principles:

Principle #1: Volunteers are real staff.

Whether or not you are comfortable with thinking of volunteers as "unpaid staff," the truth is that volunteers are an important part of the "people power" of most organizations. All the work of an organization is done by people: some are paid wages and some are not. Volunteers, like paid staff, need to be linked into the organization in ways that ensure that they are productive, that they do good work, that they are challenged and given an opportunity to grow, and that they know they are valued for what they do and who they are.

The definition of the word "volunteer" has been hotly debated in the field of volunteer program administration for at least twenty years. For the purposes of this book, we will define the word to mean any individual who is giving time to an organization without receiving monetary compensation, other than reimbursement for expenses or a small stipend. Some volunteers may come to your organization on their own; others may be motivated to sign up by a court referral, a school graduation requirement, or a welfare-to-work program. Volunteering encompasses various terms such as intern, auxilian, activist, and specific titles such as docent, tutor, or mentor. Regardless of what your organization calls such workers, their common denominators, for the purposes of this book, are that

---

[1] Throughout the book the term "coordinator of volunteers" is used to refer to the person in your organization who has overall responsibility for the volunteer program. Actual titles vary widely: director of volunteers, director of volunteer services, manager of volunteers, director of volunteer resources.

they do not receive wages, they generally work less than full time (often only a few hours a week), and they bring an enormous variety of skills and talents which may be different from those of the paid staff.

Principle #2: Volunteers aren't free.

While organizations do not pay a salary to volunteers, they do have to invest time and other resources to ensure that volunteers are effective. There are real costs associated with recruitment, interviewing and screening, training, evaluating and recognizing volunteers. Providing volunteers with effective supervision is also a necessary investment. We hope this book clearly demonstrates that it is one of the most important investments an organization can make in its volunteers. Unfortunately, it is also one of the most overlooked.

Principle #3: Supervision is about forming and maintaining relationships.

A supervisor has the challenging responsibility of forming and maintaining relationships with all the workers s/he supervises. While the content of the relationship may include tasks like training, coaching or providing feedback, its essence is a one-to-one connection between two human beings—and all the complexities and nuances that implies. Good relationships in a work setting are characterized by mutual trust, mutual respect, and mutual recognition of each person's competency and professionalism.

Principle #4: The functions of a supervisor can be shared.

All workers need supervisors, but not all supervision needs to be done by one person, nor by those formally ranked as such. Volunteers may be supervised by paid staff or by other volunteers. There may be a team of people who provide supervision to all volunteers in a particular position. Each organization must assess for itself who will supervise volunteers. In doing so, it is important to insure that all the elements of supervision are provided for. To overlook any will hamper the effectiveness of the volunteer. A word of caution, however: dividing the tasks of supervision among several people may create confusion and frustration for volunteers and, for sure, it will erode the central notion that supervision is a relationship between two people.

Some organizations may delegate the responsibility of supervising volunteers to paid workers who do not carry the formal title of supervisor and are not asked to supervise employees. Such workers, who also do not receive the higher pay that normally accompanies the supervisory function, may legitimately raise questions as to why supervising volunteers is not seen as comparable to supervising employees. How the organization responds will reflect the extent to which volunteers are perceived to be "real" staff. At a minimum, learning to supervise volunteers well is certainly an excellent training ground for assuming greater responsibility in the future.

The word "supervisor" is part of the problem because it connotes all sorts of authority and superiority. This book will not teach you to be the "boss." Better terms may be coach, staff liaison, lead volunteer, mentor, chairperson, or team leader. Someone needs to coordinate work and be "in the know." But it's a partnership rather than a hierarchy—an approach that works as well with employees as with volunteers.

Principle #5: Supervision cannot be isolated from other aspects of volunteer program management.

Supervision is distinct from, but related to, job design, screening, training, placement, evaluation and recognition. The overlap in these and other areas will be touched on throughout the book. Just keep in mind, as Linda Graff wrote in the margin when she reviewed this manuscript: "If you design inappropriate positions, recruit inappropriate volunteers, or fail to screen out inappropriate applicants, all the great supervision in the world won't solve your problems."

It is especially important that you, as a supervisor of volunteers, understand your organization's philosophy of volunteerism. Why has your organization chosen to involve volunteers? Your organization's philosophy is likely to be reflected in the type of work that is delegated to volunteers, in the wording of volunteers' assignment (position) descriptions, and even in the role and expectations it has of paid staff. I also recommend that you and the coordinator of volunteers discuss your organization's philosophy of volunteerism. Invite as many staff as possible to join you in considering the premise of the archive "Why Volunteers?" at the end of this Introduction

On the subject of philosophy, I strongly urge you to avoid saying you "use" volunteers. We use tools and things, but not people. "Utilize" is simply a longer, but equally unacceptable word. Ivan Scheier has developed a long list of acceptable verbs. Get in the habit of using your favorite:

empower	allow
count on	involve
rely on	authorize
ask	mobilize
commission	assign
enable	enlist
delegate to	request
entrust	encourage

And if you supervise paid staff, share this philosophy and this list with them, please.

Why do organizations want volunteers in the first place?

This question is absolutely basic, yet it catches some people by surprise. Isn't the answer obvious? No. Aren't agencies "supposed" to have volunteers? Not necessarily. Hasn't our organization "always had" volunteers? So what?

Did you think: "Well, we don't have enough money so we need unpaid help"? Lack of funds is one of the worst reasons to recruit volunteers because it makes volunteers a second choice, tolerated as temporary workers until more money can be raised and "real" staff hired. It is necessary to articulate the reasons why volunteers are a meaningful, positively selected strategy for strengthening your service delivery.

Imagine a "utopia" in which organizations such as yours would have all the money in the world with which to do anything they please: offer one-to-one client service, pay for all types of consultation, take the staff on a retreat to Bermuda, etc. Given such a "utopia," would your agency still seek to involve volunteers in some way?

If you play this mind game, you will identify some of the unique things volunteers offer an organization—so special to volunteers that paying a salary negates or changes them completely:

- Volunteers have perceived credibility with clients, donors, legislators, and others for the very reason that they do not receive a paycheck from the organization.
- It often makes a difference to the recipient of a service that the provider is there purely because he or she wants to be.
- Volunteers are insider/outsiders, bringing a community perspective and a wide range of backgrounds consciously different from the employees. Because they give a few hours at time, volunteers have a broader point of view than the paid staff who may be too close to the work to "see the forest for the trees."
- Volunteers extend your sphere of influence and access to additional people, businesses and organizations in the community. Even the volunteer who helps you once a year becomes another person with knowledge about your work.
- Boards of directors of nonprofit organizations are—by law—an intermediary between donors/funders and program participants, acting as "trustees" of funds from which they themselves derive no profit.
- Volunteers bring the "luxury of focus" to their work. While paid staff members must spread their time and efforts equitably among all clients and projects, volunteers can be recruited to concentrate on selected individuals and issues.
- Volunteers can be asked to work odd hours, in varying locations, and to fill special needs for which staff time cannot be justified yet which are important to individual clients.
- Volunteers often feel freer to criticize and speak their minds than employees do.
- Volunteers, as private citizens, can sometimes cut through red tape and bureaucracies more directly than employees,

who are limited by jurisdictional restrictions. Volunteers can make contacts, travel across borders, and promote cooperation in ways that governments find almost impossible.
- Volunteers can experiment with new ideas and service approaches that are not yet ready to be funded—or that no one wants to fund for a wide variety of reasons. Historically, in fact, volunteers have always been the pioneers in creating new services, often against the tide of opposition from more traditional institutions.

There is one additional "first choice" reason for involving volunteers that does, in fact, involve money. But it must be worded correctly. Volunteers do not "save" money; they allow you to spend every dollar you have—and then do more. Volunteers *extend the budget.*

Other Benefits of Volunteers

Since we live in the real, limited-resources world, what are the other benefits to an organization for involving volunteers? Volunteers offer:

- Extra hands and the potential to do more than could be done simply with limited salaried staff; this "more" might mean an increased amount of service, expanded hours of operation, or different/new types of services.
- Diversity; volunteers may be different from the salaried staff in terms of age, race, social background, income, educational level, etc. This translates into many more points of view and perhaps even a sort of checks and balances to the danger of the staff becoming myopic or inbred.
- Skills that augment the ones employees already possess. Ideally volunteers are recruited exactly because the salaried staff cannot have every skill or talent necessary to do all aspects of the job.
- Community ownership of solutions to mutual problems. Especially if your organization addresses issues affecting the quality of life, when people participate as volunteers they empower themselves to improve their own neighborhood (which is your mission, after all).
- Studies have shown that satisfied volunteers frequently are so supportive of the organizations with which they serve that they become donors of money and goods as well. They also support special events and fundraisers by attending themselves and bringing along family and friends.

So Why Pay a Salary?

Perhaps you have been thinking about the reverse of the question of why you involve volunteers, namely: "Why should we salary anyone?" It is important to recognize that the answer is not that offering a salary gets you people with better qualifications. A volunteer can be just as highly trained and experienced as can any employee. Instead, offering a salary gives the agency a pre-determined number of work hours per week, the right to dictate the employee's work schedule, a certain amount of control over the nature and priorities of the work to be done, and continuity.

SOURCE

Adapted from: *From the Top Down: The Executive Role in Volunteer Program Success*, revised edition, by Susan J. Ellis, Energize, Inc. 1996, Chapter 1.

1

What Is Supervision?

Imagine for a moment that you are a new employee in an organization. Perhaps you can think of your current position—or your very first job. The person who hired you decided you had the necessary qualifications. You have a copy of your job description. You have been assigned a space to work in. You have received some training for your position and the organization has even provided an orientation class for its new workers. So now it is your first day and you are eager to get to work.

Within a few minutes you learn that a co-worker is absent and others seem to think you should do some of her work. Should you? Then a customer calls with a serious complaint about a product that your work unit produced last month. How should you respond? Your computer isn't working properly. Do you have the authority to call for repairs?

Use your imagination to consider all the other questions or problems that might occur on your first day of work—or any other day, for that matter. You will see that, even when workers are highly motivated and have received a clear job description and good training, they still need supervision.

Supervision is, put simply, a two-way relationship between two workers. The supervisor's goal within that relationship is to empower each worker—whether employees or volunteers—to be successful in his or her work. As Peggy Wadsworth from the Chester County Library in Exton, PA notes: "*Everyone* deserves to be well supervised."

Workers count on their supervisor for many things. Look at the list below of the many essential roles that a supervisor must play so that the workers s/he supervises can be successful:

- keep things running smoothly
- organize work schedules
- assess the quality of people's work
- resolve systems problems
- plan and lead team meetings
- serve as a consultant/expert
- be an advocate for the team
- facilitate communication
- answer questions
- ensure compliance with policies and procedures
- praise
- promote team spirit
- set standards
- ensure adherence to deadlines
- determine the need for more training
- mediate conflict
- see the big picture
- set limits
- help workers connect their tasks to the goals
- serve as a role model
- eliminate obstacles
- give feedback on performance
- help people grow

If a supervisor failed to perform even a small number of these tasks, s/he would seriously impede the effectiveness of the team. While it is true that there is something innately hierarchical about the boss-worker relationship, good supervisors demonstrate that they place equal value on each person in that relationship: they monitor not only workers' performance, but also their own.

So supervision is essential if workers are to do a good job. Nonetheless, supervision is not just a matter of performing these tasks. Your attitude as a supervisor is critical to the success of the relationship you forge with your team. The ideal relationship is characterized by trust and respect. The ideal supervisor needs to act in such a way as to earn and keep trust and respect. To be an ideal supervisor you must convey that you, in turn, trust and respect each member of your team.

Supervision is not bossing people around, not constantly telling people what to do, not frequently checking up on them, not doubting their willingness and ability to do a good job. Good supervisors understand that work can be a highly meaningful and rewarding activity, that it provides individuals an opportunity to make a difference, find personal meaning, live out personal values, grow intellectually, socially and emotionally, and be challenged to give and be one's best. This is particularly true with volunteers who, by definition, have chosen to give their time to your organization. For volunteers, the rewards come almost exclusively from the work they do. Volunteers will be attracted to, and stay with, an organization that takes seriously their desire and ability to do a good job. They want work that is challenging and stimulating. Perhaps the greatest mistake in working with volunteers is to assign work that is boring or too easy.

I also challenge you to assess whether you make different assumptions about the employees and volunteers you supervise. When you approach a new employee do you tend to assume the person is competent unless proven otherwise? Do you make the same assumptions about volunteers or do you tend to think of all volunteers as unskilled? Such assumptions may seriously impair your supervisory style.

As a supervisor you must consciously and continually focus on two things: 1) your own performance, i.e., the degree to which you practice each of the necessary aspects of supervision; and 2) building relationships that are shaped by an awareness of the uniqueness of each worker. In other words, as a supervisor you must look first at yourself and then at your relationships with those your supervise.

- At the beginning, establish clearly defined guidelines for supervision and regular time to mutually evaluate the situation.
- Set goals and objectives with the volunteers and periodically evaluate their progress toward meeting these goals.
- Make sure the volunteers know what you expect of them so you do not set the volunteers up for failure.
- Consider setting up a trial period—one or two months—to give either the volunteer or the agency a graceful way "out" if it's not working out.
- Practice an open-door policy so the volunteers can speak with you when the need arises.
- Make the volunteers feel needed and an integral part of the staff.

- Hold informal group discussions with paid and unpaid staff to share ideas, air concerns and problems, and resolve any existing problems.
- Provide volunteers with constructive criticism so they can improve their skills and learn from their volunteer experience.

Volunteers are a valuable resource. As a supervisor of volunteers, you should treat them as full fledged members of the staff and encourage their input in decision making. A CONCEPT TO REMEMBER THROUGHOUT VOLUNTEER SERVICES IS THE TREATMENT OF PEOPLE, PAID AND UNPAID ALIKE, WITH DIGNITY AND RESPECT.

SOURCE

Get Organized! How to Set up a Volunteer Program, United Way's Metro Voluntary Action Center, Atlanta, GA, 1979.

The following are ten significant ways that you as a supervisor can empower your volunteers to be successful in their work. Volunteer success is important not just for the sake of the organization, but also for volunteers themselves. Success insures a good volunteer experience and the desire to remain with the organization. But also consider the impact that effective, empowered volunteers will have on your own reputation! As volunteerism becomes more important in nonprofit organizations and in governmental agencies, a worker who is widely regarded as a good supervisor of volunteers is increasingly of value to that organization.

1. Express your passion for the mission of the organization and the goals of the work unit.

All workers, and volunteers especially, need to see that their supervisor is committed to the purpose of the organization. Your ability to express enthusiastically your excitement about the whole organization and its mission is contagious and helps to give the work meaning. This kind of passion gets people through the difficult times because it enables the team to remember why the work is important. If your organization's coordinator of volunteers has done a good job in the interviewing and screening process, s/he has selected volunteers whose personal values are in harmony with the mission of your organization.

As a supervisor you also need to be enthusiastic about the purpose and goals of your work unit. You must help the whole team see the big picture: how the work of the unit supports and furthers the mission of the organization. The story is told of a traveler who walked into the city of Paris in the early years of the Renaissance. He came upon two stone cutters. The traveler asked one, "what are you doing?" The man, with a look of boredom, replied, "I am cutting stone." The traveler then asked the second worker, "and what are you doing?" "Ah," replied the man, with joy written all over his face, "I am building a cathedral."

A good supervisor wants all volunteers to know why they are cutting stone.

2. Demonstrate your competency.

In many situations, workers count on their supervisors to be experts in the work being done. If this includes you, focus on your own competency so that you can answer questions, be an effective coach, and serve as a good role model. An obvious difference between paid staff and volunteers is the amount of time each spends at work. While some volunteers may work many hours per week, most are likely to work as few as two or three. If they have questions about their work and do not obtain answers, not only will it affect their performance, but it is also likely to affect their morale and commitment.

The key is to serve as a positive role model. You may not be able to answer every question personally, but if you know how to get the answers and extend yourself to do so, you are certainly demonstrating effective behavior.

3. Reflect a caring attitude toward the whole team—individually and collectively.

Workers need a supervisor who cares. They might use words like "sensitive," "kind," "friendly," "open," "warm," and "understanding" to characterize

FROM THE FIELD

Since 1990 I have been the manager of the Patients Library at Memorial Sloan-Kettering Cancer Center. I have been blessed with a wonderful volunteer staff of twenty-four—most all of whom have been happily volunteering with me for my entire tenure. I believe that the key to their happiness and longevity lies in the axiom, "treat others as you would like to be treated."

When I began working at the Center, I was only twenty-six years old. I was aware that the volunteers I would be supervising were significantly older than I was and I knew that some of them might resent "taking orders" from someone my age. I decided to schedule a "Let's-get-acquainted Meeting." I laid out my visions and goals for the library and asked the volunteers for their ideas and suggestions. I explained that their input was very important as they had experience in the library and that this was a new environment for me. I told them that their comments were not limited to this meeting and that their ongoing input was appreciated. This meeting established that I had a direction and that they were a part of the team to create a better library for our patients. A warm and open relationship with my staff had begun.

Other actions that I believe contributed to our successful relationship include:

1.) The Director of Volunteer Resources knows how important it is for me to meet prospective volunteers before they are placed in my department. Taking the time to converse with the Volunteer Resources staff will help to eliminate bad placement choices.

2.) Getting to know each volunteer as an individual. I found out who liked to stamp and cover books, who liked to distribute magazines to the waiting rooms, who liked to work with the health and medical literature, etc. I was able to have these jobs done most effectively while also making the experi-

ence a happy and stimulating one for the volunteer.

3.) Don't reprimand volunteers—instead, teach them. Show them the way to properly sign out a book or verbally demonstrate how you want them to articulate the return policy to patients. Always be able to give them an answer when they ask you why a particular rule is in effect.

4.) Show volunteers your foibles and that you also make mistakes. Often when volunteers get angry at themselves for making, in their words, a "dumb" mistake, I will tell them that I made the same mistake. The end result is a volunteer who feels less embarrassed and will share his or her mistakes with you. Nothing is worse than mistakes being made and volunteers covering them up out of feelings of inadequacy.

5.) Never waste a volunteer's time. Always have work for them to do. Always, always thank them for their help before they leave, showing sincere gratitude. Be sure to attend recognition ceremonies and give cards to those volunteers celebrating a particular milestone.

6.) Write down and remember your volunteers' birthdays with a cake, if possible, but even a card will suffice. Thank them for their dedication and let them know that the place would not be the same without them. Always make your volunteers feel valuable.

Truly, I believe that a sincere appreciation and affection for my volunteers has contributed enormously to their longevity of service. In turn, my job has been made easier and I spend less time training new volunteers. My life has also been enriched by interacting with such a fine group of individuals.

Greg Kachejian, Manager, Patient's Library, Memorial Sloan-Kettering Cancer Center, New York, NY

the ideal supervisor. Do these words describe you? While paid staff may tolerate a supervisor who is insensitive, unkind, unfriendly, rigid, cold, and mean, working with such a supervisor may seriously affect their morale and productivity and may even result in sabotage. Volunteers who work with a negative and insensitive supervisor are likely to feel used and demeaned—and will leave.

A good supervisor encourages team members to care about each other and encourages a peer relationship between paid staff and volunteers. In practice, this may be expressed by celebrating birthdays, send-

ing a card when someone is sick, asking about the vacation when the worker returns, pitching in when a worker needs assistance, and seeking workers' input, especially when making decisions that will affect their work.

A good supervisor does not look the other way when conflicts between members of the team are affecting them and others. The supervisor mediates fairly. When conflicts arise between a volunteer and an employee a good supervisor does not prejudge with the attitude "volunteers are always right" or "volunteers are never right."

Volunteer jobs are successful when volunteers are working in jobs they look forward to and want to do. If we fail to give volunteers such a job, we will be plagued by turnover, unreliability, and low morale, because a job people want to do is the cornerstone of all successful volunteer programs. While paid people will do a job that is unrewarding because they are paid for doing so, volunteers will not for long. This has given volunteers in general a reputation among some paid staff for being unreliable. To the contrary, if the volunteer does not find the job to be personally satisfying, the volunteer can be relied upon to quit and to seek another volunteer position.

Volunteering should have the same motivational qualities that games do, to such an extent that the volunteer truly enjoys and benefits from volunteering. In designing volunteer jobs, one should strive to include the following . . .:

Turf

The first factor is "turf." By turf, we mean that the volunteer has a sense of ownership, something they can point to and say "This is mine." In the non-profit world, the turf is most often a volunteer's own client or project.

One way of thinking about turf is that it gives the volunteer something to be in charge of and hence to be proud of. One way of meeting this is to give volunteers a project of their own that they can control, or an activity for which they have discrete responsibility . . . .

The Authority to Think

The difference between a team and a collection of isolated individuals who lack ownership is that a team has the authority to plan and evaluate its work and agree on who is going to do what. With this authority the individual or group not only does the work but plays some part in deciding how to do it.

As volunteers learn the job and figure out what is going on, however, the fact that they are only doing what someone else decides begins to sap their motivation and dilute their feelings of pride in what they accomplish. They will tend either to resent being told what to do or to lose interest in the job. Either of these will increase the likelihood of the volunteers dropping out . . . . What we can do . . . is involve them in the planning and deciding process so that they do feel a sense of shared authority over the "how" of their job.

SOURCE

Essential Volunteer Management by Steve McCurley and Rick Lynch, Heritage Arts Publishing, 1989.

It is not necessary to lower expectations to be caring. Caring may mean making allowances, such as suggesting that a volunteer leave early when a snowstorm is approaching and the volunteer has a twenty-mile drive to get home. Caring means giving a word of encouragement to a hospice volunteer whose client has just died. Caring means encouraging a volunteer who is really trying hard to seek more training if you believe s/he has the ability to do better work.

4. Be accessible and approachable.

Being accessible to volunteers is a great challenge to a supervisor. Because volunteers usually do not work full time, a good supervisor needs to be deliberately accessible to volunteers to answer questions, provide feedback and information, and maintain a relationship—especially with those who work off site.

Being approachable is another matter! Carefully monitor your mood. Avoid looking harried or annoyed if a volunteer comes to you with a question. Offer alternatives if that moment is inconvenient because you are frantically at work on a project with a deadline, but assure the volunteer of your interest.

Being accessible and approachable does not mean that you must be open to unlimited socializing.

5. Aim for consistency.

Workers who experience a high degree of inconsistency in any aspect of the work environment will be confused, frustrated and unproductive. If rules or procedures are continually changing, if there is a high degree of turnover of paid staff or volunteers, if goals or assignments are suddenly and frequently shifted, if your expectations, style or mood vary widely—all these inconsistencies will have a negative affect on workers.

Volunteers, especially if they only work once a week, may be more seriously affected by inconsistencies than paid staff. Employees generally have more time to make adjustments and can, if only through the grapevine, come to understand why there is so much chaos. Volunteers, however, may feel so overwhelmed and unproductive that they will simply quit with a "who needs this?" attitude.

As a supervisor you need to create stability: a balance between the need for change and growth and the need for consistency. See that change happens in an orderly way and, whenever possible, seek input from the whole team. When this is not possible, you must explain the reasons for the change and allow workers to express their views.

Perhaps the most important form of consistency you can aim for is consistency between your words and your actions. Again, be a good role model for all of your team members.

6. Provide a job description.

If you think of a job description as a word picture of good performance, then giving one to each volunteer is essential. Without a clear job description volunteers cannot know what their responsibilities are.

Some organizations prefer to use the term position description or service assignment when describing volunteers' responsibilities. Whatever term your organization uses, it is important to give careful thought to the development of a volunteer's job description, and even more careful thought to the design of the job itself. According to McCurley and Lynch (1989), the work your organization creates for volunteers should give volunteers something to be responsible for, the authority to think, responsibility for results, and ways to measure whether the results are being achieved.

Job descriptions should be in writing and should be reviewed and updated at least annually. You and your organization's coordinator of volunteers should agree about the process that is used to review and update job descriptions for volunteers. In my view, you as the supervisor are generally in a better position to propose changes, but you and the coordinator of volunteers must jointly agree on all changes.

7. Offer top-notch training.

The interview and placement process in your organization is designed to facilitate the right match between prospective volunteers and the various jobs or positions that your organization has created for volunteers. Training volunteers reflects your belief in their potential. It further prepares them for the actual work, gives them an opportunity to integrate their knowledge and previous experience into the unique characteristics of your organization, and provides an opportunity to establish relationships with other volunteers and paid staff. Thoughtful attention needs to go into the planning of volunteer training for, without it, learning will be, at best, inefficient and, at worst, incorrect. The consequences may include serious mistakes.

There are three types of training: orientation, initial training, and continuing education/support. Some training, may be in formal, classroom style; most will be on-the-job, often coupled with coaching. As a supervisor, you will be especially responsible for initial training and ongoing support. The coordinator of volunteers will be the one offering general orientation and will provide some in-service education opportunities for all volunteers.

8. Provide feedback.

While all ten of these ways in which supervisors empower volunteers are indispensable, your obligation to provide feedback is perhaps the most important. It is the easiest to do and the least likely to be done. Put simply, giving volunteers feedback is providing simple and frequent comments on their work. It is making observations that enable volunteers to see the connection between what they are doing and the goals of the work unit and the organization. It is praising volunteers for handling a difficult interaction with a client with sensitivity and restraint. Feedback is part of coaching and dealing in a helpful way with performance problems. It is also encouraging volunteers to ask questions as well as empowering them to make suggestions. Feedback focuses almost equally on empowering for success and on building a relationship. That's why it also includes asking: "How good a job am I doing as your supervisor?"

Feedback is the tool a supervisor uses to make results a powerful motivator. Imagine that you are bowling, but that there is a large, thick cloth just in front of the pins. Time after time you roll the ball, you hear pins fall down, but you cannot see what happened. The results of your efforts are a mystery. Most likely, you will give up after a while because you don't know what you are accomplishing. Work without results is meaningless. Use feedback to help each volunteer understand how s/he is making a difference to the outcome of the unit, to clients, to other workers, and even to you!

And one final admonition: doing regular formal volunteer performance evaluations does not exempt you from the obligation to provide frequent feedback.

9. Share information.

The single most effective way to convey to workers that you trust them is to share information. Workers who do not receive adequate information are left to guess or start rumors or be guided by misinformation. Most damaging of all is the sense of betrayal that one feels when left out of the information flow in an organization. All organizations, especially those that are large, need to be deliberate in creating and maintaining avenues for sharing information.

Supervisors of volunteers face special challenges regarding the necessity to share information. If the volunteers you supervise work once or twice a week, or if you supervise many volunteers, or if the volunteers work in the field and you rarely see them, you will need to develop efficient systems for sharing information. Keep in mind that a misinformed or uninformed volunteer may make mistakes, feel isolated or devalued, experience loss of commitment, and not be motivated to give his or her best. The flow of information has powerful effects!

George Orwell said: "All animals are equal, but some animals are more equal than others." This applies to a comparison of supervising employees and volunteers. Everything that makes employees productive will also work with volunteers. But some things require special attention or emphasis when supervising volunteers:

1. Volunteers are motivated by a positive working "atmosphere."

2. Volunteers need a clearly-designated work space, including storage space for papers, supplies, and correspondence.

3. Accessibility to a supervisor or someone who can answer questions is needed during the volunteer's work shift or when s/he telephones from the field.

4. Volunteers deserve respect for their schedule. This includes having meaningful work prepared and waiting for them. It also means notification, in advance, if there is insufficient work available on any given day.

5. Supervising volunteers involves "instant accountability"—there is much less margin for error than with salaried staff.

6. Volunteers have greater freedom of choice in selecting assignments.

7. Some socializing is acceptable.

8. Recognition—both thanks and acknowledgement of input—should be continuous.

9. Courtesy and self-fulfilling prophecy are two critical concepts.

10. The point is not to treat volunteers as though they are salaried staff—it would be ideal to treat salaried staff the way it is best to treat volunteers!

SOURCE

"Special Considerations in the Supervision of Volunteers," Workshop Handout, Energize, Inc., 1985.

Over 100 volunteers worked in the pediatric playroom at Memorial Sloan-Kettering; most worked a three or four hour shift once or twice a week. They were supervised by a team of four paid recreation therapists. The recreation therapists maintained a bulletin board for communicating with volunteers. It was located in an area that was off limits to patients and families. All volunteers knew that they were expected to scan it upon their arrival in the playroom. The recreation therapists updated the bulletin board daily with information that was important for volunteers to have. Volunteers might see dated notices like this:

The key to cabinet #6 is missing. If you find it, please notify a recreation therapist right away. Thanks.

We are starting a support group for volunteers and encourage you to attend. The first meeting will be on Tuesday, April 5 from 6:30 to 8:30 p.m. in the day hospital lounge. Please sign up on the sheet below.

Evajane Oswald, the nurse manager of the inpatient unit, has received the annual Excellence in Leadership Award from the Department of Nursing. Please congratulate her when you see her.

Anthony Tompkins, a Wednesday evening volunteer, and his wife Gina, had a baby girl, Carmela Rose, on March 17. Cards can be sent to the new parents at the following address: _____

Pay special attention to communicating information about changes in policies or procedures, significant events affecting the organization or the work unit, and personal and professional news about co-workers (including other volunteers).

Besides bulletin boards, other methods for sharing information include newsletters and regular meetings, with minutes sent to those who were unable to attend. Today's expanding cyberspace opportunities open up even more channels of communication. Chapter 4 offers many creative ideas about how to keep in touch with volunteers.

10. Express your appreciation.

Most organizations that involve volunteers have annual events, such as a luncheon, to celebrate and thank volunteers. Other means to say thank you and acknowledge volunteer participation include Volunteer of the Month awards, special thank you letters, and holiday and birthday cards.

While the organization's formal expressions of appreciation are essential, continual and informal words of appreciation are equally valuable. And you, as the person most familiar with a volunteer's responsibilities and performance, have the advantage of linking your words of appreciation to the specific behaviors that are most worthy of appreciation. When you give recognition, you sustain volunteer enthusiasm.

There is a second type of recognition that is equally important for a supervisor to understand. The dictionary definition of the verb "recognize" includes not only expressing appreciation but also acknowledging something (or someone) as real or legitimate. It is in that sense that we say: "The government of the United States does not recognize the government of Cuba." Undoubtedly, this is the most important form of recognition you as a supervisor can use. It is essential that you and the paid staff in your unit see, think of, and treat your volunteers as "real" staff; to have expectations of them based not on their compensation status but on their abilities and the commitment they have made. Treat volunteers as individuals, with the same types of needs and feelings that employees bring to the work place. In short, volunteer recognition is an attitude, not an event.

One way you might assess your supervisory skills and relationships is to recall your own experiences as a paid or volunteer worker. What was your supervisor like? How did s/he help you understand the purpose of your work? build on your motivation? convey trust and respect? provide training, information, feedback and praise in ways that empowered you to give and do your best? In short, was your supervisor someone you can use as your model—or as a model to avoid? Chapter 10 offers you a checklist to help you identify your strengths and the areas you may want to improve. If you wish, you can work on this self-assessment now, and use your answers as a guide to reading the rest of this book.

So polish your skills as a supervisor of volunteers. As coach, mentor, guide, leader and supporter, your role is indispensable in making today's volunteers effective, successful and eager to give their best to your organization. Not surprisingly, the exact same statement is true for bringing out the best in employees, too.

WRAP-UP TIPS:

Don't expect less from volunteers because they're not being compensated monetarily or because you are "desperate" for help and can't afford to hire someone. Expect the best performance from volunteers because it's often what you'll get. —**Trish Kerlé**

Don't assume that all of a volunteer's free time is your time. Most people who have the time to volunteer are extremely busy. —**Ann Wead Kimbrough**

Empower volunteers by providing them with the best tools to do the job (e.g. training, mentoring, job-shadowing, evaluations, meetings, written position descriptions, etc.). —**Keri Olson**

Treat volunteers as co-workers. Encourage staff to lead, teach and recognize the volunteers' efforts and to provide constructive criticism if not as expected...Provide a good working environment...Be a role model for all volunteers—with enthusiasm and energy. —**Karen Paterson**

Make your volunteers feel that they are a part of your organization. Include them in appropriate staff and client meetings. Invite them to agency functions. Provide relevant informational training or reference materials. Use as many forms of THANK YOU as possible daily. —**Lin Spellman**

Make volunteers feel their contribution is valuable to the organization. Acknowledge when they are not there (e.g., "we missed you yesterday"). —**Debbie Walker**

Everyone deserves to be well supervised. Good work deserves recognition. Poor work deserves constructive criticism. —**Peggy Wadsworth**

Don't make volunteers sit around waiting for you to get your act together. —**Nan Hawthorne**

Smile. —**Karen Paterson**

2
Defining Expectations

Volunteers—like all workers—need to know what is expected of them. Good supervisors clearly communicate their expectations. While being authoritarian with paid staff may be permissible, it is generally ineffective with volunteers. Instead, as a supervisor of volunteers you should use positive language and be willing to negotiate in non-essential areas.

Begin with the assumption that no one volunteers in order to do a bad job. Therefore, an important part of your responsibility is to define what doing a good job is. I have already said that the volunteer's job description is a detailed picture of good performance. However, there are other topics related to the volunteer's work that you will need to review with each new volunteer.

Maintain High Expectations

If you are inexperienced in supervising volunteers you may believe that, because volunteers are not paid, you do not have the right to expect much of them. You may also, at least unconsciously, believe that unpaid workers are unable to do good work. Honestly explore your beliefs and discuss them with others in your organization who supervise volunteers or with the coordinator of volunteers.

Keep in mind that if you have high expectations of volunteers you are likely to get good results. If your expectations are low—implying that you don't believe volunteers are capable of doing a good job or cannot be trusted to do a good job—you are likely to get low results.

Don't be afraid to challenge volunteers. Moderately difficult work, even very difficult work, is more motivating than work that is too easy. That's why a bowling lane is sixty feet long, not five. The following story also makes the point. I recall speaking with a Memorial Sloan-Kettering volunteer the day after he completed his first New York City Marathon. When I asked him how it went, an anguished look appeared on his face as he replied, "It was terrible! It was horrible! It was the most difficult thing I have done in my whole life!" Then he paused, let out a huge grin, and added, "And I can't wait to do it again!" Studs Terkel once commented, "Most people have jobs that are too small for them." Again, don't be afraid to challenge your volunteers. I suspect more volunteers have left organizations because they were bored than because they were worked too hard. The exception to this observation are volunteers who feel so challenged in other aspects of their life that they seek refuge in essentially "no brainer" volunteer work (which, however, can still be extremely useful). You and the coordinator of volunteers need to understand such differences and to design volunteer assignments to meet both sets of wishes.

Let your volunteers know how much you are counting on them and be sure they understand why their work is important. Encourage volunteers to give their best. Challenge them to polish their performance, perhaps by suggesting that each time they arrive for work they ask themselves, "what can I learn today that will make me a better volunteer?" Expect the best of your volunteers and you are likely to get the best.

It is especially important that you establish a friendly but professional atmosphere that places a strong emphasis on the importance of the task at hand, on teamwork, on good manners, and on personal responsibility and accountability. Volunteers—and employees, too—should feel that it is a privilege and an honor to be a part of your unit. This has nothing to do with elitism and everything to do with pride.

This does not preclude having fun nor the necessity of having a sense of humor. In fact, humor can be therapeutic in work environments where the stress level is high or where workers are repeatedly dealing with tragedy. Volunteers may initially be startled by what seems like unprofessional behavior, gallows humor being one example. Be sure to explain how this helps people cope and give volunteers permission, so to speak, to let off steam the same way when they need to.

In addition to clarifying your expectations regarding the work itself, clearly communicate your expectations about these issues:

- adhering to an agreed-upon work schedule
- meeting productivity standards or deadlines
- following established procedures
- honoring rules regarding confidentiality
- maintaining appropriate relationships with co-workers
- reporting work-related problems
- not doing tasks beyond one's scope of responsibility

When discussing your expectations with volunteers don't forget to ask about their expectations, too. If some expectations are unrealistic, say so. But remember that volunteers have a right to expect a clearly defined job, adequate training, tools to do the job, adequate work space, cordial relations with paid staff and other volunteers, feedback (positive and negative) on their work, appreciation, and the opportunity to discuss issues or problems concerning their work. Most of all, volunteers have a right to expect that the organization is respectful of their time and that it is investing it in tasks and activities that are truly important. A good rule to remember is: never waste a volunteer's time.

Remember that each volunteer is a unique individual. You may find that you have to be more directive with young volunteers, more trusting with highly experienced volunteers. Some will need more training than others. Some will need feedback that is performance-related, others will want to hear that you enjoy working with them. Chapter 8 provides ideas about adapting your supervisory style to the individual as well as to the work setting and assignment.

Volunteer Job Descriptions

In the previous chapter, we identified written volunteer job descriptions as one of the ten most invaluable aspects of supervision. Job descriptions, whether you call them that or "position descriptions" or "volunteer role expectations," need to be developed for each volunteer position, regardless of whether the *position* is occupied by one volunteer or dozens. If, for example, you supervise ten volunteers who staff an information desk in a museum, and each volunteer has the same responsibilities, you need to develop one job description (and give each volunteer a copy). If you also supervise vol-

Attitudes/Ideas That Box Us In:

a. Volunteers work for free out of the goodness of their hearts.

b. Volunteers cannot be held accountable because they work for free.

c. Volunteers need kid glove treatment so they'll keep coming back. Staff get a paycheck.

d. If someone volunteers, you take him/her on.

e. Retention means hanging on at all costs because, if the volunteers weren't happy enough, we did something wrong.

f. If we get good enough at recruitment and placement, we will have good volunteers who stay forever.

g. Volunteers should be instantly perfect at the work and instantly compatible with staff.

h. Any generalization about ALL volunteers.

SOURCE

"Letting Go: Planning for Volunteer Release" by Jane Mallory Park, handout at Pennsylvania Association for Volunteerism Workshop, 1985.

unteers who serve the museum as tour guides, develop a job description for that position, too.

A job description has seven essential parts and two optional ones:

Title

The word "volunteer" is not a title. Give the volunteer position a title that reflects what the volunteer does: tutor, information desk specialist, driver, playroom pal, soup kitchen host.

Goals of the Work Unit

Specify the broad goals or purposes of the unit or the team of which the volunteer is a part. This helps the volunteer see the connection between his or her work and the work of the rest of the team.

Purpose/Goals of the Volunteer's Position

State succinctly why the position exists—what it is that the volunteer is supposed to accomplish.

Responsibilities

List all the specific tasks and activities that the volunteer needs to do in order to meet the described purpose/goals.

Training and Supervision Plan

Describe how the volunteer will be prepared to do the work and then supported while doing it. Your name and/or your title belongs here as "Supervisor." This reminds the volunteer that you and s/he have a partnership. You are responsible for being a good supervisor. The volunteer is bound by the parameters of the relationship, too. It is especially important to review this when you interview and/or orient each new volunteer.

Requirements

Specify the skills, background, experience, training and personal attributes a volunteer would need in order to be qualified for the position. If regular participation in team meetings or a support group is required, state that, too. Specify what you want the volunteer's time commitment to be: minimum length of commitment, minimum hours per week or month, specific hours the volunteer must be present, etc.

Benefits

Identify what the volunteer will gain from this work. Some benefits are tangible, such as a free meal or reimbursement for travel. Others are more abstract but nevertheless important: learning new skills, contributing to a cause, opportunities for input.

In addition, some volunteer job descriptions should include:

Restrictions

When applicable, state clearly what the volunteer is not permitted or authorized to do. For example, at Memorial Sloan-Kettering Cancer Center, every volunteer job description stated: "Volunteers are not permitted to give medical information or advice to patients, patients' families, or visitors." Keep the list of restrictions relevant to the job. Generic restrictions on volunteers belong in a volunteer handbook.

Length of Appointment

For some positions, especially leadership roles in all-volunteer membership organizations (service clubs, PTAs, alumni associations), it is good practice to specify how long a volunteer can occupy a position. A rotation policy decreases the likelihood of entrenched power and also ensures that members will grow into higher positions of responsibility by serving in various capacities within the organization.

To summarize, a volunteer job description is a description of what ideal performance looks like, a word picture of the ideal volunteer in action. A volunteer should be able to read it and understand exactly what s/he is expected to do. Each volunteer should have a copy of his or her job description. As the volunteer's supervisor, you can use the job description as a teaching tool, as a basis for accountability, and a framework to acknowledge growth. It is also a tool in giving recognition for good work, as a reminder about

Supervision offers volunteers the opportunity to grow through self-awareness. It provides constructive feedback on work performance from the people volunteers help (clients, paid staff), which is necessary if they are to feel an integral part of the agency Supervision also affords volunteers recognition for their work while holding them accountable for providing services. A volunteer once told me, "If I am to be given an important role, I want to be told when I am doing the job well and, more important, when I am not." In essence, this volunteer was defining appropriate supervision...

An essential part of the supervisory relationship between paid and unpaid staff is setting up an initial contract. This contract includes addressing several questions.

1. **What does each of you expect of the other?** What are your personal and professional motivations for being here? What do you need to continue? How does the other person influence your decision? How much time, energy, knowledge and skill does each party have? How can each party develop his or her talents? By when? Is the other party available at any time? Who initiates contact? Is each willing to watch and help the other grow?

2. **What does each of you have to offer?** How much time and energy? How much skill and experience as an interviewer, a diagnostician, a consultant, a supervisor, an educator? How about personal responsibilities? What are your strengths, weaknesses?

3. **How do you define your relationship to each other?** What words do you use to describe relationship, volunteers, colleagues, team, supervisor, boss, subordinate, clinician, streetworker, unpaid staff? What do they mean? Do you have to be personal friends to do the job? Can you respect each other and not socialize or even have many interests in common? Do you need to be liked by your counterpart?

4. **How are you going to handle differences or conflict?** Can you differ openly? How does each react when another disagrees? How do you avoid win-lose battles? Can you involve third parties as one technique for resolving problems? Should one party be an advocate and when? What factors are important to decision-making? What is consensus? How much are you able to risk? When does one party make a final decision? Who is responsible?

5. **How does each handle the authority component in the relationship?** When is it important to ask before acting? When can action be taken immediately? What needs to be reported, not reported?

SOURCE

"What Is Supervision?" by Dick Hodgkins, *Voluntary Action Leadership*, Spring, 1979.

restrictions, and as a reference when dealing with performance problems.

Written Contracts

Some organizations have found it helpful to have written contracts or agreements with new volunteers. We have included three examples for you. On pages 20 and 21 are the General Statement of Understanding and the Ground Rules used by Big Brothers Big Sisters of Bucks County, PA. Notice that these documents spell out the frequency with which volunteers are expected to contact their supervisor to report on the work they are doing. They also outline important policies and include the expectation that volunteers will contact their supervisor any time they are in need of support and guidance.

The one-year agreement that the Calgary Police Service asks of victim support workers (a volunteer position title) is on page 22. Note that this agreement covers many areas. Participation in initial and ongoing training is included, as is the amount of time volunteers are expected to give, notification regarding absence or resignation, dress code, professional conduct, and grounds for dismissal. No one who signs this could possibly state that he or she did not know what the expectations of the Police Service are!

On page 23 you will find the volunteer agreement of the Children's Aid Society of Metropolitan Toronto. Because this form documents an agreement between the organization (represented by a case worker), the volunteer, and the child and/or parent, all three sign the form. Note that the original copy goes to the coordinator of volunteers and that the volunteer, the case worker, and the child/parent each keeps a copy. Note also that two review times are established.

If you believe it would be helpful to develop a form similar to one of these for your area, discuss your ideas with your organization's coordinator of volunteers. You may want to include a few statements about what you are committed to doing/providing.

The Orientation Process

It is important that you establish an efficient system for discussing expectations with new volunteers.

To do that you will need to know whether your organization's coordinator of volunteers offers a general orientation class for all new volunteers (s/he should!) and, if so, what it covers. You and the coordinator of volunteers will also need to agree on who is responsible for providing training for new volunteers in your area. While one approach cannot fit all organizations, it is commonly expected that the coordinator of volunteers provides an orientation presenting all the general information new volunteers need to know about the organization and rules that apply to all volunteers regardless of what they are going to do. You, as direct supervisor, should provide an orientation to your work unit and training that will teach new volunteers the specific information and skills they will need for whatever work they will do in your area. You will have to tailor this training for each different job description and also for the experience and skills each volunteer already has.

Consider the following subjects for the orientation you conduct for volunteers you will supervise directly (unless some are already covered in the general orientation given by the coordinator of volunteers):

- a tour of the work area
- the names and responsibilities of co-workers
- your own schedule and when you will be available for questions
- where the volunteer can leave personal property
- where the volunteer will sit and can store work
- location of equipment and supplies the volunteer is authorized to use
- whom volunteers should notify when they arrive/leave each day
- rules about the use of the office coffee pot
- policies on smoking and eating while at work
- a review of how you will address performance problems
- names and titles of any VIPs you expect volunteers to be aware of

A question you might ask yourself when designing this orientation session is: "What does a new volunteer need to know to feel at home here?" No one remembers everything s/he hears, so develop a packet of written material for the volunteer to keep and review after the session.

If it is practical, orient a few or even several volunteers at the same time; they will all learn from each other's questions. You may also involve experienced volunteers in conducting part or all of the orientation. Just be sure that you are comfortable with the content and that you are involved in some way. Remember

FROM THE FIELD

Our orientation sessions for new volunteers are primarily designed to introduce them to the realities of the judicial process, which is not at all like it's portrayed on TV. We want our volunteers to know about overwhelming caseloads and the challenge of weighing what to do with a teenager who is totally out of control. We include a panel presentation by key people: judges, district attorneys, public defenders, victim advocates, etc. and we do a mock trial complete with a real judge. We give volunteers lots of written materials, including a glossary of all the legal terms they need to learn, like habeas corpus.

Janice Allen, Director of Volunteers, Boulder County Justice System Volunteer Program, Boulder, CO

FROM THE FIELD

To reduce the possibility of burning out our volunteers who serve as tutors, the education program supervisor and I have agreed that volunteers can tutor only one inmate. I also devote part of the volunteer orientation class to describing the lives of typical inmates, which is usually pretty bleak. This way volunteers are at least somewhat prepared for what they will hear and may not be quite so overwhelmed.

We made this policy decision after I almost lost a great volunteer. She had been tutoring five inmates simultaneously. But after only three weeks here she told me she wanted to quit because, in her words, "when I hear about their lives and discouragement, it just breaks my heart." She and I talked this through and decided that she should work with just one inmate. So we had two good outcomes: not only did she stay for quite a while, but this situation was also a valuable learning experience for me.

Barbara Lightheart, Volunteer Services Manager, Travis County Jail, Austin, TX

that supervision is about relationships and the orientation of new volunteers is the first day in the formation of new relationships.

Even if you have an orientation class for new volunteers you should still plan to spend time with each

continued on page 24

Big Brothers/Big Sisters of Bucks County
GENERAL STATEMENT OF UNDERSTANDING

Big Brothers/Big Sisters of Bucks County is affiliated with the national organization of Big Brothers/Big Sisters of America. As a result, we are required to follow national standards which define the minimum level of acceptable service. It is our belief that by meeting these minimum practice requirements we are providing a quality service. Thus by being in compliance with national standards, we can better serve you, protect the children we serve, and safeguard the integrity of each and every match.

National Standards require the professional staff to maintain regular supervisory contacts with volunteers, parent/guardians, and clients in order to foster and maintain the growth of the relationship and meet the client's needs. Required Procedures for match supervision include contact within the first two weeks of a match, monthly during the first year, and quarterly during year two and after.

Because of the large number of calls each case manager is required to make each month, volunteers and parents must assume responsibility to contact the agency as follows:

VOLUNTEER AND PARENT CONTACTS AGENCY
Two Weeks into Match **Monthly During First Year** **Quarterly During Year Two and After**

I am aware that it is my responsibility to be in contact with the agency as scheduled above. I realize failure to do so could necessitate the closure of my match. I also realize I have the right and responsibility to contact the agency at any time there is a problem or I am in need of support and guidance.

Date _____   Signature _____

Date _____   Agency Representative _____

Big Brothers/Big Sisters of Bucks County, Inc.
GROUND RULES

1. "Bigs" and "Littles" are friends. Parents and/or guardians are ultimately responsible for the well-being of their child. Therefore, if the child has some conflict with school, law, etc., the volunteer should not intercede on behalf of the parent/guardian. If the parent wishes help, BB/BS is available for consultation. One should always respect appropriate role boundaries.

2. The volunteer-child relationship is a one-to-one friendship. Regular contact is essential for the relationship to develop. If visitation is not possible, written or telephone contacts are essential for the maintenance of the friendship.

3. The volunteer has no financial responsibility for the support of the child and/or the child's family. Fees for activities can be an individual or shared responsibility between parent, volunteer, and child depending on the financial situation of parent and volunteer. It is suggested that money be used sparingly during activities.

4. The volunteer is not a disciplinarian on behalf of the parent or guardian. The parent may not punish the child by refusing to let the child see his/her Big Brother or Big Sister.

5. The volunteer is not a taxi or baby-sitting service. Big Brothers and Big Sisters should not feel obligated to act as maintenance or household help in single-parent homes.

6. Volunteers and parents/guardians have the responsibility of maintaining regular contact with BB/BS and should ALWAYS contact BB/BS in the event of a problem with the volunteer/child relationship.

7. Parents/guardians should be aware of and consent to all activities in which their child will participate. Parents/guardians should also be aware of the times when their child will be picked up and dropped off and at home when their child is expected unless previous arrangements have been made.

8. BB/BS policy prohibits overnight outings during the first six months of a match. After six months, the agency will approve of overnight visits where the child has a separate/private place to sleep upon notification of such plans and with the written consent of the parent/guardian.

9. BB/BS policy prohibits the use of any illegal drug and/or alcohol by either adult volunteers or boys/girls in the presence of one another. A violation of this policy will result in termination from the program.

10. Volunteers: Be yourself. Set limits of proper conduct with your Little Brother/Sister. You will both be more comfortable knowing what is expected. Do not break appointments without giving an explanation. This will encourage the child to trust you, other people, and finally him/herself. Parents/Guardians and Children: Be respectful of the volunteer's life. Give adequate notice and an explanation to the volunteer of outing cancellations and time changes.

**CALGARY
POLICE
SERVICE**

VICTIM ASSISTANCE UNIT
VICTIM SUPPORT WORKER 1 YEAR AGREEMENT

The following is an agreement between you, the Victim Support Worker, and the Calgary Police Service Victim Assistance Unit.

1. I hereby agree to participate in the full training program required by the Victim Assistance Unit and to attend at least 6 of 10 monthly training sessions.

2. I will commit myself to provide not less than one 5 hour shift per week, for a one year period.

3. Except for emergencies such as illness or family death, my attendance will be on time and regular. Before periods of absence such as vacation or other special circumstances, I will notify the Supervisor at least one week prior to the absence.

4. As a representative of the Calgary Police Service Victim Assistance Unit, I will conduct myself in a professional, responsible and courteous manner while in the service of victims of crime.

5. As a Victim Support Worker with the Calgary Police Service Victim Assistance Unit, I will present a neat and professional appearance, i.e. dress must be neat, clean and tidy. **NO JEANS, SNEAKERS OR SWEATSHIRTS.** Training Nights have been designated for casual wear.

6. As a Victim Support Worker with the Calgary Police Service Victim Assistance Unit, I understand that any misuse of Calgary Police Service equipment or abuse of privileges afforded to me will be grounds for my dismissal as a volunteer.

7. As a Victim Support Worker with the Calgary Police Service Victim Assistance Unit, I understand that my agreement commitment may be renewed yearly, and I can be dismissed immediately for any breach of the terms of this agreement.

8. I understand that I , as a Victim Support Worker with the Calgary Police Service Victim Assistance Unit, am required to supply a Unit Constable with one week written notice of my intent to discontinue my service to the Unit.

This agreement is entered into for the purpose of ensuring consistent reliable service and assistance to persons seeking help of the Victim Assistance Unit.

VOLUNTEER'S SIGNATURE: _____

DATE: _____

VOLUNTEER PROGRAM MANAGER: _____

133-6th Avenue SE, Calgary, AB
Canada T2G 4Z1 [403] 265.3330

PD 17B (R94-08)

Children's Aid
SOCIETY OF METROPOLITAN TORONTO

Volunteer Agreement

Name of volunteer_____

Name of family, child, program_____

Worker responsible for supervision _____ Ext._____

Type of volunteer assignment_____

Assignment goals_____

_____

Time commitment: How often_____   Number of hours_____

Date and time of assignment review_____
          (1 month after first meeting)

Date, time and place of assignment review_____
          (6 months after first meeting)

We, the undersigned, understand and agree to the above assignment.

Volunteer_____   _____   _____
                      Signature   Phone Number   Date

Primary worker or
Program Coord._____   _____   _____
                      Signature   Phone Number   Date
(Parent/
foster parent/
child or teen)_____   _____   _____
                      Signature   Phone Number   Date

A volunteer who does not comply with the above agreement may be withdrawn from the assignment.
Note to the worker:

1.	Please write this agreement during the initial meeting with the family, child, or program coordinator.
2.	Please phone or meet with the volunteer to review the assignment one month after this agreement is signed and be available for phone contact with volunteer, as required.
3.	Please meet with the volunteer every six months to complete the assignment review.
4.	Please write a new volunteer agreement on the anniversary of this agreement, and every year that the assignment continues.
5.	Distribute copies of this agreement as indicated at bottom of the page.

Original to: Coordinator of Volunteer Services
                    c.c. Volunteer, Client, Primary worker/Program coord.

Vol. 1\August '95 c:\volagree

I strive to make information about the minimum time requirement an integral part of the publicity and discussion about the volunteer position. Volunteers know what they are getting into from the beginning. Using this comprehensive approach, it's been my experience that when volunteers begin an assignment and then cannot complete it, they will then work with me to find a solution to make their leaving less of a disruption to the program or project. Specifically:

1. Advertise the time commitment as a requirement for all volunteers serving in the position.

2. List the time commitment in the position description.

3. Specifically ask if the volunteer can/will make the time commitment during the interview.

4. Explain why the time commitment is important to the program/project during the training.

5. Be flexible in how that time commitment can be met.

6. Discuss how well the volunteer is meeting that time commitment during your regularly-scheduled supervision talks.

(This implies that many other program practices are in place—position descriptions, interviews, training and supervision.)

Teresa Gardner-Williams, CVA, Volunteer Services Coordinator, Alexandria Division of Social Services, Alexandria, VA

new volunteer on his or her first day on the job. Develop your own checklist of the information you need to cover. Also plan to meet with each volunteer at the end of his or her first few times in your area. This gives you the opportunity to continue building a relationship, to clarify your expectations, to praise, to express appreciation, and to determine additional training needs. Ask the volunteer to tell you what the experience was like, perhaps asking specific questions about aspects of the work that you know are difficult.

At Memorial Sloan-Kettering, for example, one of the recreation therapists in the pediatric playroom would spend 15 to 20 minutes—more when necessary—with each new volunteer at the end of his or her first shift. If a few volunteers had started on the same day they would all meet together. The recreation therapist would ask the volunteers to describe their feelings about being around the children, ask what they found to be harder than expected, and what additional information they needed about their work or the setting.

Yes, this takes time. Remember that volunteers are not "free" and that investing this kind of time in new volunteers has important benefits: you are building relationships with your volunteers, showing your concern, and developing their skills. This will almost certainly increase their commitment to you and to their work.

Despite everything you do in the beginning to plan appropriately, to define expectations and to develop a good relationship with your volunteers, you may encounter performance problems or problems with attitudes or relationships. In Chapter 6 you will find ideas about how to address these.

Expectations Regarding Volunteer Time

Earlier in this chapter I stated that you need to emphasize with volunteers—especially new ones—the importance of adhering to an agreed-upon work schedule. Your organization may have standards regarding the minimum number of hours per week or per month that volunteers are expected to work. If someone cannot meet this minimum standard, s/he ought not to be accepted as a volunteer in the first place. Nonetheless, this is one area in which there is a radical difference between supervising volunteers and supervising paid staff: an organization does not have the kind of control over a volunteer's time that it has over an employee's time. An organization can require an employee to work on a specific schedule of days and hours, including necessary overtime, and fire him or her if the employee refuses. The process of committing a volunteer to a schedule is one of negotiation and adaptability. In other words, volunteers can say no with impunity—though you can certainly insist on volunteer attendance once the schedule has been determined. Likewise, an organization can place limits around how much time an employee spends on sick leave and vacation, whereas volunteers can simply tell you when they are going on vacation and for how long. It is legitimate to request that volunteers give a few weeks' notice so that arrangements can be made for coverage, if necessary. And if a volunteer is absent a lot because of long or frequent vacations, you or the coordinator of volunteers may want to meet with the volunteer to discuss the impact his or her absence is having on the organization.

As a supervisor of volunteers you will simply have to accept your lack of control over volunteers' time. An incident from Memorial Sloan-Kettering comes to mind. During the 1992 presidential campaign the Center issued a policy that employees and volunteers were not permitted to wear any political buttons on their uniforms or clothing while on the premises, nor could they hang posters, banners and the like in their work areas. A wonderful volunteer who worked about twenty hours a week in Patient Transport Service—I'll call him Joe—decided he didn't

The following techniques of effective delegation will assist supervisors of volunteers in their search for success:

...Assess their understanding. Ask volunteers to explain the assignments as they understand them. What areas are still unclear? Have you accurately communicated the tasks to be accomplished?...

Encourage decisions and suggestions. Volunteers will often avoid taking responsibilities because they are unsure of their skills. To counter this, elicit suggestions and reinforce the initiative they display in making decisions. Remember people support what they help develop.

Be reasonable and flexible. Effective [supervisors of volunteers] keep assignments within reasonable expectations of what can be accomplished, both in time and in quantity. Anticipate interruptions and obstacles and make adjustments where necessary.

Build openness and accessibility. Recognize that volunteers may be reluctant to report unfinished projects or failures to you. Encourage them to bring problems to you early.

Provide responsibility. When you delegate a task, be sure you give the responsibility and authority that goes with it. Without the proper resources and support, volunteers and the delegated projects are doomed to failure....

Monitor progress. Check with volunteers on the progress of their assignments. Do not wait until the project due date to evaluate their success. Your interest in monitoring progress of the assignments reflects your concern for their performance. Effective [supervisors of volunteers] know that they have to "inspect what they expect."

Expect improvement, not perfection. If tasks or assignments can only be done one way and that way is your way, then you are much better off to do it yourself. Otherwise, you will continually set volunteers up for failure and stifle their willingness to risk displaying initiative. In addition, it should be remembered that "success is improvement, not perfection."

Provide feedback and recognition. The most important motivation for people is feedback on their efforts. However, all too often, supervisors of volunteers forget to compliment their volunteers for specific task completion. Verbal compliments are effective and appreciated, but for some volunteers written messages count double. Remember that when you let those around you shine, you shine with them....

SOURCE

"Ensuring Volunteer Success Through Effective Delegation Techniques" by Gene Sharratt, Ph.D. , *Voluntary Action Leadership*, Winter 1988-89.

like the policy, came to my office and said he was taking a leave of absence and that he would return the day after the election, which was still several weeks off. The manager of Patient Transport was upset but recognized there was nothing she could do. We increased volunteer coverage to compensate for Joe's absence and, true to his word, Joe returned the day after the election. I always wondered whose campaign button he would have worn....

Please do not misinterpret this section as meaning that undependable volunteers must be tolerated. While you cannot control volunteer time, you definitely have the right to ask for a pre-determined schedule and to expect volunteers to be on duty when promised. The point is simply to react flexibly when volunteers responsibly request changes in their schedule.

There is, however, another way of looking at this issue of volunteers and time. I contend that being a volunteer (at least a responsible one) takes more self-discipline than it takes to be a paid worker. Workers stand to lose a lot if they fail to adhere to their work schedule: a steady source of income, for one thing. So you might say they have no choice but to go to work. If you don't have much of a choice, it doesn't require much self-discipline to do what's required: the discipline comes from outside—from the organization. Since the organization cannot exert that exact kind of discipline on volunteers, all the discipline must come from within the person. Thus, to be a good volunteer takes a lot of self-discipline. This may be less so in situations where there is another type of mandate affecting the volunteer—from a court or college, for example.

Your Organization's Coordinator of Volunteers

It is important that you maintain a close relationship with your organization's coordinator of volunteers (see Chapter 9). The coordinator of volunteers must have a clear understanding of the work you are asking volunteers to do (hence the need for you to develop volunteers' job descriptions in partnership with the coordinator of volunteers), the qualifications needed, the work environment, your supervisory style, and any special requirements that will have a bearing on which volunteers the coordinator of volunteers recruits and places in your area. Carla Lehn of the Lehn Group states it clearly: "If a volunteer doesn't have the qualifications for the position, all the supervision in the world won't change that."

FROM THE FIELD

When I conduct my workshop titled "Delegation: The Art of Letting Go While Staying in Charge," it is always fascinating that the initial reasons participants give for finding delegation challenging are control and perfection issues, but eventually someone admits that his/her greatest fear is that someone might do it better!! That always brings up an interesting discussion regarding whether the organization respects and models good delegation or good "doing." (Hopefully both, but often good delegation is not understood or rewarded.)

Most often people are from organizations that shower appreciation on the best doers and ignore or even criticize those who truly delegate and supervise well. (Good delegators don't appear to be *doing* anything— remember that may be a great compliment!) The staff and volunteer recognition goes to the one who "did it all" and "kept us afloat" rather than the one who found a great team of people to accomplish something and was the great manager.

Just a few thoughts: Delegation is how we "grow people." There is always risk. We need to learn how to minimize that risk (the unsatisfactory work). What if no one had ever effectively delegated to us? Who in our life is someone who delegated significantly and appropriately to us and what impact did it have? These are helpful questions to explore as we look at our own hesitancies to do it ourselves.

Also I believe that most of what goes on under the guise of delegation is direction or dumping—neither of which usually gets the results we are hoping for. Delegation is a complicated skill but its essence involves selecting the best person to do the job (has time, needed skills, experience, interest, etc.). Then our role as delegator involves four key tasks:

1. assigning mutually agreed upon results;
2. discussing and agreeing on an appropriate means of authority (volunteer or employee knows when to get approval and what decisions they can make independently);
3. supplying the support and resources that the person might need to be successful in this task (asking, "What can I provide that will assist you in being successful?"); and
4. designing a follow-up system which allows you to inspect what you expect.

Obviously very over-simplified, but I couldn't resist since I have been thinking about this for several hours today. I truly believe that much of the burnout in our field is due to our lack of comfort and skill in the area of delegation and I also admit FULLY that it is a great deal easier to teach this than to do it. But I become considerably more effective in delegating myself when I remember the major responsibility I have to assure the best chances of its success.

Betty Stallings, Stallings and Associates, Pleasanton, CA, posted to CyberVPM

VOLUNTEER FOCUS GROUP QUOTES

Make sure you are clear about what I am not supposed to do.

If you want the work done a specific way make that clear from the start.

Be sure to give new volunteers a warm welcome. Help them feel comfortable in their new work environment and with their new colleagues.

Expect the best from me because that will encourage me to do my best.

When I started volunteering my supervisor arranged for me to meet with experienced volunteers who were doing the same work. That was so helpful.

I want my supervisor to know he can count on me.

When my supervisor asks me if I can give extra time I take that as a real compliment.

If you have high expectations of me, then I know I am really doing something worthwhile, not just sitting around to pass the time.

I am happy to give extra time when asked because it helps the cause.

—Volunteers

WRAP-UP TIPS:

...It is important for volunteers to know that they must be accountable to someone. —**Alberta Conklin**

Help volunteers learn about the whole organization and how their specific role fits in. —**Lu Salisbury**

The more professionally your treat your volunteers, the more professionally they will approach their duties. —**Susan Cairy**

I have found that management volunteers don't like that, when they speak up and suggest something, the committee wants to give them the job. Therefore they do not offer suggestions. I have turned that around to finding out what the volunteers love to do and see if we can incorporate those gifts into our organization. —**Patricia Connelly**

Don't expect a volunteer to do something you wouldn't do yourself if you had the skills to do it. —**Nancy Roslund**

I encourage some volunteers to take leadership roles. Keep in mind that volunteers are not all alike. They have their own talents to offer. —**Carol Baker**

In our program, we are careful to avoid doing things for volunteers that they can do themselves. Tasks like buying the cookies or securing a speaker for a meeting might be easier for the staff to do, but when volunteers do them they develop leadership skills. Most important, they begin to "own" the program and increase their allegiance to the organization. —**Judy Baillere**

3
Training and Providing Support

The supervisory relationship has an end in mind: empowering the volunteer to be successful in his or her work. Nonetheless, a supervisor must pay attention to the relationship itself. One owns a car so that driving to work or taking a trip is possible. But if the car has no engine or the tires are flat, using it to go anywhere is impossible.

Consciously begin to build your relationship with each volunteer from your first day together. Think carefully about the impression you want to make as his or her supervisor. While your objective is to form a work relationship, it is nevertheless important to get to know each new volunteer as a person. Ask (don't probe!) about family, hobbies, and interests. Share some information about yourself. Be warm and genuine, showing that you care for her or him as a person.

It is, of course, essential that you know volunteers' names. Even if you supervise dozens of volunteers and see some of them only once a month, you still must know each one by name. Consider using schedules, mnemonic devices or ID photos as aids.

Tell volunteers how you want to be addressed and ask them what they would like you to call them. Probably most volunteers will want to be on a first name basis but those who are a great deal older than you may prefer to be called by their last names. Remember that many teenagers are used to addressing adults more formally in school and what they choose to call you may help them form a productive professional relationship.

Adjust your style to the temperament, age and experience of each volunteer. They are individuals. If a volunteer has a lot of experience—maybe even more than you do—don't over-supervise. On the other hand, don't neglect the volunteer either.

Training is Key

I have already said that you should give thoughtful attention to how you help new volunteers learn the information and skills they need to be effective. It is the responsibility of your organization's coordinator of volunteers to make sure that volunteers come to you with the right qualifications and with enthusiasm and willingness to do a good job. But don't expect new volunteers to come with the specific knowledge and skills they will need in your work unit (although some volunteers may indeed already have them). That's why you need to develop ways to train and coach.

The line dividing "training" from "supervising" is rarely absolute. In fact, these activities are part of a continuum that moves from learning to maintenance. Think of training and supervision as overlapping circles, such as those shown in the illustration on the following page. See how many activities fall into the center segment, common to both responsibilities.

In the beginning, with any new volunteer or employee, you will consciously be taking the role of trainer. As time goes on, you will need to do less teaching and more coordinating and monitoring. But the circles keep turning and new learning needs will surface.

While you focus on new volunteers, don't neglect the learning needs of all your volunteers. Just as you periodically attend workshops or conferences related to your field, volunteers, too, will remain motivated and will continue to improve and grow through the training and coaching you offer. Continually assess the work environment—both things and people—to ensure that it enhances productivity. Do all these things with this end in mind: volunteers, along with your paid staff, should stay focused on the goals of your work unit as well as on the mission of the organization.

INTERRELATIONSHIP MODEL: Training/Supervision*

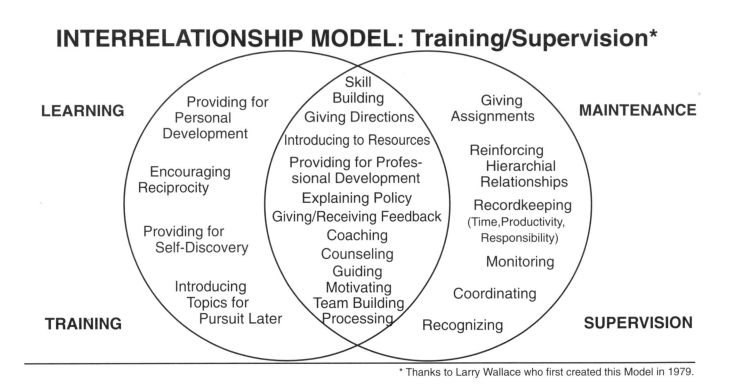

LEARNING   **MAINTENANCE**

Providing for Personal Development

Skill Building
Giving Directions
Introducing to Resources
Providing for Professional Development
Explaining Policy
Giving/Receiving Feedback
Coaching
Counseling
Guiding
Motivating
Team Building
Processing

Giving Assignments

Reinforcing Hierarchial Relationships

Recordkeeping (Time, Productivity, Responsibility)

Encouraging Reciprocity

Providing for Self-Discovery

Introducing Topics for Pursuit Later

Monitoring

Coordinating

Recognizing

TRAINING   **SUPERVISION**

* Thanks to Larry Wallace who first created this Model in 1979.

Preparing New Volunteers

Let's look first at the learning needs of new volunteers.

The training you provide for new volunteers is designed to teach them the specific information and skills they need to do their job. In order to plan this training, review the volunteer's job description and identify all the competency areas it implies. If, for example, a volunteer is serving as a receptionist, s/he will not only need to know how your telephone equipment works (a skill), but also what words s/he is to use to greet a caller (information), and what tone to use (attitude and style). Keep in mind that some volunteers will come with some or even many of the skills they need and so their training should be individualized. Linda Graff also points out:

Training is the initial opportunity to communicate policies and procedures in detail, to role play potential trouble/temptation points, and to reinforce precisely where the boundaries are on each position. Identify the consequences of breaches of policy or boundaries.

It is not hard talk about problems before they occur and in order to prevent them from occurring. You can introduce possible negatives more comfortably as you are expressing positive expectations. Volunteers will accept both as an aspect of training.

Design training sessions in an orderly fashion. Start by identifying the specific information or skill you will teach. Explain why it is important that the volunteer master the information or skill. Then use an appropriate activity to teach it. This may be discussion, role play, a skit, demonstration, practice, prob-

lem solving or a case study. Allow sufficient time for the learning exercise, especially if learning a skill is involved. One learns through practice and repetition. Give volunteers the opportunity to repeat back to you what they have learned and be sure to answer their questions. Training that is organized and well conducted builds confidence—and enhances your credibility, too. If possible, train volunteers in small groups. This is not only more efficient than one-to-one training, but each volunteer will benefit from the questions the others ask.

Janet Unger and Stephen Horton have contributed two innovative tools for reinforcing training and helping volunteers track their performance. See pages 32–3 and 34–5.

Good training takes time and effort. You would not give your car keys to your 16-year-old who has just gotten a learner's permit, and say: "Good luck, I hope you figure out how to be a good driver." You value your child—and your car—too much to do that. It is equally important to value the volunteer and the work s/he is going to do by planning training that ensures success. Training, as a subject, has many dimensions we cannot deal with here. I recommend that you consult those with professional skills in training and perhaps look at the relevant resources listed in the Bibliography at the end of this book.

Be sure that you and others in the work unit are appropriately patient with new volunteers. Nervousness as well as lack of experience may mean that it will take new volunteers a while before they are fully competent and confident. Don't be surprised if a new volunteer comes to you with the same question

Specific reasons for training are:

- It will let volunteers know why they are doing what they are doing. The agency should present a talk about their own agency's goals and objectives and should include a statement of why the volunteer partnership was established, and what the goals of the program are. Present handouts to the volunteers so that they have something to bring home to review and show to family and friends. Remember, these volunteers will be representing not only themselves, but the agency as well.

- It will give people confidence in their work and provide job satisfaction.

- It will demonstrate that the agency believes in a high standard of work.

- It will create an awareness of the safety standards and reduce potential accidents.

- It keeps the volunteer's job interesting, in that it teaches a usable skill.

- It reinforces the confidence that the volunteer program is worthwhile and that everyone can do quality work, worthwhile work and have fun at the same time.

- It provides continuity. The same method can be taught so that, if necessary, one volunteer may be able to pick up where another left off.

SOURCE

"Getting it Done with Volunteers: Recruiting, Training, Supervising and Evaluating" by Dennis Regan, in the *Proceedings* of the Symposium on Volunteers and Communication in Natural Resource Education, 1990.

during several work shifts. Most volunteers work only a few hours a week, so it will almost certainly take them a longer period to learn than it would take a new employee practicing new learning forty hours a week. While it is important that you are patient and that you answer questions, you may also urge new volunteers to write the answer down or refer to the material you gave them on their day of orientation.

Volunteer manuals are a tool that some agencies use to reinforce information. They are not a substitute for personal attention but as Trish Kerlé, Director of Cultural Programs at the Lesbian and Gay Community Services Center in New York, puts it:

If nothing else, a volunteer manual is a written document that clarifies the expectations of your organization in terms of its policies, procedures and guidelines. It also serves as a kind of surrogate for your supervision of volunteers since they can refer to their manual and, hopefully, get the answers they need to questions about the organization and its rules.

New volunteers—like new employees—will make mistakes. Good training will minimize the frequency and severity of those mistakes. But you must also carefully assess the consequences of potential errors. If these could be serious, assign a buddy (either another volunteer or an employee) to sit alongside the new volunteer as s/he begins to work. The buddy will coach, answer questions, correct, and praise. And if the volunteer is about to make a serious mistake the buddy can intervene, making it a "teachable moment."

Imagine, for example, that you supervise hospice volunteers. They have gone through an interview and have met the criteria the hospice has set for volunteers. They have completed twenty hours of classroom training and are now ready to begin visiting patients. To increase the volunteer's sense of confidence as well as to reduce the likelihood of any mistakes, arrange for each new volunteer to visit a patient with an experienced volunteer as a buddy. The experienced volunteer will serve not only as a role model but also as a coach. Encourage the two to spend time together after the visit discussing what the new volunteer observed and experienced. This could be done in a group setting with several new volunteers, along with their experienced partners, all sharing together. The next step might be to assign the new volunteer to his or her own patient, but have the same experienced volunteer go along on the first one or two visits, again engaging the new volunteer in discussion afterward.

It is a good idea for your organization to designate all new volunteers as "trainees," with the understanding that their first few weeks or months on the job are a trial period. This not only highlights that there is much to learn, but also gives everyone a comfort zone in which the volunteer can freely ask questions and all team members can observe the volunteer's work, offering feedback and suggestions for improvement.

The expectation is that the trainee will learn what s/he needs to know and then "graduate" to being a full-fledged member of the team (a great chance for recognition). However, the implication is also clear that if the volunteer seems unable to do the work—after a reasonable amount of time and a high-quality training program—s/he may be reassigned to another area in the organization or be helped to find a new place to volunteer. But consider the ethical issues here: just because you can easily ask for a volunteer trainee to be removed, this doesn't remove your obligation to provide the right environment and the right tools, especially orientation and training, that are likely to help the volunteer succeed. Volunteers are people with feelings; working with them is not like going to a shoe store and trying on one pair of shoes after another until one finds the pair with the right fit.

Continuing Education

Supervisors need to provide continuing education and support. Continuing education meets the needs of the more experienced volunteers. It provides the means for them to continue to grow intellectually, learn new information, improve their skills, prepare for more responsibility, be involved in teaching others, adapt to change, understand context and theory, and prevent burnout. No wonder it's important!

To illustrate, volunteers who work with homeless people might find it helpful to explore these topics during the course of a year:

- active listening skills

- community attitudes about homelessness

- collaborative efforts between local agencies to respond to the needs of the homeless

- the impact of AIDS on homelessness

- conflict reduction techniques with combative clients

- signs of child abuse/neglect

Think creatively about the continuing education needs of your volunteers. Ask the volunteers what their interests are. While some topics will relate mainly to your work unit, it is likely that volunteers who work in other units in your organization have many ongoing training needs similar to the volunteers you supervise. So talk with your organization's coordinator of volunteers about how you might plan in-service training together with other supervisors. Similarly, If your organization has a training department, some of the educational programs offered to employees might be attended by volunteers as well. Or, maybe the in-service programs you create for volunteers can be made available to employees, too! Suggest that your organization create an advisory committee of employees and volunteers to organize ongoing in-service training programs for everyone.

Each month at Memorial Sloan-Kettering, the Department of Volunteer Resources offered a four-hour, two-part class called "How to Be a Good Listener." An advanced course was offered periodically. Any volunteer could sign up, but enrollment was limited to ten persons. The instructor was a volunteer who was not only a licensed social worker but also a former patient. Other classes were offered on a regular basis as well. In

FROM THE FIELD

Volunteers who work fairly independently find it helpful to have access to written "Standard Operating Procedures." This is particularly important in situations such as crime victim assistance and emergency health care where procedures are critical and cannot be left to chance. Volunteers in such positions might even be asked to complete a checklist to confirm that each critical step has been followed. This discipline forces the person to examine each step in the process and, perhaps, propose how a step might be eliminated or done better. Standard operating procedures should be living documents that will change as improvements are discovered, which can be gratifying to the volunteer and beneficial to the organization and the recipients of its services.

New volunteers should be introduced to standard operating procedures during their initial group training sessions. Supervisors can also refer to them during on-the-job training. When well-written, standard operating procedures result in a minimum need for direct supervision.

Here are a few situations in which standard operating procedures are recommended:

- Flowcharts that graphically demonstrate the chain of events can be extremely valuable in planning how to execute a special event.

- A volunteer who is filing would benefit from a written guide outlining the organization's filing system.

- A volunteer who will be driving people to medical appointments will need guidelines on driving more than one person if someone has a contagious disease.

- It is helpful to post a checklist by the door indicating all the steps of closing up an office or shop when a volunteer will be the last one to leave.

On page 33 is a sample of an agency's standard operating procedures. It covers the steps volunteers must follow when answering hotline calls, during office hours and during non-office hours.

Janet Unger, President, Unger Consulting Services, Philadelphia, PA

STANDARD OPERATING PROCEDURES
for
CANCER HELPLINE VOLUNTEERS

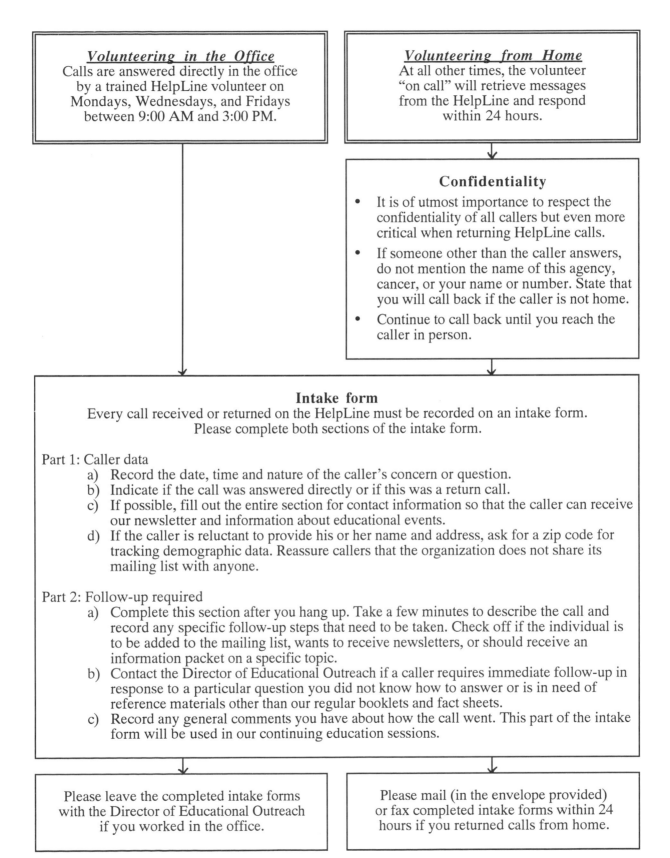

Volunteering in the Office
Calls are answered directly in the office
by a trained HelpLine volunteer on
Mondays, Wednesdays, and Fridays
between 9:00 AM and 3:00 PM.

Volunteering from Home
At all other times, the volunteer
"on call" will retrieve messages
from the HelpLine and respond
within 24 hours.

Confidentiality

• It is of utmost importance to respect the
confidentiality of all callers but even more
critical when returning HelpLine calls.

• If someone other than the caller answers,
do not mention the name of this agency,
cancer, or your name or number. State that
you will call back if the caller is not home.

• Continue to call back until you reach the
caller in person.

Intake form
Every call received or returned on the HelpLine must be recorded on an intake form.
Please complete both sections of the intake form.

Part 1: Caller data
  a) Record the date, time and nature of the caller's concern or question.
  b) Indicate if the call was answered directly or if this was a return call.
  c) If possible, fill out the entire section for contact information so that the caller can receive
     our newsletter and information about educational events.
  d) If the caller is reluctant to provide his or her name and address, ask for a zip code for
     tracking demographic data. Reassure callers that the organization does not share its
     mailing list with anyone.

Part 2: Follow-up required
  a) Complete this section after you hang up. Take a few minutes to describe the call and
     record any specific follow-up steps that need to be taken. Check off if the individual is
     to be added to the mailing list, wants to receive newsletters, or should receive an
     information packet on a specific topic.
  b) Contact the Director of Educational Outreach if a caller requires immediate follow-up in
     response to a particular question you did not know how to answer or is in need of
     reference materials other than our regular booklets and fact sheets.
  c) Record any general comments you have about how the call went. This part of the intake
     form will be used in our continuing education sessions.

Please leave the completed intake forms
with the Director of Educational Outreach
if you worked in the office.

Please mail (in the envelope provided)
or fax completed intake forms within 24
hours if you returned calls from home.

This sample of standard operating procedures was modified by Janet Unger from the protocols in use at
Living Beyond Breast Cancer which has its headquarters in Narberth, PA.

FROM THE FIELD

Supervising volunteers is easier when one starts with an attitude of success. Common problems for volunteers are feeling overwhelmed by programs, feeling guilty for not doing more and not knowing when they are successful.

Most volunteers do not have a lot of time for orientation and training, nor do they have time for long learning curves. They are also looking for a sense of accomplishment, without having been with the organization for a long time. At the same time, volunteers need to put the pieces of the nonprofit's program puzzle together one piece at a time. As managers of volunteers, we know volunteers cannot tackle learning about a whole program in one effort. We need a tool that breaks down the large picture into manageable pieces. At the Canadian Cancer Society we have devised an approach to learning called "Success Factors." [See sample on page 35.]

"Success Factors" takes each program area and divides it into four levels: beginners, learners, contributors and performers. Teams of volunteers and individual volunteers do not instantly achieve the top level. However, a volunteer can immediately know where to start and gain a sense of accomplishment by working on the first level of a program area.

The beginner level acknowledges the beginning enthusiasm of a new volunteer. This volunteer lacks the knowledge base about the organization and therefore requires leadership that gives explicit directions. The "Success Factors" are designed to be short term and quickly accomplished. So instead of managing an adult quit-smoking program, the beginner would ensure a promotion poster is faxed to appropriate organizations and doctors' offices under the supervision of the program leader. In the area of fund raising, the new volunteer would work on maintaining an existing project to attain last year's goal under the direction of the previous leader. The volunteer leader would provide specific directions, developing action plans for each step.

The learner level recognizes that the volunteer is now ready to start working with others to accomplish a program objective. The "Success Factor" is set higher or expects more teamwork from the volunteer. The volunteer leader's role is more coaching than directive, redefining goals and responsibilities and providing vision. The volunteer may ensure that all media outlets are contacted about an interview with an ex-smoker or work with another volunteer on organizing a small special event.

The contributor level appreciates the volunteer's building sense of self-motivation and ability to take on more control of programs. At this level the volunteer is encouraged to take an idea and make it work. The "Success Factor" would be to collaborate with another organization to offer a comprehensive community adult quit smoking program. The fund raising "Success Factor" would suggest some volunteer approach businesses for sponsorship. The volunteer leader's role becomes that of delegating, providing links to the larger organization and sharing information.

Volunteers who are given "Success Factors" can quickly see how each level fits into the larger picture, are able to focus on what they can do and, when ready, can move to the next level.

Stephen Horton, District Manager, Canadian Cancer Society, Prince George, BC

addition, once a year we held a free, day-long educational conference for volunteers, where participants could choose from a wide range of seminars, workshops and tours. A committee of volunteers planned and organized the entire conference.

Ongoing Support

Volunteers who are in high-risk, high-stress positions need ongoing support. Support sessions, as distinct from continuing education classes, are not formed to teach information or skills; instead, they give volunteers who do similar work the opportunity to talk about their work, especially about the feelings their work arouses. A skilled facilitator is needed to validate such feelings, help volunteers cope with a possible sense of helplessness, encourage participants to face unrealistic expectations, and bond and empathize with each other. Support groups are a powerful, effective method of reducing isolation and decreasing the likelihood of burnout, especially for volunteers in high stress assignments or whose work situations rarely allow time to process experiences as they happen. Volunteers who might especially benefit from participation in a support group include those who work with abused or neglected children, seriously ill or dying clients, people with physical or mental health problems, prisoners, victims of rape or domestic violence, and victims of accidents or trauma.

At Memorial Sloan-Kettering, the nurse manager (head nurse) and the social worker of the Critical Care Unit met bi-monthly with the twelve volunteers who

UNIT SUCCESS FACTORS

B) TOBACCO USE REDUCTION:

LEVEL 1 (BEGINNER)	RESOURCES REQUIRED
- develop a Tobacco Issues team - plan for the year's activities - develop partnership with Health Unit and Tobacco Reduction Committees - develop plan to distribute promotional and education materials - promote Smoke-Free program to schools and day cares	

LEVEL 2 (LEARNER)	RESOURCES REQUIRED
- community needs assessment - follow-up for Smoke Free and partnerships, developing action plans	

LEVEL 3 (CONTRIBUTOR)	RESOURCES REQUIRED
- lobby community governments and advocacy initiatives - liaison with Multicultural and First Nations groups	

LEVEL 4 (PEAK PERFORMERS)	RESOURCES REQUIRED
- organize adult quit smoking program (Fresh Start) - organize teen quit smoking program (PITS)	

CANADIAN CANCER SOCIETY / SOCIÉTÉ CANADIENNE DU CANCER

BRITISH COLUMBIA AND YUKON DIVISION

Northern District

District Manager:
Stephen A. Horton

FROM THE FIELD

As Training Coordinator for an HIV/AIDS hotline, I have a Head Trainer and several other Trainers under me as dictated by class size. There are also Volunteer Training Assistants who are a vital part of the training staff. Trainers are paid a small stipend and are recruited from the pool of Volunteer Training Assistants who have performed especially well. The Volunteer Training Assistants (VTAs) are sometimes volunteers who seek me out asking to take on the role, other times I recruit someone I think will do well. I prefer to have at least one VTA who is a fresh graduate of the last class. They are useful for commiserating with the new trainees about how things might be difficult or overwhelming for them, since they have very recently stood in their shoes, and expounding on the rewards of being a volunteer. All training staff are active Counselors (and often Supervisors) on the hotline as well as being training personnel.

All training staff are encouraged to monitor the progress of the trainees. Since we deal with some very sensitive subjects (sexual assault, suicide, euthanasia, etc.), we find it vital to keep track of the emotional state of trainees. After each training session, the staff stays after the trainees leave to process how the class went, were there any problems in the small groups, did we notice anyone seeming to be distracted, etc. My relationship with the training staff could be described as collaborative and supportive. The training itself is flexible. We have a solid framework for the classes, but I have the expectation that the trainers will give me constant feedback on how they think things are going and any way they could be improved upon.

If there is a problem with a volunteer in training, I consult with the training staff and we collaboratively agree on a course of action. Usually I meet with the trainee, explain the difficulty and either suggest a change of behavior, suggest they consider doing something other than counseling for us (if it's an emotional issue related to counseling), or suggest they consider doing some other kind of volunteer work with another agency that would better suit their needs.

Terry Dunn, Volunteer/Training Coordinator, Florida HIV/AIDS Hotline, Tallahassee, FL

staffed the family lounge of the unit. They updated the volunteers on clinical issues, listened to volunteers' suggestions about the needs of families, led role playing on how to handle difficult interactions with families, and simply took time to maintain relationships.

If you provide such ongoing support for volunteers, make participation mandatory (this can be specified in the "requirements" portion of the job description). Because there will still be times when a volunteer will be unable to attend, keep attendance records and follow up with those who are absent. Have an open discussion with each volunteer about the reasons s/he missed the meeting. Is it simply that the session was held at an inconvenient time or are there some issues regarding the work that the volunteer is unwilling to share in a group setting? This is a time when your knowledge of the volunteer and the quality of your relationship will be essential in determining how to proceed.

Group Meetings

If you supervise many volunteers, schedule regular meetings. Understand that some volunteers' work shifts may not coincide each time, but rotate the meeting day and hour to accommodate as many people as possible. You may have to hold more than one meeting. These face-to-face meetings can be used for three purposes:

- *To share information with volunteers:*
  Update volunteers on changes in the work unit and organization and on progress towards established goals.

- *To discuss their questions and concerns:*
  Establish a way that volunteers can let you know beforehand what they would like to discuss so that you are prepared with the information they need. Include an agenda with your meeting notice so volunteers can see how they will benefit from attending. If you build in time for socializing, do it after, not before, the meeting.

- *To collect and discuss volunteers' reports about their work:*

  If volunteers are responsible for preparing reports about their work, it is essential that the report serve a purpose the volunteer can see. Compliance with the reporting requirement must have some benefit to the organization, the volunteer personally, and/or to other volunteers. For example, hospice volunteers will probably be more inclined to complete reports on their patient visits if the content of the reports are discussed in supervisory meetings than if volunteers are told that they must write reports to meet a Medicare requirement. Besides, you

...Support needs will vary from volunteer to volunteer, even amongst those engaged on the same task and, furthermore, will change as the volunteer's needs and motivations change in the course of doing the voluntary activity. The support process is not only fluid but is constituted from many elements which may be used either singly or in combination with each other depending on the needs of the organisation and the volunteer. We can list some of these elements as being:

- Sharing work
- Giving approval
- Good communication
- Giving time
- Constructive supervision
- Relevant training
- Sensitive timing
- Facilitating groupwork
- Clarifying ideas
- Responsive to needs; both emotional and practical
- Sharing anxieties
- Maintaining objectivity
- Providing a sense of being needed
- Relieving pressure when appropriate
- Providing reassurance
- Providing opportunities for growth and development

...We can distinguish between seven broad categories of support within which the elements listed above can be offered. These are:

- **Giving Advice.** Offering somebody your opinion of what would be the best course of action based on your view of their situation.
- **Giving Information.** Providing volunteers with the information they need in a particular situation (e.g., about legal rights, the whereabouts of particular agencies, etc).
- **Direct Action.** Doing something on behalf of the volunteer and relieving pressure.
- **Training.** Helping someone to acquire knowledge and skills.
- **Systems Change.** Working to influence and improve systems which are causing difficulty for volunteers. Working on organisational development rather than with individuals.
- **Personal Support.** Helping volunteers to explore problems and alternative ways of dealing with them.
- **Facilitating mutual support.** Enabling volunteers to support each other (e.g., group support).
- **Supervisory Support.** Giving feedback on volunteer performance.

SOURCE

Managing Volunteers: A Handbook for Volunteer Organisers by The Volunteer Centre UK, 1992.

can exert a little peer pressure by actually collecting the reports in the presence of others at the meeting!

One note of caution here: make sure these meetings are of genuine value to the volunteers, not just useful to you for giving and getting information efficiently. Linda Graff notes that "a volunteer generally volunteers to do a job, not to go to meetings about doing the job." Helping you to improve the overall program may be something volunteers agree to do once in a while, but they signed on as workers, not consultants. The best way to avoid this pitfall is to involve volunteers in structuring and leading the meetings—and to cancel a meeting if there is nothing worthwhile to discuss beyond your "announcements." Send postcards or e-mails instead.

Develop an efficient system for notifying volunteers about these meetings. In addition to postal mail,

consider e-mail and phone trees. Be sure to allow plenty of notice; it's not likely that your volunteers are able to go to a meeting at the drop of the proverbial hat. If volunteers' schedules permit, consider standardizing the dates and times for your meetings for, say, the second Tuesday of each month at 8:00 p.m. Be sure to send out reminders. If you have a special reason for wanting specific volunteers to be at the meeting, personally telephone them. Be direct: "At our meeting next Wednesday for library volunteers we are going to discuss our new computer system for cataloguing books. You told me last week that you are having some trouble mastering this new system so I want to be sure that you attend this meeting. Can you be there?"

Ask volunteers to RSVP. This not only gives you an opportunity to plan but you can also follow up with individuals whom you want to attend. Be sure to have a contingency plan that enables you to get information from the meeting to volunteers who, despite your efforts, were unable to be there.

At OMNI Youth Services, where volunteers are matched with youth referred to us by the schools, police, and OMNI counseling staff, we have experienced success supervising volunteers in groups. Each of my staff of three has his or her own group of volunteers to supervise. These groups meet on the last Wednesday of each month from 7:00 P.M. to 8:30 P.M. We have kept that day and time consistent in order to make it easier for the volunteers to arrange their life and have that evening for OMNI. During the training we emphasize how important the meetings are to them, the volunteers, for support, and to the agency, for supervision. We talk a lot about the fact that this is an important part of the commitment, not just to the youth, but to the agency also.

Attendance, until approximately 6 months ago, was about 40%. At this time it has risen to about 60% because of some new strategies we are trying. In the past we did not hold the volunteers accountable in a structured system, and now they are being called immediately the next day if they did not show up and had not responded that they would not be able to attend.

During this call we reiterate the importance of the meeting, let them know they were missed (other volunteers asked about them), and tell them we will send them the business of the meeting by mail. It seems that when they are held as accountable as paid staff, and told that others asked about them and how their youth was doing, they begin to realize the importance of the meetings.

Also, if they were not at the meeting and did not hand in their monthly report (which is fairly simple to fill out), they then are asked to get that to us immediately. This report is necessary to satisfy our funding requirements regarding how many hours the volunteers spend with their youth and, of course, to let the supervisors know the same, in addition to assessing how the relationship is developing.

[If a volunteer is lax in reporting] we contact the parent once a month just in case the parent has some concerns or observations to share with us.

Lu Salisbury, Director of Volunteers, OMNI Youth Services, Buffalo Grove, IL

I supervise three groups of volunteers who meet on a monthly basis. Each group consists of five or six volunteers sharing information about the clients they visit.

Problems or concerns are discussed first among group members, and then brought to the attention of case managers if there are issues that need to be resolved. Case managers visit their clients on a quarterly basis. Volunteer Senior Companions, however, visit their clients on a weekly basis; they are often made aware of problem situations before the case manager.

One of the most difficult situations that volunteer Senior Companions encounter is the need to set limits with their clients. At one recent group supervision meeting, a volunteer mentioned that her client was low on money, and she agreed to give her $50.00. This client had already convinced the volunteer to do several things that were against program rules. I mentioned that I understood the volunteer's need to help her clients, but it was important that the volunteer learn to set limits with all her clients. When I followed up with the volunteer outside of the group, she reported that the client was accepting of the fact that the volunteer was prohibited from giving her money and no further intervention was needed. The value of group supervision is apparent when situations such as this arise.

Susan Brown, Volunteer Coordinator, Elder Home Care Services of Worcester Area, Inc., MA

Being in Charge

Regardless of all the warm, fuzzy notions of relationship building, there are times when you, as supervisor, must actually supervise! Don't be afraid to do so. It is your right and obligation to observe and monitor performance, to ask those affected by a volunteer's work for feedback, and to assure that standards are maintained. Ironically, being serious about work performance is one of the most effective forms of volunteer recognition. You send the message that volunteer contributions matter and that you assume a mutual desire to provide the best possible service. Everyone can learn and improve. As a supervisor, you intend to help all your workers do just that.

You do not have to choose between "nice" supervising and "serious" supervising. Being serious is part of being nice. It's the fact that you have built good relationships that allows you to monitor as well as support your team.

Tips on Supervising Volunteers in the Field

The supervisory relationship is more challenging if the volunteers you supervise do not work side by side with you. Examples of volunteers who work in the field are mentors, Scout and other youth group leaders, home hospice volunteers, petition drive coordinators, and AIDS buddies. Be intentional about setting up systems that effectively substitute for both the casual and structured meetings you would have if the volunteers worked on-site.

First, concentrate on maintaining your relationship with each volunteer. Know their names. Establish regular phone or e-mail contact and determine who will initiate it. If the agreement is that volunteers will phone you monthly, keep a simple checklist so that you can easily see who didn't call. Then be sure to contact the volunteer right away. The greatest mistake is simply letting the volunteer fade away. Of course, be sure that all volunteers know that they can—and should—call you anytime they have a question or concern. You will certainly need voice mail for this. Be sure to return their calls promptly.

Second, set up periodic but regular meetings with the off-site volunteers you supervise. Set the dates far in advance so that volunteers can make plans to be there. Arrange for child care if possible. The agenda should allow time for work-related discussion and also for socializing afterward (which reinforces the feeling of belonging). Create the expectation that volunteers will come prepared. Encourage them to keep a log to jot down problems or questions as they arise off site so that they can make the best use of these group meetings. You may also want to devote some of the meeting time to continuing education. Periodically invite a guest speaker, show a videotape, or give volunteers the opportunity to visit a facility that relates in some way to their work. Girl Scout leaders, for example, would certainly want to visit a new campsite that the organization has acquired.

Third, do things that remind volunteers that they are a valued part of the team. Put them on the mailing list for your organization's newsletter or develop a simple, newsy letter that you send regularly to each volunteer. It could even be sent via e-mail. Send thank you notes and birthday cards. If you hear a positive comment from a client about a volunteer, be sure to immediately pass it on to the volunteer. The point to remember is that no volunteer should feel isolated.

Chapter 4 offers additional ideas for maintaining communication with off-site volunteers, including those whose work may be done at a far distance electronically via the Internet.

FROM THE FIELD

"Share the Care" volunteers go for four hours each week to the home of someone with Alzheimer's disease so that the usual family caregiver can have a respite. Alzheimer's disease is progressive and debilitating. Volunteers who work with this client population will experience few victories in terms of seeing clients improve. The family members they become close to are in an extended grief and loss experience. To help the volunteers maintain some perspective, support their own mental health and make them more effective volunteer caregivers, Sunnyside provides extensive professional support. Regular, individual supervision by the social worker is complemented by a one-hour support group meeting/in-service training session that meets approximately every six weeks. Run by the Coordinator of Training from the Alzheimer's Association and a Sunnyside staff social worker, the support group is a place where volunteers can discuss client behaviors and diminishing capabilities. They hear how common their AD patient's experience is. They learn about the progress of current research in the field. They are encouraged, supported, educated, and inspired by one another.

Occasionally one of our volunteers is "without a client" for a brief period of time—because the client has been institutionalized, died or was otherwise removed from the venue where we provided care and support. Almost always, the volunteer, who has indicated a wish to have another client after a brief time to mourn, rest, or otherwise prepare, has continued to participate in the support group meetings. A staple of the meetings is "reporting in" when each volunteer shares, briefly or sometimes at length, about his/her activities and the well- or not-so-well-being of the client. Even when volunteers lack this major element to contribute, they find the support group stimulating, nurturing and worthwhile.

Jane Richardson, Volunteer Coordinator, Sunnyside Community Services, Sunnyside, NY

Keeping Volunteers Focused on the Goals

Why does your work unit exist? What business are you in?

Your ability to provide clear answers to these questions is critical if your volunteers are to find meaning in their work. Doing work that has personal significance is a powerful motivator. This point may be obvious, but can easily be overlooked. Its importance begins back when you develop the volunteer's job description and when the coordinator of volunteers goes through the recruitment and placement process. A clear articulation of your work unit's purpose assures that you receive volunteers who are personally interested in that purpose.

For example, volunteers who are tutoring first graders should know the goals of first grade, which might be: ensure that each child masters the first grade curriculum; help each child develop socially and emotionally, especially in relationships with his/her peers; and help each child develop good feelings about school and learning. The volunteer tutors who have these goals as a part of their job description will understand that they are not only helping children with reading or arithmetic but, perhaps even more important, are helping to create positive feelings about school and learning.

While the goals may be clear and attainable, as a supervisor you must also help volunteers see the way in which their work contributes to reaching these goals. If, for example, you are supervising the volunteer tutors above, you would want to share any observations about how the students are progressing academically (increased participation in the classroom) and socially (improved relationships with classmates). Remember how important it is for all workers, but especially for volunteers, to see the results of their work. While it will take time on your part to do this regularly, it is not wasted time. Perhaps the most significant factor that determines whether volunteers stay with your organization is knowing that they are doing something worthwhile. And, as we indicated in Chapter 1, your ability to communicate excitement about the goals of your work unit is quite contagious.

VOLUNTEER FOCUS GROUP QUOTES

"I had gotten very attached to the patient and his family and my supervisor knew that. When the patient died, my supervisor attended the funeral, even though the weather was lousy and she probably had lots of work to do. But she knew what I was going through and wanted to be there to support me. I was so touched. It kept me going.

I really like it when we have speakers at our volunteer meetings. Not only is it informative, but it also shows that the organization is really interested in my growth and development—that they want to help me be a really great volunteer.

My supervisor knows how to raise my spirits and she just intuitively knows when I need that.

Getting together with other volunteers is so helpful. We compare notes and encourage one another. I'm so glad our supervisor makes these meetings possible.

I work with AIDS patients. If I didn't have a supervisor who provides emotional support, who listens to my ideas and concerns, I'd have burned out long ago.

Develop my skills by giving me new tasks.

If I am experiencing some difficulty learning a new task, give me some time. I may not learn as fast as you do.

If you are teaching me something, stay with me until I get it right.

I need to feel valued and respected, not only for what I do but also for who I am. Nurture my enthusiasm. Don't stamp it out with too many negatives.

In this organization it's very important for volunteers to be part of a team. We don't want to be Lone Rangers.

When my sister died my supervisor sent me a card. I knew then that I wasn't just a worker whom she was obligated to supervise but that I was someone she really cared about.

Volunteers should be invited to staff meetings so they can learn, exchange ideas and offer input.

Getting a card or note when I am out sick means so much."

— *Volunteers*

In addition to identifying "what business are we in?" you should also ask: "How's business?" or "How well are we doing our work?" This question leads naturally to an assessment of individual performance as well as the performance of the team as a whole. By setting annual objectives together you empower the whole team—employees as well as volunteers—to identify ways in which they can contribute to meeting those objectives. During periodic meetings you can then discuss the progress that is being made. Use these meetings as a time to praise individuals for the work they have done that has contributed to progress on annual objectives. Meetings should be used not only as a time for working out solutions to problems, but also as a time to celebrate progress.

Also help volunteers to understand who your "customers" are. In a human services organization your customers are obviously your clients, but you might also think of clients' families as customers, too. For a zoo or museum, the customers are those who visit the facility. The customers of a library are the researchers and book borrowers. In an animal shelter, the customers are cats, dogs, and perhaps other creatures, as well as humans who come to the shelter to adopt a pet.

Your customers may also be employees or volunteers in other parts of your organization. At Memorial Sloan-Kettering, for example, the volunteers who staffed the reception desk in the Admitting Department certainly knew that their primary customers were arriving patients and families. But because the volunteers also kept the records on who had checked into the hospital each day, their customers were also hospital doctors who would periodically call or stop in the Admitting Department to learn whether their patients had arrived.

Your staff—paid and volunteer—should keep in mind that the aim of their work is the benefit of the customer, whether seen or unseen. Putting a face, human or otherwise, on the work is also a powerful motivator for excellence. Encourage everyone to reflect on what they would want if they were in the customer's place.

WRAP-UP TIPS:

Give instructions slowly and carefully. Don't try to teach too much. Spread the sessions out over a few days and, at some point, have a group session to review so that one volunteer can help another. —**Jay Weinberg**

When teaching something complicated, encourage volunteers to take notes. They will write it in a way that makes sense to them. —**Alberta Conklin**

We experienced problems getting troop leaders to show up for meetings. In order to be respectful of their busy schedules, we developed and followed a concise agenda, keeping the meeting to no more than an hour. Those who wanted to socialize could stay and do so after the meeting. —**Sheila Williams**

Keep a log of calls and meetings with volunteers and refer to [the content of] previous calls/meetings. Write down personal information volunteers tell you and refer to it later ("Did your son get into the college he applied to?"). [This] impresses volunteers and makes them feel special. —**Joel Cohen**

All paid staff pitch in and help the volunteers do their job if things get busy, dropping whatever we're working on. After all, the volunteers are serving the public and that takes precedence over whatever administrative thing we're working on. —**Terry Dunn**

It is important to think of volunteers not only as service providers but also as part-time staff. Accordingly, if we are providing more training opportunities for staff, it makes sense to do the same for volunteers. —**Bob Smith in Department of Corrections Manual, Waterbury, VT**

On-The-Spot Coaching

Help Line, a crisis and suicide hotline in New York City, operates 365 days a year. The hotline is staffed by 120 volunteers who work 12 hours a month. They receive 50 hours of training, including closely supervised time on the line. We also provide on-going education and supervision year round.

When I sense a volunteer needs support during a tough call, I will listen in on the call and, if needed, pass the volunteer a brief note of guidance and encouragement. Sometimes a volunteer will wander away from the active listening guidelines and I will pass a note to refocus the conversation or a reminder to avoid certain road-blocks. All notes have a drawing of a smile to soften any hard feelings.

When the call is over we have a debriefing which is solely for the volunteer to express his or her feelings on the call and clear any doubts or questions which might come up. Debriefing is always available for difficult and emotional calls. I never want any of our volunteers to walk away after a shift to process a disturbing call on his or her own.

I have high expectations of our volunteers, as I do for myself. Professionalism is very important for the well-being of our callers and maintenance of our service.

—*Anne R. Wild, Supervisor of Volunteers for Help Line and Cheering, Help Line Telephone Services, New York, NY*

Here are examples of the role I played in two typical calls:

Example #1

Caller:	Gail
Story:	Suicidal. Single parent. Lost her job due to downsizing. Bouts of depression. Mother cares for Gail's child.
Volunteer:	Panics for a split second. Then remembers the value of using reflection skills. Volunteer reflects hopelessness, fear, agitation, worry and Gail's desire to end her life.
Caller:	Feels understood and cared about, but is threatening to take sleeping pills.
Volunteer:	Waves at supervisor to listen in. Volunteer seems at a loss, but continues to focus on options and seriousness of suicide threat.

Supervisor's positive note: (*pictured to right*)

Hi Bill,
You are doing wonderfully. You really have identified with her feelings and she trusts you.

Volunteer:	Starts to focus on the whereabouts of the pills; reflects again the content of the problem and the harshness of death with deep compassion for the caller.
Caller:	Breaks down in loud sobs and does not speak for a minute. Caller then shares her love for her son and says she doesn't have the nerve to commit suicide. More uncontrollable crying and blowing of nose.
Volunteer:	Reflects this intense pain and anguish. Reflects the pressure of this outburst as a letting go of the anxiety and blame.

Supervisor's positive note: (*pictured to right*)

Hi Bill,
Beautiful summation and understanding of the caller's sobbing and quiet moment. You really know how to track her and be supportive. Job well done! Come see me after the call.

Caller:	Regains composure long enough to say she was offered a part time job that she didn't want but at least she could make some money while looking for another job. She thanks volunteer, says she feels better and hangs up.

Volunteer and supervisor discuss the call. Volunteer really needs to talk about his terror at first and the transition to gain control of his emotions. Much discussion, sharing and compliments for the volunteer.

Example #2

Caller: Bob

Story: Child molester. Tells the volunteer, who is very new, details about his urges to find children to molest.

Volunteer: Shocked and appalled. Despite training, not prepared for her first call to be from a child molester. Says, "You need to get help. Don't you have any guilt about what you did?" Waves supervisor to listen in.

Supervisor's negative note: *(pictured above)*

Hi Susan,

I'm hearing how upset you are. This will help. Calm yourself...and detach.... Then ask him what he is doing to prevent this from happening again. You're going to be OK.

Volunteer: Lowers her voice and says, "So the reason you called is that you are feeling powerless about these urges and you need some help and support. What have you done in the past that has helped?"

Caller: I need to get ahold of my parole officer and let him know so he can put me back in prison before I strike again.

Volunteer: So it sounds like your goal is to contact your parole officer. Is this something you can do after we hang up?

Volunteer and supervisor discuss the call during a debriefing in the supervisor's office. Supervisor asks the volunteer how she is feeling. Volunteer unloads for five minutes, grateful for the chance to vent how irate she feels. Supervisor listens actively and without judgment. Supervisor asks the volunteer how she will handle this the next time. We discuss many options and review the three parts of active listening. We also role play the call and see how voicing personal opinions drew her into the problem so that she became ineffective.

FROM THE FIELD

Volunteer sites can be microcosms of community life, providing opportunities for involvement, a place to interact with other people, a place to be known, a place to belong, a place to make a difference: in short—a community. In 1990 the Carnegie Foundation for the Advancement of Teaching published a report entitled "Campus Life: In Search of Community." The following are six Carnegie Report principles modified to apply to volunteer settings, as well as recommendations for implementing each of the six principles.

• **The Purposeful Community**

A purposeful community is one in which all volunteers, regardless of position or placement, are knowledgeable about the institution's goals and participate in the furthering of these goals. It is important that staff and the volunteer office regularly convey how volunteer contributions help the institution achieve its goals. Long-term or new volunteers can also participate in the establishment or revision of goals. A clear definition of purpose, communicated and articulated clearly, is key in any recruitment effort and should also be included in all recruitment mailings and volunteer orientation sessions.

• **The Open Community**

An open volunteer community is one in which volunteers are encouraged to express opinions, contribute ideas, express frustration and voice feedback. While anonymous suggestion boxes allow volunteers to vent frustration, they do not encourage the ownership of opinions. Volunteer forums provide an open environment where dissenting opinion is heard and valued. Establishing ground rules for criticism and feedback at such forums helps reduce their sting and ensures that "civility will be powerfully confirmed," as stated in the Carnegie Report. Guidelines such as "offer some solutions when you identify an issue" and "critique the behavior, not the person" can set boundaries without prohibiting free and constructive expression.

• **The Just Community**

The Carnegie Report defines a just community as one "where the sacredness of the person is honored and where diversity is aggressively pursued." After intake and orientation, do the unique characteristics of volunteers become obscured by the roles they play? It is important to cultivate relationships with volunteers as individuals, cognizant of the fact that each volunteer has a life outside the volunteer setting.

Volunteer administrators universally desire a more diversified volunteer pool. Perhaps the answer to diversification comes first by examining why the pool is not diverse. Institutions cannot fall victim to a common tautology: we can't recruit diverse volunteers because our volunteers aren't diverse. Underrepresented populations must be actively recruited and given active attention following recruitment in order to avoid feelings of tokenism and isolation.

• **The Disciplined Community**

It takes self-discipline to volunteer in the face of an over-committed world and to continue to do your best work throughout one's tenure as a volunteer. The onus is on volunteer administrators to be actively aware of potential pitfalls, such as burnout, which prevent volunteers from fulfilling their original commitment. Volunteer administrators must also hold volunteers to a reasonable standard of expectation which may take the form of a minimum service commitment or a minimum amount of hours pledged. All volunteers should also be held to the same standards, with reasonable allowance for individual differences.

• **The Caring Community**

Since volunteers are caring people, administrators are charged with caring for those who care. Caring may take the form of inclusion, enthusiasm, positive regard and, most of all, attention to the volunteer as a person. It may mean a call to a sick volunteer or even a minute spent at the beginning or end of the day. Introducing volunteers to each other and encouraging team meetings and events all foster caring on the part of participants and leaders. Mentoring programs in which newer volunteers learn the ropes with an established volunteer, not only build care by minimizing new volunteer jitters, but also by entrusting an experienced volunteer with the important job of mentoring.

• **The Celebrative Community**

This sixth and perhaps most important principle emphasizes the importance of rituals and tradition for building community. Volunteer training class graduations, end of the year parties, incentive programs, and award ceremonies all formally express the institution's deep gratitude for service donated by volunteers. Nominations of volunteers by other volunteers should be incorporated as part of any award decision-making process. Celebration need not be time- or money-intensive in order to remind participants that their efforts are valued by the community. A mention in a newsletter or speech, a sign in the volunteer lounge, certificates, or even verbal praise of a job well done in the presence of other volunteers or family members are all forms of celebration. National Volunteer Week can spur other institution-wide activities which should not substitute for ongoing efforts. It is critical that volunteers are thanked and celebrated often and publicly.

Most volunteers are motivated by a desire to give back to the community. However, many people live isolated lives and have no sense of belonging. The need for community—the opportunity to establish strong bonds with people and places—is truly a pressing one. By facilitating community, a volunteer administrator can maximize opportunities for individuals to grow by virtue of their association with the volunteer community in addition to the benefits derived from volunteering itself.

Maureen Crawford, Director of Volunteer Programs and Internships, New England Aquarium, Boston, MA
Source Cited: The Carnegie Foundation for the Advancement of Teaching. *Campus Life: In Search of Community.* Princeton, NJ: Princeton University Press, 1990.

4

Communicating Effectively

I have repeatedly emphasized the need to maintain good communication with volunteers. A volunteer must not feel isolated or like an irrelevant extra. When you build effective systems for communication you are building trust. The systems you build need to be two-way: you will regularly have information to share or questions to ask; and volunteers will have information for you, reports to submit, or questions and issues they want to discuss.

Maintaining good communication is likely to be challenging because many volunteers fulfill their assignments away from your worksite. Some, like Girl Scout leaders, Big Brothers, or literacy tutors work in the field where their youngsters or learners are, so you may rarely see them. Other volunteers may do their work at home and communicate via conference calls and e-mail. In fact, a whole new area of service has been invented to make use of the Internet: "virtual volunteering." The volunteers are real, but their assignments involve work that can be accomplished in cyberspace. Finally, in organizations that are national or international in scope, almost by definition local volunteers are widely scattered, both from the main office and from each other. Some volunteers may never meet their supervisors in person.

Here are various systems for communicating, many of which are newly available through the wonders of computer technology. And it's likely that, by the time this book is a few years old, even newer ways to communicate will be commonplace. As you read about each system, consider which one(s) would operate most effectively in your unit. Then work with paid staff and volunteers to set up the mechanism(s) of your choice.

Bulletin Boards

In Chapter 1, I described the bulletin board which the recreation therapists set up for the 100 or more volunteers who worked in the pediatric playroom at Memorial Sloan-Kettering Cancer Center. It was located in an area that was off-limits to patients and families and was primarily used by staff as an efficient method of sharing information with volunteers.

You may need a whole bulletin board dedicated to volunteers or a designated portion of an existing bulletin board may be sufficient. Give thought to the location. It should be in a spot that is regularly accessible to volunteers and low enough that volunteers in wheelchairs can see it. If you are posting sensitive or confidential information, that will be a factor in where you place the bulletin board. To ensure privacy, fold notes to individuals over (or seal them in an envelope) and write the recipient's name on the back. This also saves space.

The items you post can be general ones or messages to specific volunteers. Just keep in mind that there will be a time delay—from a few hours to a few weeks or longer—between the time you post something and the time all volunteers see it. If the message is important or timely you may need to telephone the volunteers or mail the item to them.

The bulletin board can also be used to facilitate communication among volunteers by encouraging them to leave messages for one another. Attach a pad and pen to the board and be sure there are plenty of push pins available. You might also want to design a message form or a special request form and keep a supply near the bulletin board. This will allow everyone to leave complete messages in a uniform manner.

If the bulletin board is used in this way by many volunteers you may want to designate sections for alphabetical groupings or for different volunteer assignment clusters. Have you ever looked at a message board at a conference and wondered if you overlooked a message left for you because the board was so cluttered and disorganized that it was virtually impossible to read each name?

Communication encompasses all human behavior that results in an exchange of meaning. How well you manage depends upon how well you communicate in this broad sense. These "Ten Commandments" are designed to help you improve your skills...of communication with superiors, subordinates, and associates.

1. Seek to clarify your ideas before communicating.

The more systematically we analyze the problem or idea to be communicated, the clearer it becomes....Good planning must consider the goals and attitudes of those who will receive the communication and those who will be affected by it.

2. Examine the true purpose of each communication.

...Identify your most important goal and then adapt your language, tone, and total approach to serve that specific objective....The sharper the focus of your message the greater its chances of success.

3. Consider the total physical and human setting whenever you communicate.

...Consider, for example, your sense of timing—i.e., the circumstances under which you make an announcement or render a decision; the physical setting—whether you communicate in private, for example, or otherwise; the social climate that pervades work relationships within the company or a department and sets the tone of its communications; custom and past practice—the degree to which your communication conforms to, or departs from, the expectations of your audience....

4. Consult with others, where appropriate, in planning communications.

...Such consultation often helps to lend additional insight and objectivity to your message. Moreover, those who have helped you plan your communication will give it their active support.

5. Be mindful, while you communicate, of the overtones as well as the basic content of your message.

Your tone of voice, your expression, your apparent receptiveness to the responses of others—all have tremendous impact on those you wish to reach....Similarly, your choice of language—particularly your awareness of the fine shades of meaning and emotion in the words you use—predetermines in large part the reactions of your listeners.

6. Take the opportunity, when it arises, to convey something of help or value to the receiver.

Consideration of the other person's interests and needs—the habit of trying to look at things from his point of view—will frequently point up opportunities to convey something of immediate benefit or long-range value to him....

7. Follow up your communication.

...This you can do by asking questions, by encouraging the receiver to express his reactions, by follow-up contacts, by subsequent review of performance. Make certain that every important communication has a "feedback" so that complete understanding and appropriate action result.

8. Communicate for tomorrow as well as today.

...[T]hey must be planned with the past in mind if they are to maintain consistency in the receiver's view, but, most important of all, they must be consistent with long-range interests and goals.

9. Be sure your actions support your communications.

...[G]ood supervisory practices—such as clear assignment of responsibility and authority, fair rewards for effort, and sound policy enforcement—serve to communicate more than all the gifts of oratory.

10. Last, but by no means least; seek not only to be understood but to understand—be a good listener.

...Listening is one of the most important, most difficult—and most neglected—skills in communication. It demands that you concentrate, not only on the explicit meanings another person is expressing, but on the implicit meanings, unspoken words, and undertones that may be far more significant. Thus we must learn to listen with the inner ear if we are to know the inner man.

SOURCE

"Ten Commandments of Good Communication" by the American Management Association, 1955.

Encourage those who post items on the board to date them so that you can more easily determine when something can be discarded. Keep the bulletin board uncluttered and consider regularly posting something humorous or thought-provoking as a way of drawing volunteers to the board.

Ideally, intra-office memos and communiqués from administration should be routed individually to all volunteers. But if this is not feasible, at least post these memos on the bulletin board. Also be sure to post the most recent monthly report from your unit and/or from the volunteer services department. After all, the volunteers contributed to what was accomplished and so deserve the chance to review the report.

You can even use a bulletin board to develop silent "discussions." Post a question at the top of a free space dedicated for this purpose. Encourage volunteers (and anyone else passing by, for that matter) to post their responses on index cards provided. They should tack their cards up in sequence, or tack them next to whichever card they want to answer, debate, or support. You could even color code "pro" and "con" cards. Over time, you will have a lively interchange spreading across the board. And at the end, you can keep the index cards as a record.

Cubbies or Mail Slots

If you have a smaller number of volunteers, you may be able to set up cubbies or mail slots for each one. Consider the size of the mail before purchasing a system so that the individual units are large enough. In the Department of Volunteer Resources at Memorial Sloan-Kettering we had two systems for our staff, which included several volunteers. Telephone messages, which were written on small message pads, went into a small holder on the secretary's desk. The location prevented the secretary from having to get up whenever she took a message. Each of us had a section in the holder. Mail and other larger items were put in stacking in-boxes; again, each of us had our own. Everyone knew that it was my expectation that the in-boxes and message slots needed to be emptied out frequently.

Incidentally, you can use mail slots or cubbies for surprise thank you items: a Hershey's Kiss®, a small gift, or a personalized note of appreciation.

Routing Systems

Custom design a routing pad for each person on your team, including each volunteer by name. Attach it to the document you want to circulate amongst the team, indicating whether everyone or just certain people should see the item. As team members finish reading it, they simply check off their name and pass it on to someone else on the list. If you want a response from any or all readers, or you want them to know the item will be discussed at an upcoming staff meeting, you can write that on the routing slip below the

names, so be sure to design a form that allows for messages like this. On the bottom of the form have a place where you can check whether you want the item returned when all have read it or whether the last person should throw it away.

It is valuable to show volunteers that you are thinking of them. If you receive a memo that relates to the work a volunteer is doing, be sure to route it to him or her as well as to the unit employees. Similarly, if you read an article in a magazine that is applicable, share a copy with the volunteers. And encourage volunteers to be on the lookout for materials the rest of the unit might find helpful, too.

Notebook or Log

You may want to keep a notebook or log on or near your desk so that volunteers can leave you notes when you are not available. You can use the same page if a reply is warranted. This is a particularly good system if volunteers routinely work when you are not there and you want them to write you a short summary of what happened during their shift. Keep in mind that this system does not allow for confidential communication and that there is the possibility that the log book will get misplaced.

The notebook system can be combined with volunteer time sheets. For example, Energize consulted with a school system trying to monitor what volunteers did each day in the classrooms. They eventually designed a form that was 8 $\frac{1}{2}$" x 11" and fit into a loose-leaf notebook. Each teacher received a notebook for his or her classroom, with a separate page for each assigned volunteer. The pages were designed in columns. The first column was for the date of service and the second column asked for in and out times. A much wider third column provided space for the volunteer to enter a brief description of the tasks completed during that shift. So the pages became a sort of diary for the volunteer—and a source of useful information for the teacher and the volunteer office. Each month the completed pages were collected and replaced with fresh pages by the coordinator of volunteers. At the bottom of the form was space for "Questions to the Teacher" and "Response." Since volunteers often left for the day while the teacher was busy with the class, this allowed for direct communication between the two of them—as long as the teacher read the logbook daily.

Suggestion Boxes

Suggestion boxes may be an effective method for getting ideas from volunteers, especially those not inclined to speak up at meetings, provided that you continually promote use of the suggestion box and have a system for reviewing and evaluating the suggestions that are submitted. This could be done by a small team of employees and volunteers. Be sure to

Even if you already publish a newsletter, it's never too late to go back to the basics. Effective newsletters begin in the planning stages, so if you never took the time to determine your newsletter's goals, objectives and key audiences, do it now...every planning decision you make directly affects your content and design, as well as your choices about printing and distribution.

Here are three steps to help you...map out an effective newsletter strategy:

1. Establish clear-cut goals for your newsletter. Your goals will guide your content, design and budget, so choose them carefully. Don't try to accomplish too much with one newsletter—aim for a maximum of two or three major goals. Any more than that and your newsletter will lack focus.

2. Determine measurable objectives. Your objectives will provide the results your newsletter should yield for your organization and the benefits your readers should receive...

3. Define your target audience. If you remember nothing else from this special report, remember this: keep your target audience in mind during every step of the newsletter production cycle. Plan your content with your audience in mind. Write with your audience in mind. Choose appropriate graphics with your audience in mind. If you're producing a newsletter to please a committee or board of directors rather than to meet the needs of your audience, you're setting your newsletter up to fail. (You're also wasting your time and money!) ...

Don't try to appeal to too many audiences. Aim for one or two key audiences, such as volunteers and donors. Although you might have many audiences with whom you need to communicate (i.e., staff, community leaders, government agencies, local businesses, religious groups, etc.), they each have very different information needs. A one-size-fits-all newsletter usually doesn't work.

Once you've tackled these planning basics, you'll be prepared to plunge into the two major elements of producing an effective newsletter—content and design.

SOURCE

"A Nuts & Bolts Guide to Non-Profit Newsletters" by Lisa Beach, Editor, *Non-Profit Nuts & Bolts*, 1998.

give public recognition to the author of any suggestion that is implemented. And if your organization has a program that pays bonuses to employees who submit successful cost-reducing proposals, ask whether volunteers are eligible for such a reward for their ideas, too.

Remember that volunteers, especially those who are new, may have a fresh perspective on organizational practices and may see things that paid staff, who have gotten used to the way things are, can no longer see. On page 103, Terry Dunn provides a fascinating example from the Florida HIV/AIDS Hotline, where volunteers' perspective on the work environment resulted in some dramatic improvements that benefitted the whole organization.

Newsletters and Memos—On Paper and Mailed

Even if your organization has a newsletter for volunteers you may want to consider developing one especially for volunteers in your unit, particularly if you have many or if they work in the field. Another option is to ask for a designated space in the organization's volunteer newsletter.

Paper memos and newsletters are usually received as one-way communication. While you may ask for a response, it is rare to hear from many readers. There are ways to improve your feedback rate, however. Try the following:

- Highlight items of special importance by boxing the text or placing a star next to them. Then *state a specific* question and give a date by which you'd like a response. So, instead of "please let me know if you have any suggestions," try "by the end of the month, tell me two things you like about this idea and two things that worry you."

- Attach a pre-addressed (and even pre-stamped) postcard or envelope to make it easy for the volunteer to jot down a reply.

- Make the last page a response form. Save your questions for the end and give volunteers the space to answer. If they don't have to hunt for paper, you increase the chances for a response. A similar idea is to provide a response column alongside the entire newsletter. Rule off about two inches on the outside margin of each page and encourage volunteers to jot down notes as they read. They can then either photocopy the entire piece and send it back to you or they can cut off the response columns and send back only these strips.

Always acknowledge the responses you received to the previous mailing, to set up a feedback *cycle*. Indicate the number of volunteers who returned the form, thank them, and summarize their opinions. Over time, the message will get through that you do indeed read the responses and take action on them. This, in turn, will stimulate more feedback.

Newsletters and Memos—Electronic Communication

Printed newsletters are a slow and expensive method of sharing news with volunteers, so consider developing an electronic edition. First ascertain how many volunteers have access to e-mail. For a while (maybe a long while), you will probably have to produce both a paper version and an online version. But even if only a few volunteers receive the electronic communication, you will save money on printing and postage. As time goes on, however, more and more people will be "wired."

The beauty of electronic newsletters goes beyond cost savings. For printed editions, it is customary either to wait until enough news accumulates to warrant the mailing or to add items of minor importance just to fill the pages. Online, you can send news when it is newsworthy. Even a short item can be communicated instantly. In fact, people prefer receiving brief, pithy e-mails more often than scrolling through a very long e-mail sent periodically.

Furthermore, because you are using e-mail to send your message, a simple "push" on the reply button allows all readers to send you a response! Use the same principles as described in the previous section for eliciting useful feedback: highlight items needing a response, ask specific questions, give a deadline, share responses received.

Meetings

In Chapter 3, we discussed why and how to hold meetings with the volunteers you supervise. These can be one-to-one or group meetings, with either all or some volunteers, depending on what you want the session to accomplish.

When planning meetings remember the key principle: never waste a volunteer's time. Plan an agenda, preferably in consultation with those who will attend the meeting, putting the most important items at the top of the list. Determine in advance how much time you want to devote to each item and allow participants to add topics important at the moment. If individuals are expected to give reports, notify them ahead of time to make sure they are prepared.

Don't use meetings exclusively to convey information to volunteers. Show your respect for their time by distributing written reports that they can read at home or during a free moment at work. If the content of this material is a subject for discussion, make sure volunteers receive the report in advance. Meetings can then be used for problem solving, for in-service education, or for reports and questions from participants. If you develop a reputation for running interesting,

FROM THE FIELD

From 1978 to 1980, I served as the first chair of Professional Development for the Association for Volunteer Administration. I was assigned a "committee" of 45 people scattered across 33 states! And we had no way of meeting face-to-face, except once a year at the AVA conference, and even then not everyone was present.

How was I going to get this "committee" to function? I hit upon a method that, over the years, I've modified and used in other distance coordinating situations. And today, the very same approach can be used through e-mail.

I initiated a bi-monthly mailing that combined disseminating information from me with gathering input from the committee members. I designed a masthead and gave the mailing a consistent look throughout the two years. In each mailing I outlined issues needing committee deliberation and tasks awaiting someone to take them on. There were three important facets to my approach:

1. I presented issues by outlining the facts and then asking for SPECIFIC responses like: "Identify three contacts who might be able to help with this." All items were numbered and in order of importance. When appropriate, I drew their attention to things with boxes, arrows, or stars.

2. I formatted the pages so that there was a "response column" next to the text throughout. So, as committee members read my questions, they could jot down their answers immediately. I even put the question numbers and the number of lines matching what I had requested.

3. The opening of every mailing was a report on their responses from the previous mailing. I told them how many people had answered and what they said. This reinforced my sincerity in wanting their replies. It gave recognition to everyone who contributed and gently reminded those who did not reply that they were missing from the discussion.

I kept a log of the responses over the two years. About five to seven people answered every time—my angels. About five people never answered (despite personal handwritten notes on later mailings) and so these people were not reappointed. The remaining 30 to 35 people averaged a response every two to three months. So, over time, I did indeed get input from just about everyone, and certainly whenever members were truly interested in a subject.

When I announced "openings" for specific assignments, I included details about the work to be done (sort of a mini-job description). Someone always came through. Once these individual committee members were assigned to their projects, I used the telephone to monitor their progress, reporting to everyone in the bi-monthly piece.

Once I taped a shiny new penny to the first page—for their thoughts. I tried to use humor, too. And I always included thank you's during National Volunteer Week.

Susan J. Ellis, President, Energize, Inc., Philadelphia, PA

FROM THE FIELD

The following are three quite different approaches to newsletters posted to CyberVPM on the same day in response to a colleague's question about newsletters.

> > We feature volunteers in our agency wide newsletter about three times a year.... January when we celebrate staff and volunteer achievements, April when we celebrate National Volunteer week, and July when we highlight the summer youth volunteers. We also do an article on the Library Foundation Board and the Friends of the Library.

I prefer to have it in a broader focus newsletter so that the staff get to see the articles, and I believe it makes the volunteers feel more connected to the organization (and vice versa). I distribute the newsletter every month to all the volunteers' work places so that they get it when they come to work, and there is no mailing expense. I send a stack to each branch rather than trying to put name labels on them. It is much easier and less time consuming....

Ann Stafford, Volunteer Services Coordinator, Austin Public Library, Austin, TX

> > When I started this job nearly three years ago, almost the first thing that I did was to start a newsletter. We have (now) 200+ volunteers scattered over the west of Scotland and most of the volunteers work in their local areas. A bi-monthly newsletter was started to keep the volunteers involved with what was happening at base. Initially it was simply two sheets of paper stapled together, now it is a 28-page newsletter available in print, large print and on tape. Volunteers help produce it, and volunteers are encouraged to write articles. The feedback from volunteers has been great,

and I consider it one of my easiest yet most successful achievements!...

Jennifer Roe, Volunteer Projects Co-ordinator, Glasgow and West of Scotland Society for the Blind, Glasgow, UK

> > We mail out a volunteer newsletter (for telephone counselors) with the monthly schedule. It includes pieces about our work, office reminders and policy updates, announcements of events, articles by volunteers (sometimes challenging policy), contact information for people who leave, and whatever else we can think of.

The newsletter is regarded as a confidential document. Trainees do not start receiving the newsletter until they are ready to start their apprenticeship, so that it's a small rite of passage for them. People on leave continue to receive it, to signify that we expect they'll return soon. It should not reach other persons at all; we ask that volunteers do not leave their copies where others might see them. (That is partly because some of the content is sensitive and partly because phone counselors' names appear, and our phone counselors are to remain anonymous.)

Several years ago, our then executive director started a more elaborate quarterly newsletter for the public. A good idea in itself, but she tried to replace the internal newsletter for volunteers with the public newsletter and a sheet of office reminders. The result was rage and anguish (and reinstitution of the newsletter for volunteers)....

Ruth S .McCreery, Board member, Tokyo English Life Line, Yokohama, Japan

Posted on CyberVPM, Summer 1998

---

productive meetings that always begin and end on time, you are likely to have fewer problems with attendance.

Minutes and Special Reports

Since it is unlikely that all volunteers will attend each meeting you plan for them, develop a simple system for summarizing the meeting and quickly send it to everyone who was absent. We have repeatedly emphasized the importance of having high expectations of volunteers and here is an opportunity for you to demonstrate them. By sending minutes or a report, you are conveying that you expect volunteers to be interested in knowing what they missed. The first time you see a volunteer who was not at the meeting, be sure to ask whether s/he received the minutes and then ask him or her an open-ended question regarding

the contents. In other words, not: "Did you read about our plans for a spaghetti dinner?" Rather: "What suggestions do you have to add to our plans for the spaghetti dinner?" If volunteers come to expect you to ask for their comments about the reports/minutes, they are likely to get in the habit of reading them.

When your meeting is for a committee or a board with leadership authority/responsibility, distributing minutes may not be enough. I recently served on a board that, within a few days of each monthly meeting, also sent everyone a document called an Action Report. It listed each action that a member of the board had agreed to take responsibility for during the last meeting, the person's name and the date by which the action was supposed to occur (vague entries like "as soon as possible" were not acceptable in this column). At the following meeting, we reviewed the Action Report and carried over onto the new one any tasks that were unfinished. This was an effective version of peer pressure: most of us would not dare come to a meeting where we would have to admit to our peers that we had not done the work we had agreed to do!

Maximum Use of the Telephone

Features such as voice mail, pre-recorded messages, teleconferencing and speed dialing make telephones a versatile medium for communication. Give thought to the situations where the telephone may be preferred over meetings or mailings. If you have to get news out quickly or make a decision quickly, phoning is ideal. Especially with volunteers in the field, the telephone is the vital link in your feedback cycle. Establish how often you need to speak and when it is most convenient for both of you. Whenever possible, encourage volunteers to save their questions for this telephone appointment. While you will be glad to help in an emergency, the idea is to avoid drowning in phone calls.

If you have more than a few volunteers assigned to your unit, consider developing a team leader position. This can either be a permanent assignment or can rotate among volunteers for a few months at a time. The team leader is the communications link. Rather than speaking with you every time, volunteers discuss their needs, give reports, etc. to the team leader who then covers all the items with you (and then, in turn, shares your responses with the volunteers). Obviously it is more efficient to deal with one or a few team leaders than trying to call every volunteer every month. However, it is a good idea for you to make personal contact with a different sampling of volunteers each month. This keeps you directly involved and demonstrates your interest. Make it clear, as well, that any volunteer can call you directly if there is a problem or concern—or to share a success story!

If you ask volunteers who work off site to report by mail, you may find yourself faced with a lot of follow up calls. An alternative is to require telephoned (or e-mailed) information. It may be useful to set up a telephone answering machine or a voice mail box specifically to receive volunteer reports. Give volunteers a "script" for leaving their message so that phoned-in information can easily be transferred to a paper form at your end. A sample:

"Hi, this is _____ and today's date is _____. I am reporting that I met with my _____ on the following dates: _____. Here are some of the things we did together:_____. The major success of the month was: _____. A problem I encountered was (or a question I have is):_____."

FROM THE FIELD

Whenever a volunteer took leadership of a project or big committee, I made one file folder for the volunteer and one for me. I put post-it notes inside both files and gave the one with my name to the volunteer and kept the one with the volunteer's name for myself.

Then I scheduled weekly meetings with the person (at the volunteer's convenience). For both the volunteer and me, the folders became the repository of questions, comments, suggestions, ideas, and contacts. Using these files kept the staff person and the volunteer from picking up the phone and calling "whenever" they had a thought about the project. We wrote our ideas on the post-it notes and saved them for the planned meeting.

I was repeatedly told by volunteers that they appreciated the weekly face-to-face and the fact that I wasn't harassing them during the week with issues that could easily wait until the regular meeting. I also appreciated someone coming with ideas to a meeting, rather than shotgunning it during the week.

In addition, this system allows both the volunteer and the staff member to be well-informed, able to field questions, and ready to prevent trouble from interfering with the progress of the project.

Nancy Macduff, President, Macduff/Bunt Associates, Walla Walla, WA

The volunteer can be trained to include a request to be called back if necessary—and when is a good time to call. To make this system work, you'll need a volunteer to transfer the messages onto paper forms or directly into a computer file.

A more personalized form of this system involves designating a special volunteer who likes the assignment of collecting and maintaining records. In this scenario, off-site volunteers are told that, within a certain range of days, the "Data Collector" (or some other creative name you dream up) will call. The Data Collector has a set of forms in front of him or her and walks the field volunteer through the questions, recording the responses. Of course, the volunteers must know in advance what information will be required. Again, as supervisor, you should call a few volunteers at random yourself each month, and the Data Collector should be trained to encourage field volunteers to call you if they have something special to discuss.

I had a stunning reminder this morning of the need to keep in touch with volunteers.

At 3 p.m. today, a coalition of ten rural communities across our state will be considered for a $44,150 anti-violence, anti-drug grant from the state. Our proposal involves 100 adult mentors and 200 teen-age peer role models who will impact more than a thousand at-risk kids in 20 neighborhoods statewide.

Since I was injured in a car accident and still have a few weeks before I am allowed to travel, I put out the word a month ago that we needed volunteers to go to today's interview. I put together handouts for the review committee, graphics for a flip chart as well as a stirring final closing to be presented by our spokesperson.

This morning I was called by a member of the four-person delegation that emerged, the 14-year-old chairman of our youth advisory council. He was all excited about going to the state capital and getting an excused absence from school. In the hearing, he will talk about his former membership in an inner-city youth gang, show off a bullet scar from a drive-by shooting, and testify how being mentored last year in our pilot project helped him turn himself around. To my surprise, I learned that his telephone call woke up one of the adult members who should have been preparing to give him a ride to the capital.

Although I thought everything was lined out, just to be sure, I checked in with the other two adults of the delegation. The first I called—who lives two hours away—was stunned and apologetic, but said that since he and I had last talked seven days ago, he and his wife had planned a large yard sale and he really couldn't leave her all day to go to the state capital tomorrow. I dug out paperwork and verified that it is today. He began rearranging his schedule and vowed he would be there—even if he was a tad late.

I am confident the hearing will go well. It convenes in an hour. But I wish I had stayed in touch a little better with these volunteers. What was important to me completely slipped one guy's mind and, without this morning's wake-up call, our spokesman would have showed up Saturday afternoon, 24 hours after the fact, puzzled that a state agency was locked up over the weekend when he was sure they were holding grant interviews.

In short, it pays to keep in touch with your volunteers.

Rob Kerby, Public Information Officer, Northwest Arkansas Economic Development District, Green Forest, AR

It may be old-fashioned, but telephone trees do work. For snow closings, special ticket availability, and other last minute or quick notice items, calling a few people who then call a few people, who then call a few more people, spreads the word quickly and with a minimum of effort on any one caller's part. The idea is to establish the tree in advance so that everyone knows his/her set of telephone numbers, how the system works, and what to do if s/he cannot reach the next person on the list. If communication is blocked close to the trunk, so to speak, the folks on the tips of the branches will never get the message! And be sure, of course, that the message is correct when it is first sent out. Remember to add new volunteers (and employees) to the tree, and to delete people who have left.

More on Cyberspace

We've already dealt with the wonders of electronic newsletters and memos. Now let's examine even more ways to tap the potential of the Internet. Cyberspace allows you to communicate to volunteers en masse quickly and cheaply. It also gives you a way to encourage volunteers to communicate among themselves and to educate themselves independently.

A more sophisticated form of newsletter is called a "listserv." It requires special set up, but then automatically handles itself. For volunteer supervision, a listserv could be developed for all volunteers in the agency or separate listservs could be created for your unit or various clusters of volunteers. The value of a listserv is that it allows everyone on the list to communicate instantly with everyone else. When someone posts a comment or query, it is automatically sent by e-mail to everyone on the list. By hitting "reply," anyone can add his or her comment and send it out to everyone. So a listserv becomes a wonderful way to share experiences among volunteers. Since people can access their e-mail whenever it is convenient, you never have an "attendance" problem. Listservs can be archived so that past discussions are stored and can be searched by key words. In this way, you have an ongoing record that newcomers can read.

If your organization maintains a Web site, there are numerous ways volunteers can be supported by it. Web sites can accommodate "private" pages accessible only by those who know the direct URL (http: address) or even by password. If your organization is willing to designate a special area for volunteers, you can use the electronic medium to provide all sorts of information, both timely and timeless. For example, you could post:
- organization policies, history, and other orientation information
- news items relevant to volunteers
- a calendar of meetings and training events
- special recognition and awards
- success stories
- changes in procedures

Remember that site visitors can always print out paper copies of any Web page, so you are allowing volunteers their choice in whether or not they want to read the material off-line.

Web site capacity (if you have a cooperative Web master) allows you to include such immediate communication options as "RSVP now for the next in-service education class," providing an electronic "form" e-mailed directly back to you.

There are all sorts of distance-learning options available. Electronically post handouts from past training sessions. Or post any type of material for volunteers who were unable to attend the last meeting. After they have read the material, include an electronic "quiz" to assess their learning—again instantly returned to you by e-mail. Explore the possibility of scheduling live "chat room" discussions. Invite small groups of volunteers to come online with you and each other to discuss (virtually) recent activities.

Electronic "bulletin boards" are very useful. These are usually arranged by subject "folders," in which volunteers can post questions and respond to one another (and you can answer questions, too). The entire "thread" of the discussion is accessible to any new visitor, so the learning is continuous. You can recruit a volunteer to be the site manager, monitoring postings for relevance and timeliness, organizing the posts into new folders if necessary, and generally stimulating interaction. This can be a "virtual" assignment, done from the volunteer's home or office computer.

As of today, the quality of audio on the Internet has improved significantly, with free downloads of programs that allow almost any computer to run sound clips. This means that you can audiotape meetings, training sessions, or even a direct message from you and make it available to all volunteers online. And wait until *video* quality meets our expectations of television! This *will* happen in the near future. Think about all the ways you can use video (taped and live transmissions) to communicate.

Finally, become skilled at using e-mail more effectively. Send brief messages and be clear about what action, if any, is needed and by when. Use the message bar to your advantage. When people receive a ton of e-mail, they scroll down their mailbox and use the message bars to prioritize what they will read. Develop a standard message bar vocabulary and encourage everyone to get into the habit of using it. For example:

- First, decide on an acronym for your organization and use it as the first item consistently. So, the Department of Human Services might become: DHS.

FROM THE FIELD

How to maintain communication with off-site volunteers? Create a volunteer liaison position.

Jeanette volunteered as a mentor for two years. During that time, she met once a week for one-to-one activities with an elementary school-age girl. When the match ended, Jeanette did not want to be matched with another girl because of the long-term commitment but wanted to stay involved with the program. After talking together about the program's needs and her time availability, Jeanette volunteered to call her volunteer colleagues on a regular basis to remind them of volunteer in-service trainings, group trips and activities and to call as needed when special activities became available (i.e., availability of donated tickets to an upcoming performance).

After volunteering in this capacity for several months, Jeanette and I realized the impact of her calls and communication. Attendance at activities increased and volunteers voiced their sense of feeling more connected even though they did not see all of the mentors on a regular basis. Jeanette and I realized the need for this, or a similar kind of, intense on-going communication. Jeanette proposed the idea of a program newsletter and served as its first editor. Jeanette has since ended her volunteer work with the mentor program. The newsletter continues to be published quarterly. And other volunteers in a similar situation of having limited time but still wanting to volunteer have filled the volunteer liaison role.

This volunteer liaison position is great because it fills a program need, creates a position for an interested volunteer, keeps active volunteers better informed and frees the volunteer administrator's time for development of trainings, activities and other responsibilities in the office. I think it works best if the liaison volunteers or grows into this position over time. The volunteer administrator must be willing to delegate this responsibility and listen to ideas the liaison returns from the other volunteers. The liaison worked so well for the mentor program that my goal is to have a volunteer liaison for each program that I am responsible for.

Teresa Gardner-Williams, CVA, Volunteer Services Coordinator, Alexandria Division of Social Services, Alexandria, VA

I find that what keeps volunteers motivated is the communication and the feeling that they are part of something bigger. What about biweekly chats on the computer where people can share their successes, frustrations, concerns and questions? If a "real-time" chat room is out of the question, you could at least set up a listserv.

I find the extra effort to keep people informed helps a lot, too. A weekly mailing, fax or e-mail message with everything from program updates to birthday wishes is usually appreciated. It also helps people do their jobs better.

Maybe assign everyone a buddy. Have the buddies call back and forth regularly.

Use a newsletter that highlights at least one aspect from everyone's area. People can read what others are doing and get ideas for their area. Include pictures of the volunteers so that people can attach names to faces.

Have contests for the "best system-wide...."

Most helpful, if you can find the money, is to bring everyone together at least once a year (more if possible). Use that time to set goals together, train people, build teams, and have fun. That last point is really key.

Posted to CyberVPM by Terrie Temkin, Ph.D., NonProfit Management Solutions, Inc., Hollywood, FL

- For general information e-mails, the message bar might say:

  DHS INFO: < subject > < date >
- If you need a response quickly, you might say:

  DHS: RESPONSE NEEDED!
- If this is information requested by the volunteer individually, say:

  DHS: Your information as requested.

This will also allow volunteers to save important e-mails in computer files matching the message bars—which means that everyone will be storing them in the same way. For committees or boards of directors using e-mail communication, this can be a very useful way to systemize files.

Of course, you can quickly become inundated with too many e-mails. One idea is to create a separate mailbox specifically for interchange with volunteers.

This will free your main mailbox for other messages and will allow you to set aside time to focus on all the volunteer-related messages in the other box. It also leads to another volunteer assignment: e-mail opener! By segregating volunteer e-mails, you can train an interested volunteer to read them, deal with standard inquiries without your involvement, and alert you to items needing your attention. Again, this could be done virtually.

Emphasis on Off-Site Volunteers

It's important to remember that communication is your primary supervision tool when volunteers work in the field, physically separate from you and often from any other volunteer, as well. As we've already noted, with distance and limited contact, it is easy to feel isolated or, worse, ignored. Only the most self-motivated volunteer will persevere endlessly without a sense of connection to the organization.

The exciting emergence of "virtual volunteering" adds a whole new dimension (and meaning) to "off-site volunteers" (see Chapter 8). While you will almost always meet field-based volunteers in person at some point—at the initial interview, in training, at a recognition event—it is quite possible that you may never meet face-to-face with someone helping you in cyberspace. So finding ways to interconnect is a vital challenge.

The business world has a comparative situation with telecommuters. Many industries have developed ways to integrate employees who work at home all or some of the time. Technology is a great aid to this process, but whether or not telecommuting is successful depends more on the ability to form interpersonal relationships despite physical distance than on modem speed.

Designated Supervisor

Whenever you are away for a conference or vacation, designate someone else on your staff to answer volunteers' questions and to share important information with them. Be sure that you properly brief your substitute and are clear about his or her authority should a serious problem arise in your absence. Ask the designated supervisor to keep notes on happenings pertaining to volunteers that you can review together when you return. Then follow up as appropriate in a timely manner.

If you are away from the office for a day or less, it is still extremely important to designate someone to answer questions that can't wait for your return. As already noted, because volunteers may only be in for a work shift once a week, missing the chance to ask a question might effectively waste that entire period.

On the other hand, many questions can wait for your return—provided the volunteer can leave you a message. Consider using special forms to facilitate this

66

I need to be well informed.

———

Keep me up to date about what's going on.

————

I especially appreciate the annual meeting for the volunteers, when the heads of all the departments come and give us an update on what's happening in their areas.

————

Meetings, newsletters and so forth demonstrate that I am part of the team.

————

Use mailings, training, notes, phone calls, meetings—whatever. Just keep me informed.

————

If you going to notify me by mail about a meeting, please send it out on time.

99

— Volunteers

type of communication and leave a pile of these on your desk or in a folder attached to your office door— with a place to put it when the volunteer has filled it out. Design the form to elicit as much information as possible so that you can act or answer without a lot of additional questions. For example, include lines for such things as: specific action requested; deadlines or due dates; contact information for whoever made the request (particularly where s/he can be reached the next day).

The communications systems you create must work effectively for you and for your volunteers. They are the bridges that maintain relationships. Without these systems you do not have a team, just a collection of individuals. Effective communication systems build trust and enhance your reputation as a caring supervisor.

ARCHIVES

Nothing frustrates a volunteer more than dealing with a poorly organized group. If you send a volunteer the wrong equipment—or the right equipment two days after a collection date—you send the message that the program is not working and the volunteer's efforts are wasted. Probably the worst sin is losing the data that volunteers braved storms, dogs and mosquitoes to collect

...Late is better than never—but not by much. Promptness in replying to volunteers' inquiries and in analyzing and reporting results demonstrates to the volunteer that someone is overseeing all the details efficiently.

...Your volunteers should know that they can turn to you for advice or troubleshooting. An [Acid Rain Monitoring (ARM) Project volunteer in Massachusetts] who was losing interest in the project because she thought acid rain was no longer a problem happened to confide her misgivings to the ARM coordinator during a routine phone call. An explanation or the importance of long-term trend monitoring was all the volunteer needed to restore her commitment.

SOURCE

"Credibility with Volunteers: How to Establish and Maintain It" by Marie-Francoise Walk and Jerry Schoen. *Volunteer Monitor*, (Volunteer Water Quality Monitoring Newsletter), Fall 1992.

WRAP-UP TIPS:

We publish a newsletter just for our off-site volunteers which is devoted exclusively to their work. It is timed to arrive between quarterly issues of the agency newsletter. Volunteers love it! —**Mary Teresa Gray**

The time [sign-in] book is located in a convenient space outside my office where the door is always open. —**Lucy McGowan**

Coaching and Encouraging Your Team

Coaching is a powerful approach to supervision. Marilyn MacKenzie describes this beautifully in her book, *Dealing with Difficult Volunteers* (1988):

> *I am increasingly committed to the notion of the volunteer manager as coach rather than supervisor. A coach is someone who can help you do something that you cannot do by yourself. The coaching relationship is one of equals. The coach sets standards, assists in the development of strategies, adjusts those strategies to accomplish the goals, but the doing is the responsibility of the volunteer. The volunteer may surpass the coach in actual skill performance or achievement, but it is the coach that has provided the guidance to allow this to happen.*
>
> *Contrast this with the concept of a supervisor. Even in the most enlightened relationship, it is the supervisor who is in charge, who is responsible and ultimately accountable for the activity. When volunteers are encouraged to take responsibility for their actions, they do act more responsibly. When volunteers believe that any failure to act on their part will be compensated for by the manager, they are less likely to act responsibly.*

Volunteers who work with a supervisor who practices coaching can count on honest feedback. They also have a powerful role model who consistently demonstrates confidence in each individual as well as the whole team. As Sarah Elliston of the United Way Resource Center in Cincinnati, Ohio notes: "A coach is one who teaches you basic skills, helps you practice them and helps you work towards your eventual excellence. The goal of a coach is to develop each player to

FROM THE FIELD

I found that paid staff feel less awkward in the role of a coach. Being a coach enlarges their perception of their relationship with a volunteer. If the paid staff person is an individual who wants to just give the work to the volunteer and walk away, seeing themselves as a coach helps remind them that they do have a responsibility to nurture the relationship. If the staffer is a controller who wants to micro-manage every step of the work being done by the volunteer, the term coach reminds them that the goal is empowerment of the volunteer to be able to do the work by themselves.

The volunteers have the same reaction to the term: a dependent person who wants to be told what to do at every step is encouraged to believe that independence is possible. At the opposite end of the spectrum where the volunteer doesn't want any guidance at all, the concept of a coach reminds the volunteer that somebody is paying attention and it is important to report in periodically.

The same holds true for all-volunteer organizations. Just substitute committee chair for paid staff person and the same results occur.

A well-managed volunteer program in any organization functions best as a group of people working together for a common goal, i.e., a team. People working with the volunteers in a supervisory capacity have the potential of developing an exceptional team when they become the coach.

Sarah Elliston, Professional Development Associate, United Way & Community Chest of Greater Cincinnati, OH

the highest ability and a team to function at its highest level."

As a coach you may also have to help volunteers learn to say "no." Some volunteers, those who are especially caring and those who are over-achievers, may be inclined to take on more tasks or work more hours than they should. Your knowledge of each individual, as well as the quality of your relationship, will aid you in determining when and how to step in. In these situations it is important that the volunteers see you as an ally or protector, someone determined to ensure that they are not abused or used by the organization or its clients. If part of your job as supervisor includes asking volunteers to give extra time, keep individual vulnerability in mind when deciding whom to call.

Coaching will also be essential in assignments that place volunteers in one-to-one situations with clients, especially in the first weeks and then again around the time when those relationships are about to come to an end. Volunteers in one-to-one assignments, for example, may need your help identifying and processing their feelings as the relationship with their assigned client ends.

Finding time for coaching is a special challenge. Because volunteers may work in your work unit just a few hours a week, you will need to be deliberate in making time for them. Another obstacle will be meeting with volunteers whose work schedules do not overlap yours. Encourage them to leave you notes with their questions. Be sure to reply promptly. Call them at home at a mutually agreed upon time.

Foster Communication

Be a good listener. You cannot form a two-way relationship without listening.

Pay attention not only to words but to the feelings—and history—behind the words. Because you need to count on volunteers listening to you, model your expectations. Use body language and facial expressions to convey your interest and affirm understanding by restating what the volunteer has said to you. Remember that all feelings are valid. Good listeners never say, "you shouldn't feel like that." Accept feelings; only correct facts.

Be trustworthy. Keep your promises. If you are unable to do something you said you would do, explain why you can't and what you are going to do next. Don't say one thing and do another. Develop a reputation for integrity. Never talk behind people's backs. Never play favorites. Be friendly—but not personal friends—with those you supervise. Demonstrate genuine interest in each volunteer's personal joys and sorrows outside your setting.

Be accessible and approachable, being careful that your mood is consistently positive and unruffled. Imagine how workers, especially volunteers, would try to avoid a supervisor who is calm and happy one day, stormy and explosive the next! While your work will inevitably have frustrations (perhaps caused by *your* supervisor!), never take your frustrations out on those you supervise. While paid staff may be forced to tolerate this, it is unlikely that volunteers would do so for long. If you have an unusually bad day (your dog died and your favorite team lost the Super Bowl and you had a dead battery when you started your car this morning) you might be in a very uncivilized mood. Let the team know. They can steer clear of you. Or perhaps they'll try to console you!

While being accessible is very important, please give careful thought to whether or not to give your home phone number to volunteers. If you do, you may be inviting more than a work/professional relationship. You may also dislike interruptions of your personal time, which may then adversely affect your attitude about volunteers.

When interacting with volunteers, use positive language. If, for example, a volunteer knocks on your door when you are about to leave for an important meeting, instead of saying, "I can't see you now," say, "I'll be back in an hour, can we meet then? How much time will you need?" Instead of "you can't use office supplies without permission," try "whenever you need office supplies, see Janet. She is in charge of distributing our supplies." The use of positive language is respectful. It empowers people by providing solutions rather than withholding them. It also creates a work environment that is responsive rather than adversarial.

Seek suggestions from your volunteers, making an effort to ask for ideas about aspects of your program that you know specific volunteers have an interest in. This will not only build your relationship by demonstrating confidence but may also result in major improvements in your program.

Praise

"Catch people doing something right," exhort Blanchard and Johnson in *The One Minute Manager*. Praising your volunteers is a critically important behavior. Praise motivates. It reinforces. It inspires. It helps people through the tough times and encourages them to do even better. It helps people feel valued and valuable, and it means their work matters.

To be most effective, praise needs to be linked to specific actions. Not, "You're a great volunteer," but, "I noticed how patient you were with the client who was so upset. You're a great asset to our department. Thank you." Not, "We really like you," but, "You are always so punctual and reliable. And you have such a positive attitude about your work. We really enjoy being around you."

Some volunteers will especially appreciate comments related to their personal strengths—that they are warm, outgoing, caring, nice to work with. Others

ARCHIVES

There are four principles in supporting volunteers:

The first is to create the **climate** which allows volunteers to ask for help. Volunteers have no monetary incentives and so will seek other rewards from their work. Paradoxically however the ability of volunteers to ask for help may be impaired by personal inhibitions. Some volunteers can feel that people who do voluntary work should do so out of the goodness of their hearts with no expectation of reward and that their sole thought should be to help others. The offer of support needs to be made in such a way that volunteers can expect it as a right and not experience guilt by asking for it.

The second principle follows on from the first and concerns **accessibility**. It is obviously pointless to make volunteers feel that support is available when it is not readily accessible to them. Support must be made available at appropriate times and places for volunteers. This means sometimes taking support to volunteers and offering it on their terms even though this may mean making further demands on the resources of the organisation. This is particularly important in terms of developing an equal opportunities approach to supporting volunteers.

The third principle is about **flexibility** and the need to accommodate the needs of individual volunteers. It may suit the organisation to plan for quite a rigid support structure but which may be quite inappropriate for some of its volunteers. Again it is a matter of taking support to the volunteer and tailoring it to that individual's requirements. Most organisations will need to take on board the culture or language needs of different groups and provide support according to those special needs.

The fourth and final principle is the question of **appropriateness**. The support given must bear some relationship to the work that volunteers are being asked to do as well as being obviously helpful to them. A balance should be maintained between the primary need of the organisation for the completion of tasks and delivery of services on the one hand and, on the other, the personal needs of the volunteer. Volunteering is not therapy although much of the activity may be therapeutic for the volunteer.

SOURCE

Managing Volunteers: A Handbook for Volunteer Organisers by The Volunteer Centre UK, 1992.

FROM THE FIELD

At Families First some volunteers—called Family Support Mentors—are matched with single moms. The mentor and mom make a one-year commitment to each other. Mentors, who must be women, help the client develop living skills, such as how to open a checking account. The mentor also empowers the client by helping her see and explore her options.

All our family support mentors are supervised by one of our licensed clinical social workers who has experience in supervising volunteers. When he matches a mentor with a mom, he either gives the mentor specific goals to work on or he may ask the mentor and the client to develop some goals together. This gives their relationship focus.

The supervisor offers tips to the volunteers on relating to our clients. He advises mentors to act like a friend, neighbor or interested cousin, not as a therapist or parent. He also sug-

gests addressing the small problems that their mentees are going through, and allow him to address the large problems....

Each volunteer keeps detailed notes of what she is doing to achieve goals, how the relationship is developing, her observations about the client, and her own feelings. These notes are turned in monthly. The supervisor then talks with the mentor, either in person or by phone, to offer suggestions or encouragement. Such accountability contributes to the progress of each case. When it is time for closure, the supervisor works with both the client and mentor to bring the relationship to a positive end for both.

Marty Atherton, Coordinator of Volunteer Services, Families First, Atlanta, GA

who are more achievement-motivated would prefer praise that acknowledges the quality of their work. Still others will consider a promotion to a position of more authority to be the kind of praise that has the most meaning. As you get to know your volunteers, aim to use the form of praise that holds the most meaning for each one.

Be deliberate in looking for behaviors to praise. This may feel unnatural at first, but it is extremely important. In fact, your paid staff members need to be caught doing something right, too. Experts on motivation say that the ratio of praise to negative feedback needs to be four to one. If you are in the habit of praising, it will not be so difficult for you—nor so difficult for the volunteer—if you have to discuss a performance problem later.

Experts on motivation also say that when a worker is brand new and just learning the information and skills needed for the job, the ratio of praise to negative feedback must be twelve to one. With new volunteers it is important to acknowledge effort, good questions, improvement in performance, a positive attitude. Your coaching of new volunteers needs to be liberally seasoned with praise so the volunteer won't give up. But be sincere!

Praise is an important part of a feedback cycle, as is evaluation. Some organizations have developed formal performance assessment programs for volunteers (see Chapter 7). If you want to evaluate volunteers in your unit, first talk to your organization's coordinator of volunteers who will have access to resources you can use. It is also likely s/he will want to work with you to develop the evaluation instrument.

Regardless of whether you conduct formal evaluations of volunteers, informal evaluation must go on continually. Consider evaluation—and all feedback—as a benefit of volunteering. See the comments made by Jill Friedman Fixler on the necessity for evaluation and feedback (page 95-6). Workers who get no feedback on their performance may assume the worst. It is also like working in a vacuum.

Some folks just seem to have the gift of discouragement. You probably know some of them. They never have a kind word for anyone and they're always spreading bad news. They whine and complain. When someone excitedly shares good news with them, they blandly—and insincerely—mutter, "that's nice." They don't readily give compliments and rarely smile. Those with the gift of discouragement don't make good supervisors of volunteers. How do you rate?

Expressing Appreciation

In the Introduction I pointed out that the dictionary defines "recognition" as acknowledging the existence, legitimacy or genuineness of something. You can practice this type of recognition in many ways: first and foremost, acknowledge that volunteers are a

---

FROM THE FIELD

The Captain Kirk Model of Supervision

For many years, I've been including a module in workshops on supervision that centers on what we can all learn from Captain James T. Kirk of the Starship Enterprise® (in the "classic" first series—actually, there's a lot to observe in the manner of Captains Picard, Sisko and Janeway, too, but Kirk started it all). Once my participants stop laughing, they acknowledge that it's possible to analyze just about any Star Trek® episode from the perspective of management style. So, if you've never watched Star Trek®, consider this a homework assignment to do so (it's still in re-runs in all U.S. markets and most of Europe, too)!

Major Lessons from Captain Kirk:

1. Star Fleet is a military model. The Captain can command all the time, if he chooses. But he rarely does so. In fact, he issues a command so rarely that, when he does, he sometimes has to add: "That was not a request, gentlemen." Kirk only uses command style in battle and other emergencies. Or when he gets mad.

2. Kirk is most comfortable with the "consulting" style of leadership. Before making a decision, he wants all the information possible. So, no matter what the situation, the first thing he does is turn to First Officer Spock and asks: "What do you think?" He respects Spock's superior scientific knowledge and his logical assessment of the facts. Then—usually for no reason apparent from the problem—he asks Dr. McCoy for his opinion. The doctor usually offers an emotional outburst with little data, but Kirk needs to see all sides of the problem. Then, he uses the intercom to ask Commander Scott what the situation is with the engines. This leads to:

3. Kirk's use of positive self-fulfilling prophecy. I have never heard Scotty say anything other than: "The engines canna take it, sir!" To which Kirk always replies: "You can do it anyway, Scotty." And, of course, he does.

4. When Kirk really wants to motivate his crew, he uses persuasion techniques. On Star Trek®, you'll always know when this is happening because the music swells up. He'll say something like: "I can't order you to let these aliens take over your bodies, but isn't this what we came into space to explore? Etc., etc." By the end of his fervent speech, the crew acquiesces—happily—to whatever he wants.

Although Kirk is not half as interesting a character as the Captains who succeeded him, he would have made a superior director of volunteers! He sets the tone of enthusiasm and wonder. He always looks for the best in his crew. He acts quickly when mistakes are made, but he is just as quick to acknowledge good performance. People want to do their best for him. We could have a worse role model.

Susan J. Ellis, President, Energize, Inc., Philadelphia, PA

real part of the people power of your organization. If at all possible, involve volunteers in your staff meetings. If space prohibits all of them attending, then develop a rotating invitation system. As stated earlier, volunteers who work in emotionally stressful areas need regular support. Such support is also a form of recognition.

Taking volunteers seriously, having high expectations, being open to their ideas, being sensitive and supportive—all these reflect volunteer recognition.

The second definition of recognition is acknowledging as worthy of praise—that is, saying thank you. It is important that you thank your volunteers both formally and informally.

Each year the President of the United States, through the Points of Light Foundation, designates one week in April (usually the third week) as National Volunteer Week. In England, they celebrate a similar week in June. The United Nations also has an International Volunteer Day, usually December 5. These are times when organizations like yours can publicly thank volunteers for all their work. If your organization does not hold formal volunteer recognition activities, then work with your coordinator of volunteers to develop one or more events to coincide with such official dates. If there are formal events, think about what you and the paid staff in your work unit can do to thank the volunteers on your team more personally. Even a small gesture, like giving each volunteer a thank you card that has been signed by each employee, means a great deal. Volunteering is a gift of time and it is simply good manners to say thank you.

Informal thanks are also important. If the weather is bad, but your volunteers made a special effort to get to the work site, be sure to thank them. If you had a big job to do and the presence of volunteers made the difference in meeting the deadline, say thank you. When volunteers return from vacation, ask about their trip and say: "We missed you." That, too, is a form of thank you.

All workers—paid and unpaid—need praise and recognition. Volunteers will especially appreciate praise and recognition, provided it is truthful and sincere, because it validates what they have chosen to do with their leisure time. It conveys that their work is important and that they are important. Good supervisors know that praise and recognition fulfill deep human needs. They consciously develop the habit of seeing and honoring the good work done by each volunteer.

Promote Teamwork

In addition to focusing on the relationship between you and each volunteer, focus on the relationship among volunteers themselves and on the relationships between volunteers and paid staff. In other words, build a team. Some work groups never see themselves as a team but only as a collection of individuals. This may be especially true when some mem-

FROM THE FIELD

KOLOA, KAUAI, HI
THE LEHN GROUP

United Way of Sacramento Area, where I recently worked, offered training programs for board members of non-profit agencies. All of our trainers were volunteers who were selected for their experience as trainers and as board members, and completed a twenty-hour training program.... After the program had been in place for a few years, three challenges emerged:

• Agency requests for services focussed on three of the eight workshop topics, placing too high a demand on some trainers, while leaving others with too little to do.

• The number of volunteer trainers grew to over twenty, placing a heavy burden on staff to maintain individual contact, while also carrying responsibility for supporting additional programs.

• Our first recognition reception for the volunteers was a flop—nobody came! We were crushed, but resolved to recognize these volunteers whether they liked it or not!

Once over the shame of our failed recognition event, we surveyed the volunteers, asking how they like to be recognized. What we learned surprised us, but it shouldn't have: their motivation for volunteering for this program was the opportunity to *learn about and to do training!* They said they would feel recognized by getting opportunities to do more of both.

We made three changes in response. First, we began scheduling periodic in-service sessions, where the trainers could come to learn a new technique, or see fellow volunteers demonstrate a training exercise they found worked particularly well. This met their desire for additional training, the staff's need for periodic supervisory updates, and eventually also became a place for informal recognition.

Next, we recognized outstanding performance by promoting volunteers to teach a second workshop topic. This met both the staff's need for additional trainers in some topics, while giving volunteers the opportunity to teach a new topic and train more often.

Finally, we established the position of lead trainer in each topic. The job description included mentoring newer trainers to ensure quality control and maintaining close contact with those in the group. The position was viewed as a promotion for long-time outstanding performers.

Implementing these measures over time solved all our identified problems: some trainers with too much work; others with too little; staff with too little time to supervise the growing number of volunteers; and our desire to provide meaningful recognition for the good work the volunteers were doing...In the end, we achieved our goal of providing high quality training to community agencies through the involvement of these outstanding, highly motivated volunteers.

Carla Lehn, CVA, Principal Consultant, The Lehn Group, Koloa, Kauai, HI

FROM THE FIELD

Each month I scan through the volunteers' time sheets to look for outstanding accomplishments or no activity recorded and attach one of my famous "love notes" to let them know I am keeping in touch. I use these as a mark of acknowledgment or an expression of praise for outstanding performance. Here are some examples.

Lucy McGowan, Lake Oswego Public Library, OR

VOLUNTEERS STICK TO IT

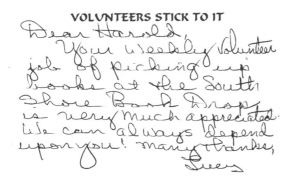

IN RECOGNITION FOR 50 HOURS OF VOLUNTEER TIME AND DEPENDABLY PERFORM-ING A REGULAR DUTY OF SATISFACTORY WORK DURING THE YEAR, YOU ARE ENTITLED TO THE PRIVILEGES AS A BONUS VOLUNTEER

Please complete attached card for com-puter records and return card to my box

(The above may be clipped and used as a book mark.)

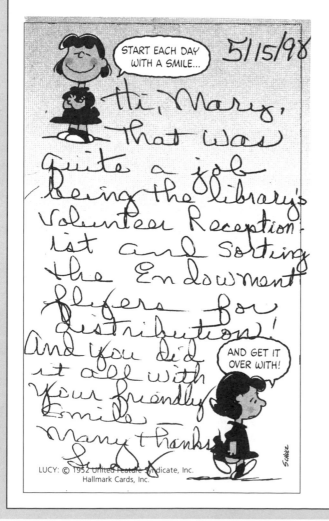

One goal during the monthly supervision call is to find out if the volunteer has any concerns or frustrations with the match relationship with the Little Brother or Sister. I basically ask how the match is going and see what they say. For example, one Big Sister was feeling frustrated with her Little's behavior because he was not listening to her. I spoke to Big Sister for a long time about establishing limits and boundaries for her LB and having realistic expectations for an eight year-old. When a volunteer is feeling frustrated, I try to find out what is the underlying concern. I have the Big look for other ways the Little is communicating that they like them (excited to see them, calling them, bragging to their friends and family about their Big). I try to clarify what the volunteer is truly feeling. I also give the volunteer examples of other Bigs who have experienced the same thing and tell them how that Big handled the situation. The key to resolving match conflicts is for the case manager to help the Big initiate communication with their Little. I have already brought a Big and Little into my office to discuss the concerns within their match relationship....

When a Big Brother or Big Sister is feeling unappreciated in their match relationship, I call up the Little Brother or Little Sister and speak to the child about sending their Big a card. I also encourage Littles to draw their Bigs a picture and especially to remember them on their birthday. For example, I had a Big who felt her Little did not like her so I had a conversation with the Little about it. Anyway, the next time the Big saw her Little the Little thanked her and told her how much she enjoyed spending time with her.

Susan Bartels, Case Manager, Big Brothers Big Sisters of Bucks County, Jamison, PA

bers of the group are employees and some are volunteers.

There are several things you can do to promote teamwork. Help each worker to understand the way in which his/her work connects to the work of others. Then it will be easier for each person to think about the consequences for others if s/he does a bad job. If a volunteer who is filing understands that misfiled records will result in significant delays for a client to see a caseworker, s/he is likely to be more careful. Of course, the caseworker needs to recognize that correctly filed records are the result of an attentive volunteer and make a point of periodically thanking the volunteer both privately and publicly.

Encourage every worker to get to know the rest of the team on a personal level. While some members may be outgoing and others reserved, it is still important to find time to acknowledge important personal milestones: birthdays, new babies, a death in the family. These personal ties will help your workers pull together when facing difficult challenges. It also helps people think "we" instead of "me."

You can also encourage teamwork by fostering an employee/volunteer relationship characterized by mutual trust, mutual respect, and mutual recognition of the expertise of each person. This begins during the orientation of new volunteers to your work unit, when you should include an introduction to paid staff. Likewise, the orientation you conduct for new paid staff should include information about volunteers: what they are doing in the work unit and why, your expectations about how volunteers are to be treated and, of course, personal introductions.

Remember the importance of sharing appropriate information with every member of the team. This conveys that you trust your workers and helps each person feel valued. Include volunteers in staff meetings if possible. If conflicting schedules or other logistical problems make this difficult, think creatively about how you can still communicate information that others learned at the meeting. Perhaps an employee who attended the meeting would prepare a written summary for the volunteers who were absent.

Solicit input from volunteers about things you can do to help them feel more included. Some of their suggestions may be for activities that you could delegate to other paid staff in your work unit.

Encourage volunteers and employees continually to look for ways in which the whole team can do a better job. Use staff meetings as an opportunity to solicit and discuss ideas. Even if the ideas are not always feasible, give thanks and recognition to those who suggested them (not disingenuously, but in appreciation of their effort to problem solve).

Foster pride in the team by frequent praise, again emphasizing "we" and giving public recognition to any special efforts the team made under difficult or unusual circumstances. In the Department of Volunteer Resources at Memorial Sloan-Kettering we spontaneously created the "Alert Award" when many years ago someone (no one can remember who now) did something to prevent a mistake that would have caused a serious problem. From then on, each of us—

...Recognition is part of the central core, an ongoing process as fundamental to managing as oxygen is to breathing. When babies are learning to walk, we don't wait until they enter the Boston Marathon before we encourage them. They pull themselves up, we squeal in delight. They fall, we pick them up, hug them, and urge them on. We call grandma. We hold them by the hand.

It should be the same for the volunteer. Any step toward the goal is worthy of praise. (Hugs are all right, too!) Keep it focused on specific behavior that is appropriate. Examples of specific recognition are:

- "A very thorough report"
- "You've developed a splendid team"
- "A creative plan for fundraising"

Look for opportunities to find your volunteers "doing something right."

SOURCE

Dealing with Difficult Volunteers by Marilyn MacKenzie, Heritage Arts Publishing, 1988.

Classic research by Torrance (1962), Torrance and Myers (1970), Mackinnon (1978), Amabile (1984), and VanGundy (1984) have led to a number of theories regarding creative problem solving. This article presents some of the major principles of their studies.

"THE ENVIRONMENT CONDUCIVE TO CREATIVITY"

The following list of...suggestions...provides recommendations to...shape an atmosphere conducive to creativity and innovation. The items...are necessary for creativity to take place, although other factors may need to be present as well.

1. Provide freedom to try new ways of performing tasks; allow and encourage individuals to achieve success in an area and in a way possible for him/her; encourage divergent approaches by providing resources and room rather than controls and limitations.

2. Build a feeling of individual control over what is to be done and how it might best be done by encouraging individuals to have choices and involving them in goal-setting and decision-making processes.

3. Provide an appropriate amount of time for the accomplishment of tasks; provide the right amount of work in a realistic time-frame.

4. Provide a non-punitive environment by communicating that you have confidence in the individuals with whom you work. Reduce concern of failure by using mistakes as positives to help individuals realize errors and meet acceptable standards and provide affirmative feedback.

5. Recognize some previously unrecognized and unused potential. Challenge individuals to solve problems and work on new tasks in new ways. Ask provocative questions.

6. Create a climate of mutual respect and acceptance among individuals so that they will share, develop, and learn cooperatively. Encourage a feeling of interpersonal trust and teamwork.

7. Listen to and laugh with individuals; a warm supportive atmosphere provides freedom and security in exploratory and developmental thinking.

8. Encourage a high quality of interpersonal relationships and be aware of factors like: a spirit of cooperation, open confrontation and resolution of conflicts and the encouragement for expression of ideas.

SOURCE

Scott G. Isaksen, The Creative Problem Solving Group, Buffalo, NY: 1998.

there were five employees and several volunteers in the department—looked for opportunities to bestow the Alert Award on one another, accompanied by applause and thanks from everyone else. (We also had a Swiss Cheese Award, which was given for a dumb mistake. It was rarely given, and usually it was the recipient who gave it to herself!) Help your workers—including your volunteers—develop effective methods for handling their conflicts. Mediate conflict when necessary.

Maintaining a Work Environment that Enhances Productivity

You will remember that we defined supervision as a relationship in which you, as the supervisor, take actions that empower those you supervise to be successful in their work. Perhaps the most important action you can take regarding the work environment is to remove obstacles to success.

Do your volunteers have adequate work space? Is the work space organized, well-ventilated and well-lighted? Do they have the supplies they will need for their work? Is the equipment they use in good working order? If making telephone calls is a major part of their work, do they have regular, uninterrupted access to instruments and outgoing lines? Is there a place they can store their work in between shifts?

What do volunteers see when they look around? Are others—especially paid staff—motivated? energetic? productive? cooperative?

If volunteers must bring personal property to your area, is there an adequate and safe space for coats, purses, and wet umbrellas? If not, you can see that a volunteer may feel like an "extra" rather than like an integral member of your team. They may also have their minds on whether their property is safe rather than on their work.

The safety of the volunteers themselves should be of concern to you. Are volunteers doing activities with a high risk of injury? Are they working in or traveling through an environment that is unsafe? Might the clients be a source of any danger? Work with your organization's risk manager to address these situations openly and honestly. You may need to provide special risk-reduction training or institute policies such as having volunteers travel in pairs.

Ask volunteers what they need to do their job well and what environmental factors might prevent them from doing their best. Ask about equipment and supplies, access to information, and the rest of the team. If you can't immediately address every issue, explain why and keep working on them. Let volunteers know what you are doing so that they see that you keep your word. If there are problems you can't solve, explain why and then explore with your volunteers methods to either get around the problem or to cope with it.

Simply stated, **retention is the art of keeping volunteers in your program**...In a practical vein, here are some practices that have been shown to improve volunteer retention:

- Ongoing training for volunteers, including college and university courses, attendance at meetings and seminars, and visits to other volunteer programs. Self-improvement is a motivation for many volunteers, and continuing education and training makes the volunteer more valuable to you. An invitation to participate in such training is also a compliment to the volunteer. (It's ideal if this is paid for by a community organization or your program, of course.)

- Procedures for explicitly crediting the volunteer for the work that was done. This means keeping complete and businesslike records that tell not only how many hours were spent volunteering but specifically what kind of activities the volunteer performed. Keep the records in such a form that the volunteer can use them as a part of a resume in future applications for paid or volunteer employment. (Many states and corporations now take volunteer services into account when they evaluate applications for jobs.)

- Procedures for documenting to volunteers the value of their work in reducing drug abuse. Beyond general praise many volunteers want to know what effect they've had on drug abuse, dropout rates, school attendance, etc. If these are given to prospective volunteers as the reasons the coalition seeks their services, they have a right to know how the effort comes out. Giving volunteers an opportunity to make suggestions in a meeting or conference when such results are discussed, may provide some valuable insights and volunteers will feel like full participants in the drug education process for which they were recruited.

- Emphasis on training staff to work with volunteers. Coordinators of other volunteer programs or staff people working with volunteers in their organizations could serve as trainers for your coalition's program. You may want to approach the local university or community college to create courses in the use of volunteers. College courses are a wonderful way to institutionalize and legitimize your volunteer program.

- For those who want it, make volunteering an upwardly mobile occupation in which volunteers can take on additional responsibilities as they become more experienced and competent. In other words, reward continued service!

SOURCE

A Practical Guide to Creating and Managing Community Coalitions for Drug Abuse Prevention by the National Association of Partners in Education, 1989.

For example, if you manage a food distribution pantry, volunteers may become frustrated if clients continually ask for items that are not available. If the clients take their disappointment or anger out on the volunteers, the volunteers may become defensive, feel guilty, or be so sympathetic that they routinely buy the missing items themselves. To remove any sense of being victimized, either research how to obtain the items being repeatedly requested by clients or help the volunteers cope. Suggest ways to speak to clients who are unhappy. Use a group supervision session to allow the volunteers to express their pain over the plight of the clients.

Volunteer Retention

One of the legitimate worries of supervisors of volunteers is high turnover. We often hear supervisors say, "I just get the volunteers trained and they leave" or "my staff hardly gets to know our new volunteers before they're gone."

The truth is that, eventually, every volunteer will leave, as will every employee, including you, dear reader. What you must do, in partnership with your organization's coordinator of volunteers, is to manage the turnover rate so that it is at an acceptable level. You cannot do anything about volunteers who leave because of an unanticipated crisis at home or because they move across the country, but you can, and should, minimize the factors affecting retention over which you do have control.

It is also useful to note that retention is an *outcome*, not an activity. In other words, while you can "supervise" as a set of tasks, you cannot "retain." Retention occurs when all the pieces are in place—it's a result of having meaningful volunteer work done by the right volunteer in a welcoming environment. Also, there is no external standard for volunteer retention. Susan Ellis defines retention as "a volunteer remains on the job for whatever time he or she originally committed during the placement process." In other words, if someone offers you the month of July, works as scheduled each day that month, then leaves, the volunteer has not "dropped off" or left unexpect-

My supervisor says "thank you" before I leave. She never forgets. That's so wonderful.

———

I like it when my supervisor passes on to me positive things he's heard about me from the client I'm working with.

———

I like it when my supervisor is specific about what he likes about my work. Hearing "You're doing a good job" somehow doesn't ring true.

———

The supervisor in my department is in the habit of sharing good words with the whole team from what he

calls "the mother ship" (the main office of this multi-site organization). We laugh—and we love it!

———

My supervisor is so good at reminding me that what I am doing is important, that my work really counts.

———

One day my supervisor said, "You do such a nice job. I know I can trust you." It was great to know she felt that way.

———

When I have doubts about my own abilities it helps when my supervisor encourages and compliments me.

My supervisor gave me a photocopy of some nice words a patient's family wrote about me after the patient died. It was so nice of her to share them.

———

If I didn't get positive comments I think I'd continually be wondering if I was doing a bad job.

———

It's so nice when my supervisor says, "I don't know what I'd do without you."

—Volunteers

---

edly. In fact, s/he was "retained" as planned. Retention is relative to each assignment and to each volunteer.

Review all the factors that may right now have a negative effect on volunteer retention. You might conduct exit interviews with volunteers, either in person or via a form. Ask them to be frank about:

- how realistic their job description was
- volunteer-paid staff relations
- working conditions
- meaning or value of the work
- degree of difficulty of the work
- quality of the training
- personal comfort level with clients
- whether they felt appreciated
- feedback they received on the quality of their work
- access to supervision

It is especially important to ask volunteers to talk about ways in which the work differed from what they expected. Maybe it's time to redesign the job description for that assignment. On the other hand, if volunteers bring unrealistic expectations, the work will be different than they imagined and they will lose motivation. The answers you get from current volunteers

can help you to explain the work more accurately to new volunteers.

Three times a month at Memorial Sloan-Kettering the Department of Volunteer Resources held a 90-minute session called an "open house," to which we invited most prospective volunteers who had called to inquire about volunteering. Part of the agenda included a presentation by two seasoned volunteers who talked not only about what they liked about working at Memorial, but also what was difficult. We asked them to be very candid. At the end of the open house we gave packets including an application form to all who attended and asked them to call for an interview if they were interested in applying. Only about fifty percent followed up. The open house gave participants the opportunity to assess whether volunteering would be different from what they expected. And those who followed up had very realistic expectations and were therefore highly motivated. Had the others become volunteers it is probable that our turnover rate would have been higher.

Volunteer retention is a consequence of doing things right. It is the outcome of an ongoing, focused relationship between those who supervise volunteers and the coordinator of volunteers who are mutually committed to creating the conditions that enable volunteers to be productive, valued and valuable members of the organization.

FROM THE FIELD

When trying to improve volunteer retention, we need to consider the culture and the times in which we live. The lives of many people are characterized by recurring crises, sit-com concentration spans and sound-bite mentalities. They may feel far more comfortable saying "yes" and staying with a task when given bite-sized (or should I say byte-sized?) assignments, trial periods for exploring the placement, and tasks which expand incrementally, not exponentially. Likewise, frequent reminders and periodic updates help sustain interest.

Of course, certain courtesies are always important. Remembering the volunteer's name and being prepared demonstrate that you value the person's involvement and recognize that the volunteer's time is as important as yours.

On the other hand, it is important to remember that burnout is in the eye of the beholder. There are a surprising number of burnout stories that emerge from under-challenging volunteers. Some persons are hunting for a truly consequential task that requires the best of their abilities and a long term commitment.

Either way, all volunteers deserve periodic check-ups that let them know that you care about what is happening and that you want to keep them from experiencing either extreme: being over-committed or under-challenged.

Sarah Jane Rehnborg, Ph.D., CVA, Director, Volunteerism and Community Engagement, Charles A. Dana Center, University of Texas at Austin, Austin, TX

WRAP-UP TIPS:

Enjoy your volunteers. Enjoy their satisfaction in their labors when the job is done. —**Eve Breeden**

Stay attuned to your volunteers' feelings. It's one thing to get the job done. It's something else to recognize how your volunteers feel about what they're doing. —**Susan Cairy**

The most important assets we have in our volunteer program are the volunteers—people. I try to keep that right in front of me always. It is very easy to hide behind my desk. I continue to remind myself to always make time for the volunteers: to talk, listen, validate feelings—because that is the most important part of my job. — **Donna Dandrilli**

The most effective off-site supervision technique I use is training experienced volunteer Buddies to serve as leaders in the program. They are in weekly contact with their team members and...handle any immediate supervisory need...I am available if situations arise that they are unable to handle. —**Alison Bernstein**

Sometimes "promoting" volunteers through a career track can be the highest form of recognition they receive. —**Carla Lehn**

When we get a letter from a client or his/her family praising a volunteer we always send a copy to the volunteer. —**Rhoda White**

Our agency sends a personal letter from the executive director to volunteers identified as having done something special. —**Mary Teresa Gray**

When a good volunteer leaves, be gracious. Express appreciation and regret (in moderation). Do nothing (including too much regret) which makes the person feel like a "defector." —**handout by Jane Mallory Park**

Inexpensive Recognition Ideas

Saying "thank you" on a regular basis to the volunteers who are part of our government in the City of Cottage Grove, OR is very important. Each month we distribute postcard-size notes that are appropriate for the time of the year. Many have a treat attached. These notes are easy to print. The masters are in black and white, four to a page. I usually print them on colored cover stock, if color printing is too costly. Volunteers are thanked in this way on a monthly basis. More personal thank you's are given individually.

I distribute these notes to the volunteers in a variety of ways, depending on the different City departments in which they work:

- Police Department: placed in their individual mail boxes or delivered personally if they are working days
- Fire Department: given to Fire Chief to deliver at their regular drill meeting
- Finance Department: personally delivered
- Public Works: given to supervisor to deliver personally
- Library: given to Librarian to deliver personally
- Committees, City Council (not a paid position in Cottage Grove), Planning Commission: given to City Liaison assigned to them to deliver personally

For School Volunteers, I meet with our school volunteer coordinators (who are also volunteers) on a monthly basis to put together the thank you's. They place them in baskets next to the volunteer sign-in book for their volunteers to pick up. The coordinators are given their thank you's at our monthly meetings.

Below is a list of possible themes for the cards along with a sample of several of the designs.

Judy Cunningham, Volunteer Coordinator, City of Cottage Grove, Cottage Grove, OR

Monthly Theme Cards (print four up on card stock)

January	Our volunteers are like a cup of hot chocolate on a snowy day (attach a packet of hot chocolate mix) There's SNOW one like our volunteers Volunteers...warm HUGS on a winter day (Hershey Hugs®)
February	Our volunteers have such warm hearts (heart shaped chocolate) You are a work of heart (heart shaped chocolate) Our volunteers make our hearts sing (heart shaped chocolate)
March	We found the pot o' gold when we found you (bag of chocolate coins) You're worth a mint to us (mint wrapped in green paper) We are real lucky to have you as a volunteer. You are a lifesaver. (Lifesavers® candy)
July	Things are really poppin' around here with your help (Tootsie Pop®) You really make thing "POP" around here! (Tootsie Pop®)
October	It's a real TREAT to have you on our team (Halloween wrapped chocolates) We wouldn't stand a GHOST of a chance without your help (Tootsie Pop® ghost) It would be real scary without you as our volunteer! (Tootsie Pop® ghost) Thank you for giving us a hand (plastic glove filled with popcorn wearing a black spider ring)
November	Our volunteers give us so many reasons to be Thankful (cornucopia made from a sugar cone filled with fall candy, e.g., candy corn, candy pumpkins, chocolate wrapped in fall colors, etc.) When we count our blessings, we always count on you (paper basket filled with fall candy) As we count our blessings, we always begin with you (paper basket filled with fall candy)
December	We cane't do it without you (candy cane) Our volunteers are heaven sent (angels made with Hershey Kisses®) Our volunteers are heaven scent (packet of potpourri, scented candle, etc.)

General Cards　No clowning around...we would be NUTS without you! (packet of peanuts)
We are NUTS over you! (packet of peanuts)
We are on a ROLL with your help! (Tootsie® rolls)
You make us smile! Thank you for being our volunteer. (Snickers® bar)
We are all smiles with you as our volunteer. (Snickers® bar)
We would go to PIECES without you. (Reese's Pieces®)
Here's a HUG for you! (Hershey Hugs®)
Here's a KISS for you! (Hershey Kisses®)
A KISS for our volunteers (Hershey Kisses®)
Take as needed: red for patience, blue for relaxation, orange for energy to continue volunteering, green for blocking flying arrows, yellow for smiling in the face of adversity, brown for attending another meeting (prescription envelope filled with M & M's®)
Thanks a-latte! (certificate for a cup of latté)
You are a real LIFESAVER (roll of Lifesavers®)
Our volunteers are out of this world (Milky Way® bar)
Our volunteers make a world of difference (Milky Way® bar)
Things are much brighter with you around (Starburst® candy)
Pep pills (jelly beans in prescription envelope)
Our volunteers are noteworthy (notepad)
Our volunteers are like a symphony (Symphony® bar)
Roses are red, violets are blue, we are successful because of you. (Red roses made from Hershey Kisses®)

6
Solving Performance Problems

Your organization may be held liable if the volunteer makes a mistake that causes harm. This alone should give you reason to be certain that the job is clearly defined, that volunteers are well-trained and that performance problems are addressed promptly and professionally. Moreover, you will lose the respect of other volunteers and employees if you don't deal with volunteers' performance problems.

But the best reason for handling performance problems is that it reflects your respect for volunteers—the importance of their work, their sincere desire to do good work. Poor performers can affect the morale of the whole team. As a supervisor, your ability to handle problems in a sensitive and caring manner is very important, not only to the volunteer who is making mistakes but to the whole team. It's an expectation they have of you.

Diagnose Why Problems Occur

The story is told of a woman who, on a very hot summer day was delivering a rare penguin to a zoo. She was driving a specially equipped van. Unfortunately, the van broke down several miles from the zoo. Being an extremely conscientious person, the woman flagged down a passing motorist and said to the driver, "Quick, take this penguin to the zoo!"

Hours later when the van was fixed, the woman drove to the zoo just to make sure the penguin was OK. No penguin had been delivered! The woman, enraged by the irresponsible man, frantically drove all over town looking for him. Eventually she spotted him walking down the sidewalk with the penguin right behind.

"What are you doing?" she demanded. "I told you to take the penguin to the zoo!"

"I did," the man replied, "and we had a wonderful time. Now we're on our way to a movie."

The moral of the story is that not all performance problems are the fault of the performer. Look at the diagram on the next page, "Analyzing Performance Problems." This may help you assess what you need to do to prevent further occurrences of unsatisfactory performance. Has the volunteer received good training? Is this his or her first day at work? Are there special circumstances—a recent death in the family, for example—that might be causing a normally capable volunteer to make mistakes?

If, after a fair and objective assessment, you conclude that there is a performance problem that is worth addressing, then do so promptly. Remember that failing to deal with a performance problem is itself a performance problem. As hard as it may be, as a supervisor you have the responsibility to talk with your volunteers about errors in their work.

It will be easier for you to offer constructive criticism if:

- you have maintained a good relationship with each volunteer

- you have been generous—and honest—with your praise (remember the four to one rule)

- during orientation and training you discussed what you will do if a volunteer makes errors; and

- your motive is to correct, not to punish.

Humility helps, too. Keep in mind that you have also made your share of mistakes and will continue to do so—and that we tend to judge ourselves by our intentions and others by their actions.

ANALYZING PERFORMANCE PROBLEMS:
WHAT IS INFLUENCING UNSATISFACTORY PERFORMANCE?

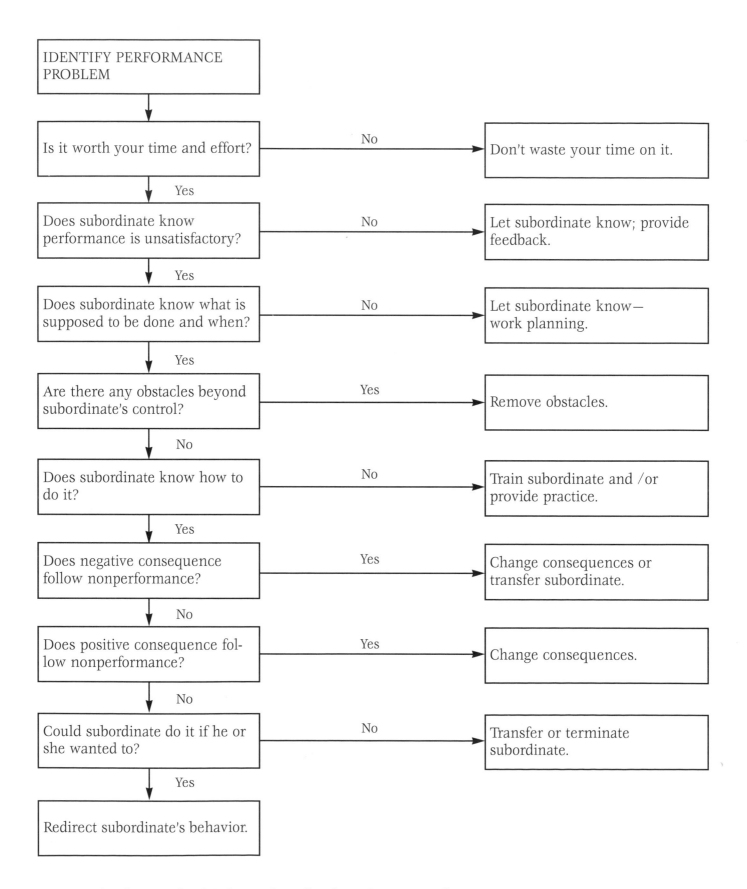

Source: *Coaching for Improved Work Performance* by Ferdinand Fournies, McGraw-Hill, 1988.

I have a Russian volunteer who is in the process of learning to speak English. He was matched with a woman that he visited once a week for several hours. In our monthly supervision meetings, he mentioned that he was vacuuming for his client, a home-making task that volunteers are not allowed to do. He also mentioned that he drove this particular client in his car, another "no, no." When I attempted to communicate with him, it became obvious that he didn't understand my meaning. Grabbing a sheet of paper (my creative skills are minimal), I drew a man pushing a vacuum cleaner, with a big X over the picture. I also drew a very crude picture of a car with the same X. A grin crossed his face, as he indicated that he understood. We had, indeed discovered a universal language.

Susan Brown, Volunteer Coordinator, Elder Home Care Services of Worcester Area, Inc., Worcester, MA

Performance problems are likely to be one of four types:

1. Quality of work
The quality of the work being done by the volunteer does not meet stated expectations. This may include things like submitting incomplete reports, answering the phone inappropriately, giving out inaccurate information, interacting with clients aggressively or with indifference.

2. Quantity of work
The quantity of work being done by the volunteer does not meet stated expectations. This may include things like delivering fewer flower arrangements to hospitalized patients than is typically expected within a given shift or not assembling the required number of meals for homebound clients.

3. Timeliness
The problem is not with quality or quantity but with adhering to schedules or deadlines. This may include things like coming to work late or turning in a report after the deadline.

4. Rate of Improvement
You expect new volunteers to take some time to master their work, especially if it is complex. Nevertheless, you do expect improvement from week to week. If you sense that a volunteer is taking an excessively long time to develop competency, you have a rate of improvement problem.

As a volunteer myself, I was helping a performing arts organization to involve its corps of volunteers more effectively. For the annual mass mailing to all ticket subscribers, I dutifully rounded up about fifteen volunteers who normally filled other assignments but were more than willing to spend a few hours on this necessary group project. I made sure that the General Manager and the volunteers were settled in before leaving for a previously-scheduled appointment.

That evening, the General Manager telephoned me and angrily announced: "Those volunteers did the mailing all wrong! They messed up all the zip codes and everything is lumped together—we can't send out a bulk mailing that way."

I then asked a pertinent question: "Did you TELL them to put the pieces into zip code order?" He responded indignantly: "Well, EVERYONE knows to do that!"

At which point I said: "Oh, you're right. These people gave up about six hours of their time doing this volunteer work and then—after putting everything into the order you wanted—decided to throw the envelopes into the air, mess them all up, and put them out of order just to annoy you."

The General Manager paused and asked: "You mean they DIDN'T know to put them in zip code order?"

Bingo! And, to make matters worse, I then discovered that he had left the volunteers on their own about twenty minutes after I had departed—and did not return until after they had gone home. So, in this "teachable moment," I helped the General Manager learn:

1. The importance of giving good instructions (especially for a very concrete, specific task) cannot be overemphasized!

2. Do not assume knowledge. It is possible to include simple details in an explanation of tasks without "talking down" to anyone.

3. Develop written checklists for projects that occur regularly, but with time in between during which people can forget procedures.

4. If you have scheduled a one-time activity during which volunteers must finish a project, don't leave! Or, if you have to go out, designate someone else on site to be accessible to the volunteers! And to approve the work and say thank you before they leave.

Susan J. Ellis, President, Energize, Inc., Philadelphia, PA

1. **Try to handle problems promptly.** Problems won't disappear if you just ignore them. In fact, they are likely to get worse. Don't "store up' problems, but deal with them as they occur.

2. **Don't try to confront difficult situations when you're so upset that you're not rational.** (Could this be you—not rational?) You need to be at your best—calm, under control, and ready to listen to the response of the volunteer. You want to be as open and honest as possible. If you're very upset, you'll be defensive and perhaps accusatory. It's better to rehearse what you want to say. I find writing down the key points helps me focus and clarify my concerns.

3. **Serious reprimands should be carried out in a one-to-one setting.** The Japanese are right about "saving face." You may feel it important to have a second person there to imply that this action has the blessing of a higher authority (your supervisor, the agency's president, or a senior volunteer) but the interview should be conducted by only one of you, with an observer. You may want to indicate that you have checked this action out with the appropriate authority, if they are not present. "I have talked to Mrs. Smith about this yesterday and she agrees that...."

4. **Describe what you have observed.** Evaluate or interpret as little as possible. I find it helpful to have the example of the problem behavior that I have observed recorded, with the date as the basis of my concern. If I can't confirm a behavior that is reported to me by a third party, I usually will not act on it....

5. **Use the job description to identify expected behaviors.** Sometimes it is important to separate the individual from the function or position in order to make a fair decision. Is the person able or willing to do the job as assigned?...

6. **Indicate a shared commitment to finding a solution to problems.** The volunteer should not hear: "This is your problem. What are you going to do about it?", but rather should hear: "How can we work together to lessen or eliminate this problem?" or "How can we develop a plan for dealing with this issue?"

7. **Arrange for follow-up.** This is part of the coaching assessment and recognition activities that are so important in assuring that problem behavior doesn't recur and that solutions are being worked on. Set a specific date in the near future not more than three weeks. Put it on your calendar right then. Do the follow-up. Have the volunteer come to your office or talk on the phone. Review the plans and the progress. Remember to look for movement towards the goal, not perfection.

SOURCE

Dealing with Difficult Volunteers by Marilyn MacKenzie, Heritage Arts Publishing, 1988.

Dealing with the Problem

In each situation just outlined, there is a defined expectation—a standard—for how the work is done. A performance problem is simply a gap between what is expected and what is happening. So you need to talk with the volunteer in order to identify the reasons for the gap. This is best done privately when you and the volunteer have adequate time. It is also very important that you remain supportive and concerned. If the volunteer's mistake has really angered you, either wait until you are calmer or ask someone else to talk with the volunteer.

When you talk about performance problems it is important to select the right words, express your feelings calmly but clearly, and ask pertinent questions. Some of the suggestions below are based on a process for communication outlined in *Personal Power* by Arlene Labella and Joy Dolores Leach (1985).

Begin by stating clearly what the mistake was: "I noticed this morning that you told a few callers that the Monet exhibit opens on March 21, when actually it opens on March 2." Or, "The last three weeks you have arrived at or after 9:45, although your shift in the children's playroom begins at 9:00."

Limit your words to a description of what you (and/or others) heard or saw. Avoid making comments about the volunteer's motives, emotions or feelings. For example, referring to the sentence above, don't say: "The last three weeks you have arrived at or after 9:45, although your shift in the children's playroom begins at 9:00. I guess you feel you can come and go as you please."

Then state the impact the behavior or mistake has on you and/or others. You certainly can express your feelings, but be calm and measured in what you say. Don't blame the volunteer for the feelings you have. No one can make you feel the way you do. For example, you might say: "When you are late the rest of the team has to pitch in and do your work. I end up feeling rushed and frustrated."

Here are some . . . tips on talking to volunteers about a problem:

- Hold your discussion immediately after you have observed his or her performance (in a meeting or at an activity) or as soon as you are informed of a problem; for example, by a parent or member. Don't delay with difficult situations; they get worse when they are ignored.

- Before sharing your comments, ask the volunteer to evaluate his or her own performance and how he or she feels about it (self-observation).

- Begin by focusing on strong points—the things you both agree were done well.

- Explore the problem together: The first step in changing behavior is accepting that a problem exists. Share with the volunteer your negative observations or the complaints you have received; e.g., "Here's what seems to be happening." Begin by asking for his or her views on the situation. Remember, sometimes there is more to the story than what you or others can observe.

- Give examples of how you or other volunteers have handled similar situations in a more effective way.

- Agree on what steps will be taken and when you will check on progress.

- Always end on a positive note, thanking the volunteer and urging him or her to call whenever help is needed.

When you're considering firing a volunteer, ask yourself these questions:

- Was the volunteer informed of specific examples of unsatisfactory performance in the past and given the opportunity to improve with the understanding that lack of improvement would result in release?

- Based on the volunteer's level of experience, should he or she have known better, or is this a typical "new volunteer" mistake?

- Was the appropriate behavior or procedure explained to the volunteer during training?

- Is this a one-time occurrence or a recurring pattern of behavior?

- If based on a complaint, was the complaint investigated? Was it substantiated by more than one person?

SOURCE

"YMCA Teen Leadership Programs" by Mary B. Zoller, 1992, in *The Seven Rs of Volunteer Development* by Celeste J. Wroblewski, YMCA of the USA, 1994.

Next explore with the volunteer the reasons for the gap. Do this by asking open-ended questions. Confer, don't interrogate. Listen patiently and calmly. Be quick to listen, slow to speak. Remember that the purpose for discussing performance problems is to prevent them from recurring, not to punish or make the volunteer feel bad. By discussing the reasons together, you are in a position to decide together what the remedy is. Consider what you concluded when you applied the "Analyzing Performance Problems" chart to this situation. Perhaps additional training is in order; perhaps certain facts need to be put in writing so that the volunteer does not need to trust his or her memory.

After you have conferred about the reasons for the gap, specify what behavior you want to see or what action the volunteer needs to take. Be specific. Also be sure that what you are asking for is realistic. Suggest only actions or behaviors that the volunteer is likely to accomplish relatively quickly or easily. Asking for enormous changes all at once is setting the volunteer up to fail. For example, you might say: "I'd like you to be on time in the future but, for a start, let's aim for 9:15. Can you do that?"

Once you have agreed on the area of improvement, state both the positive and negative consequences of future actions. "If you are on time, you will have the opportunity to get the playroom ready for the day and greet the children as they arrive. If you continue to be late I will wonder about your commitment to the children and to our team and I may have to ask you to resign."

If the volunteer is defensive or angry, stay calm. You can validate feelings, but you also need to stay focused on the facts. It may also help to ask the volunteer, "How important is it to you that we resolve this matter?" The volunteer's response may offer insight as to how you will proceed.

Also be sure to let the volunteer know that you will want to meet with him or her once or even a few times in the future so that you can together confirm that the problem has been solved or that there has been improvement. If there has been improvement, be sure to say so. Remember to catch people doing something right.

If, on the other hand, you and the volunteer decide that s/he is in the wrong position, that s/he does not have the aptitude to learn the information

Sometimes you need to distinguish between the upset customer with a legitimate problem and the chronic complainer who consumes your time with unreasonable demands.

First, determine if you're dealing with a *chronic* complainer. *How to tell:*

- Chronic complainers gripe about the way others speak and act toward them and about anything else they happen to think of.
- They blame everything on someone else and don't think what they can do to correct the situation.
- They often fail to discuss their problems with the right people. Instead, they grumble to those who can do little about their complaints.

To deal with chronic complainers:

- Don't hesitate to politely interrupt them. Empathize, but don't take sides. Rephrase what they say to show you understand. "I realize you're upset because you're dissatisfied with our efforts to correct the problem."
- Realize that chronic complainers usually exaggerate problems and are masters of the sweeping generalization. To deal with that, try to get them to face the facts. "You said you tried to see her all day. How many times did you try?"

- Don't apologize if you're on the receiving end of the complaint. Complainers don't think about solving the problem. They seek to blame someone. Try questions such as "Would giving you a replacement solve your problem?"
- Try to force complainers to solve the problem. One [good] way to do this is to limit the time you'll spend dealing with the complaint. "I have to leave in fifteen minutes. Can we get this solved by then?"
- Walk away if all else fails.

If you *aren't* dealing with chronic complainers—and they have legitimate complaints, you should:

- Listen to them and take them seriously.
- Compensate them or make restitution.
- Communicate a sense of urgency; handle their problems quickly.
- Avoid further inconvenience for them.
- Treat them with respect.
- Make sure that the person responsible learns that a problem occurred.
- Assure them that the problem will not reoccur.

SOURCE

Adapted from "37 Quick & Easy Tips You Can Use to Keep Your Customers" and "The Guide to Customer Service" by *Communication Briefings*, in AVA *Update*, Sept./Oct. 1994.

---

and/or skills required, you then need to explore with your organization's coordinator of volunteers whether there are other assignment options within the organization for the volunteer.

Show respect by never discussing issues pertaining to a volunteer's performance problems with your other volunteers or with your paid staff, for that matter, unless you are seeking their input or corroboration of your observations.

In this chapter you will find several brief "Archive" articles that may also help you develop a style of talking about performance problems that doesn't cause the volunteer to feel personally attacked and keeps the conversation focused on the problem, not the person. I encourage you to study the principles offered and then develop an approach with which you are comfortable. This may necessitate change on your part! Try to look objectively at how you have handled performance problems in the past and how you felt before and during the discussion. You may want to review this with a colleague. If your tendency, for example, is to blame others for your feelings, you will

need to work on changing that. Or if you tend to beat around the proverbial bush so that the volunteer cannot clearly grasp what you want to say, practice being direct. It may even help to role play with a colleague or family member.

It is also important that your feelings—like your words—be neutral. There will inevitably be some volunteers that you don't like as much as others. Can you try to be objective in evaluating their performance, or do you find yourself picking on them? Or perhaps you are less supportive and professional when you do discuss problems with them. You will also need to be honest with yourself about how you deal with volunteers who happen to be friends or relatives. You may be inclined—perhaps without even knowing it—to look the other way when they make mistakes. See if you can recall situations from your own work history in which someone was known to be the boss' pet—or the boss' scapegoat. How did you feel? How did others feel? Your reputation and your credibility as a supervisor rests, in part, on your fairness.

Q. Why do volunteers burn out? What are the common causes?

A. People volunteer for complex reasons, and many of those reasons are tied to their emotions. People who volunteer are particularly connected to the mission of the organization. Also, [some] people who volunteer don't have a lot of training in the particular field they're working in. So their attitudes, values and expectations of what they will get out of this work are very idealistic and often unrealistic.

And when you have people who are connected to the mission without a clear sense of realistic expectations, you have people who are very prone to burning out..

The common causes of burnout are lack of reward, too much work, not meeting expectations, lack of training, inadequate supervision and direction, lack of funds to accomplish goals, too many difficult tasks....

Q. Are there any signs to warn you that a volunteer is in danger of burning out?

A. Anything you see that's a real shift in the original way the volunteer came to you is important to look for.

Listening is the first step toward understanding, reducing and preventing burnout. It's very important you ask people how they're feeling about their work, how the work is affecting them emotionally. You should ask that all the time and develop ongoing training or group sessions to get that information....

Q. After volunteers burn out, what's next?

A. Coming to some understanding of what is happening to them is vital. Ask what were the values and attitudes that brought them to this point. What were some of the aspects of the volunteer job that led them to be disillusioned? Talk about their frustrations, their expectations. Tell the volunteer that he or she is a very important and valuable person who's behaving in a negative way.

Then you can negotiate. You may grant a brief leave of absence, telling the volunteer that you value and want him or her and encouraging him or her to come back.

You may decide to monitor the volunteer's performance for a period of time. Agree that if the volunteer is still having problems, he or she can change volunteer assignments. If the volunteer's behavior is very destructive, then that volunteer may not be cut out for the work....

SOURCE

"How to Prevent Volunteer Burnout" by Martha Bramhall, interviewed by Donna Hill, *Voluntary Action Leadership* Winter 1985.

Warning and Documenting

If the problem you are addressing has occurred many times before, you may want to talk with your organization's coordinator of volunteers before speaking with the volunteer. The coordinator of volunteers may want to be present (some organizations have a policy that two staff persons must be present when serious problems are discussed with volunteers). This would also be the appropriate method if you know or suspect the problem is due to declining health. You may also want to confer with the coordinator of volunteers if the volunteer is/was mentally ill, has been a volunteer with your organization for a very long time, has little or no support system at home, or has strong personal ties to those in high leadership positions in your organization. The coordinator of volunteers has probably dealt with these problems before and may want to be involved with you in determining a course of action.

On page 78 you will find the corrective strategies of the Courage Center in Minneapolis. Note that the supervisor has the responsibility—and unilateral authority—to re-supervise, re-train and accommodate. Decisions to revitalize, reassign, refer and retire are made with the coordinator of volunteers.

You also need to know your organization's policies regarding documenting performance problems and warning volunteers if problems are serious enough that they may result in removal from the position or termination from the organization. You and your organization's coordinator of volunteers must be clear with one another regarding both the extent and the limits of your authority.

Your organization may also have a policy that volunteers can be suspended for a serious offense while the matter is being investigated and while discussions with the volunteer and others are taking place. If your organization does not have policies delineating supervisory responsibility/authority, and policies on documentation, warning, suspension and termination, I encourage you to work with the coordinator of volunteers and with other supervisors to develop them.

CORRECTIVE STRATEGIES

SUPERVISOR OF VOLUNTEERS:

Re-supervise

Clarify your role in relationship to the volunteer, that your commitment is to the organization and that organizational policy must be followed. Mission, values and goals may be helpful tools.

Re-train

Some people take longer than others to learn; some require a different training approach than a traditional one (video, one-to-one mentoring, hands on)

Accommodate

We are all individuals with different needs, perhaps there is an accommodation that would make a volunteer successful.

WITH COORDINATOR OF VOLUNTEERS:

Re-vitalize

If a long-time volunteer's performance is unsatisfactory, perhaps they need a rest or a change of pace.

Re-assign

Try the volunteer in a new setting. Their skills and interests may have been incorrectly assessed or there may be a personality conflict in the current environment.

Refer

The volunteer may need to be referred to an entirely different agency that is a better fit with their skills, interests or style.

Retire

A volunteer may simply no longer be able to do the work and, in fact, may be a danger to him/herself or others. It may be time to suggest retirement, giving them the opportunity to depart with dignity.

Staff training handout, adapted from original material on page 52 of *101 Ideas for Volunteer Programs* by Steve McCurley and Sue Vineyard, Heritage Arts Publishing, 1986. Reprinted with permission of authors. *Developed and submitted by Lisa Taylor, Director, Volunteer Services, Courage Center, Minneapolis, MN*

It is also important that your organization have a grievance policy for volunteers so that they can have an objective, fair hearing if they feel there are issues affecting them that you as a supervisor have not properly or satisfactorily addressed. This, too, is a matter to discuss with your organization's coordinator of volunteers.

At the end of this chapter there are several "discussion starter" stories, some of which were contributed anonymously. I encourage you to read them, not only for the insight they will provide, but also for encouragement: you will see that others have successfully handled performance problems, some of them quite serious. You can, too!

Burnout and Performance Problems

Christina Maslach and Michael P. Leiter, the authors of *The Truth About Burnout: How Organizations Cause Personal Stress and What to Do about It*, state:

> *Burnout is the index of the dislocation between what people are and what they have to do. It represents an erosion in values, dignity, spirit, and will—an erosion of the human soul. It is a malady that spreads gradually and continuously over time, putting people into a downward spiral from which it's hard to recover.*

Thus, burnout may be a cause of performance problems. While burnout is usually the result of long term exposure to emotionally difficult work, burnout may also be the result of an unacceptable gap between a volunteer's expectations—sometimes unconscious—and reality. A person may have offered to volunteer in a nursing home with the expectation that s/he would somehow be able to cheer people up. The reality the volunteer experiences, however, is that residents don't even appreciate what s/he is doing; in fact, they may take their frustrations out on the volunteer!

Supervisors need to be sensitive to the signs of burnout. Here are a few examples:
- headaches
- insomnia
- fatigue
- mood swings
- easily discouraged
- loss of meaning
- apathy
- forgetfulness
- negative attitude
- confusion
- isolation
- resentment
- lashing out

FROM THE FIELD

My work involves inviting and training members of this 4,200 family church to volunteer in various outreach programs. Sometimes volunteers develop a zeal in their service to others and they overextend their energy and commitment to a particular program or effort. I pay close attention to the hours my folks devote to certain projects. I encourage volunteers to keep in contact and always to share with me their concerns, joys and struggles. If I sense that someone is burning out, I step in. We discuss how it may be time to move into another program or to step back and reflect about their service experience over a relaxed period of time. I remind them of the passages from Ecclesiastes, Chapter 3 that teach that there is a time for everything, a time for beginning and ending, a time for change. This provides comfort and assurance that letting go is OK.

Burnout rarely happens in our volunteer programs because, as policy, I encourage a rotation of leadership responsibilities. When this does not happen I pay closer attention to the particular situation and the respective volunteer(s). I also urge the leaders to work with co-chairs or co-captains in each outreach program so that there are no "Lone Rangers." When volunteers are isolated they are more likely to burn out.

Joseph H. Soncrant, Christian Service Coordinator, St. Andrew Catholic Church, Rochester, MI

Volunteers who are burned out need to be encouraged—perhaps even mandated—to take a leave of absence or switch to a "behind the scenes" position for a while. If you supervise volunteers whose work may subject them to burnout, discuss with your organization's coordinator of volunteers what policies and practices you need to put in place to protect your volunteers. For example, volunteers who worked in the pediatric playroom at Memorial Sloan-Kettering were not routinely allowed to work more than twice a week nor were they allowed to maintain contact with a child or his family outside of the hospital setting. We were concerned not only about burnout but about over involvement, too. Again, if you devise policies aimed at preventing these kinds of problems, they are less likely to occur.

While I was Director of Special Services (the volunteer program) of the Philadelphia Family Court in the early 1970s, I accepted a college Sophomore into the program for a two-day a week, one semester assignment. He was bright and enthusiastic, and looked like every other college student we had at the time. This meant a bit disheveled, in casual clothes. The semester started out fine, but within a few weeks we all noticed a problem: body odor. Strong body odor.

When three different volunteers complained to me about the smell, and when his supervisor professed great dismay at broaching the subject, I girded my loins and scheduled a conversation with him. (Note that today I would probably have counseled his direct supervisor to try first.)

Now it helped that I really liked this young man and that he had much to offer in his assignment. So, I took a deep breath (through my mouth) and said: "This is as embarrassing for me as for you, but I want to help you make this placement work. So I have to ask if you are aware that you have body odor?" He was visibly dismayed, but also sheepish. It turned out that he was living in an apartment with about six other guys and hygiene wasn't high on their list of priorities. He sometimes skipped bathing and really hadn't thought much about going to the laundry room.

As we spoke, I realized that, although he was blushing and uncomfortable, he was also grateful to me for taking the time to talk with him. He had noticed that people were treating him distantly (literally and figuratively) and very much wanted the chance to do better.

On his next shift, he arrived in a suit! We had never seen him so well groomed! Everyone piled on the compliments. He assured us that he wouldn't "dress up" every day, but wanted to show us that he could. He remained a volunteer for several months beyond his original commitment.

So this turned out to be a story with a happy ending. I might have offended him beyond saving. But I had an obligation to his co-workers who were affected by his habits—and to him. My direct approach conveyed the message that I wanted him to stay, but we had to correct the problem.

Susan J. Ellis, President, Energize, Inc., Philadelphia, PA

The Need for Attention

Does it surprise you that workers sometimes deliberately—although perhaps unconsciously—make mistakes in order to get your attention? If you suspect a volunteer is doing that, then you need to assess whether you have been giving this person an appropriate amount of attention, particularly praise for good work and credit for good ideas. If the need for attention is insatiable or unreasonable, assess whether you can discuss that with the volunteer. Validate feelings while at the same time being clear about what you can reasonably provide. If the volunteer is lonely but otherwise does good work, can you—or the organization's coordinator of volunteers—find other volunteers s/he can socialize with during lunch or after hours? Or perhaps there are resources in the community that would help.

Some problems are not incident-related but affect overall performance and so must be addressed. Concerns about declining health, mental or emotional stress, hygiene problems, or sudden, unexpected changes in behavior or ability are clearly issues that require attention, whether by you or the coordinator of volunteers. For the safety of the volunteer, clients and staff, do not allow this type of situation to fester. Ideally, the volunteer will be relieved when you discuss your concerns openly; s/he may have felt deficient and not known how to approach you about it. In some cases, especially if the volunteer is resistant to your observations, you might need to involve a volunteer's family or physician.

Conflicts over Personal Style

Much as we might wish that only nice people volunteer, the fact is that some volunteers (who are, of course, people) have all the worst traits that one can see in humankind. Some are bossy, rude, arrogant, lazy, untruthful, and selfish. Ideally, your organization's interviewing and screening processes should spot these traits and help these applicants find another, more appropriate organization. However, despite you best efforts, you may occasionally have to deal with difficult volunteers.

Difficulties may also arise from changes—temporary or permanent—in a volunteer's circumstances. The unexpected loss of a job is likely to have an impact on a volunteer's attitudes and behaviors, as would situations like a family crisis, legal problems, financial problems, personal illness or illness in the family.

While the approach for dealing with conflicts over personal style is similar to the approach for dealing with performance problems, it is complicated by three factors: your feelings; the volunteer's feelings; and the inability of all of us to make radical, overnight changes in our personality. So if you want to confront a volunteer who is doing a good job but is, let's say, a very negative person, you will have to deal with these three factors and possibly others.

FROM THE FIELD

Here is a supervision question posted on the CyberVPM listserv along with the helpful responses of three other listserv subscribers. While the specifics involve volunteers online in virtual assignments, the situation—and strategies proposed—are completely applicable to dealing with any volunteer who does not follow through on commitments.

> > *Question:* I am encountering a problem that I hope others who have faced this can advise on. I work with about twenty online volunteers at any given time. They are, for the most part, fabulous—they get the task done, they do the task well, they often do more than I have even asked for, and they provide me with terrific insight on ways to improve Virtual Volunteering.

But there always seem to be about three or four that, after they've filled out the online application, gone through the orientation/evaluation process, agreed to all the commitments for volunteering and been given an assignment, come back two weeks later with the most heart-wrenching stories of tragedies as the reason they can't complete a task. At this time they let me know that these circumstances actually preceded their signing up to volunteer, but they didn't think it would be a problem.

After I give them sincere sympathy and a break, and then give their assignment to someone else to complete, I often hear from them in a month or two wanting another assignment. When I give them another assignment, almost without fail, a tragic circumstance interferes with their attempts to complete this one as well.

It's obvious that they take on more than they can handle, despite my systems that are supposed to screen out such people. And matching people to assignments is time-consuming! How do I say "no" to someone who, in my opinion, cannot take on an assignment, without hurting that person's feeling? I tried saying no, and tried to gently and honestly explain the reasons why, and now I have two people very upset with me....

Jayne Cravens, Manager, Virtual Volunteering Project, Impact Online/ University of Texas at Austin

> > *Response #1:* Consider setting a policy that in order to get another assignment the volunteer must complete one assignment successfully. If someone fails to complete an assignment for whatever reason they must wait six months to one year for another chance. An alternative is that they could serve as a team member on another project in the meantime (if teams are an option).

I don't think we hurt the feelings of others as much as they hurt their own feelings. I do not take responsibility for others' feelings in these matters. Reasonable people would not have a problem with your decisions as you describe them. People are always going to be mad about something and you "can't please all the people all the time," etc.

Jerome Scriptunas, Board President, Big Brothers Big Sisters of Monmouth County, Inc., Eatontown, NJ

> > *Response #2:* Take into consideration those volunteers who have completed their project—and then have to turn around to finish someone else's project! I'd far and away rather have a non-productive volunteer upset with me than one of my "faithful few" who do everything I ask (and then some!). If you keep saying "yes" to the non-productive ones and then have to ask someone else to finish, are you not sending a negative message to the productive volunteers?

Cindy Petty, Director of Planning & Marketing, Gibson General Hospital, Princeton, IN

> > *Response #3:* Having a policy, preferably up-front, is the easiest way to go—then folks don't think you are singling them out or picking on them. Something like a "three strikes, you're out" concept. If they are forewarned, then they cannot come back and plead ignorance.

I have recently set up a policy for clients who stand up their volunteer drivers: if they stand up a driver then they are responsible for their own transportation for thirty days. This illustrates to them that there are not a lot of daytime volunteers to spare (and to send on futile wild goose chases).

When you are training your volunteers, consider doing some boundary setting exercises with some strong "I messages" such as "When you leave me hanging on an online project, it causes the project to fall behind." Be honest with them and let them know the challenges their behavior gives the program and see if they want to work with you to make a more realistic workload. It goes back to the concept that, if you treat volunteers as professionals, they have to behave professionally. Could they get away with that at their workplace?

Wendy Lavine, Director of Volunteer Services, Triad Health Project, Greensboro, NC

In 1990 the Monterey Bay Aquarium established the Volunteer Emeritus status in order to recognize retiring volunteers for long, faithful and distinguished service to the aquarium.

To qualify, a candidate must have given 1,000 hours or five years of service. Candidates are nominated by their supervisor, who may be a volunteer or a paid staff member. The application form asks the nominator to document examples of distinguished service and/or special contributions. Applications are reviewed by a committee that consists of myself, a member of the Interpreter Program Department and three volunteers, who serve on the committee for a one year term. While there is no limit to the number of persons who can receive Volunteer Emeritus status in a given year, the understanding is that this is to be a small, select group of people. The number so honored each year has ranged from one to ten. New recipients of the Volunteer Emeritus status are given a special name badge, a photo identification card and an aquarium pass for themselves and one other person. They are honored in an appropriate way by paid staff and other volunteers on their shift.

Our volunteer manual stipulates that volunteer retirement may occur under two circumstances: volunteer-initiated or staff-initiated. Staff initiated retirement occurs when the volunteer is no longer able to perform the duties outlined in his or her job description; or when the circumstances are such that the volunteer causes hardship or strain on other members of the team (paid staff or volunteers) or to visitors.

Most retirements that are staff-initiated are accompanied by a nomination to the Volunteer Emeritus status, as the vast majority of our older volunteers have truly served the aquarium with distinction. By having the Volunteer Emeritus status the end of a long, meaningful affiliation is, for both the recipient volunteer and the aquarium, positive and pleasant rather than painful.

Ruth M. Buell, Manager of Volunteer Resources, Monterey Bay Aquarium, Monterey, CA

Before you even speak with the volunteer, reflect on your own feelings. Why is the behavior upsetting you? It might be helpful to discuss this with a trusted friend or colleague. Total candor is necessary. Perhaps the offensive behavior links the volunteer with someone in your past whom you disliked, so those feelings are surfacing. The volunteer may only be the trigger for a flood of unpleasant memories. Or you may discover you have strong views on, say, laziness, due to your own upbringing. If so, even a hint of laziness may rile you. Check your feelings out through a confidential discussion with a colleague who also works with the volunteer. This will help you assess whether you are being objective. Through honest explorations of your feelings you may conclude that the volunteer's behavior is really not that bothersome.

Second, consider the volunteer's feelings. It is said that hurting people hurt people. Arrogant behavior may be a cover-up for deep insecurities. Laziness may cover up lack of self-confidence. Bossiness may be a manifestation of an insatiable need for perfection. And someone who has sudden outbursts of anger may be coping—unsuccessfully—with deep fears. While I am not suggesting that you become an amateur psychiatrist, I do believe that it is essential in these situations to show—and feel—respect for the person's feelings. That doesn't mean you have to agree with those feelings. However, your professionalism demands that you act with sensitivity and restraint.

Third, accept the fact that, even if you speak with great kindness and the volunteer can see your point of view without being defensive, it may be many weeks or months before the volunteer will seem to be changing. The lazy person mentioned above will not, overnight, become energetic and enthusiastic after your chat. The changes you see will be incremental, so you must acknowledge them publicly or privately as s/he gains more self-confidence. Just remember the four-to-one rule and lavish praise on the volunteer when you see even small changes.

When dealing with difficult volunteers whose behavior is the result of a temporary hardship outside your organization, consider suggesting that the volunteer take a leave of absence for a month or two. In certain circumstances you may want to insist on a leave of absence. Check with your organization's coordinator of volunteers about what the policy and procedures are regarding leaves of absence for volunteers. And be sure that you and the volunteer both understand the agreement you made with each other before the leave begins. Perhaps an informal written note for each of you is necessary. Be clear about these questions:

- Will the volunteer get his/her same shift back?

- Who is to initiate reconnecting the volunteer with the organization, you or the volunteer?

- What if the original problem is still evident?

HOW TO FIRE A VOLUNTEER AND LIVE TO TELL ABOUT IT:

1. **Provide clear forewarning and notice to volunteers that they may be terminated:**
   a. have clear agency policies on termination.
   b. make the policies reasonable and related to the work to be done.
   c. include a policy on suspension.
   d. tell volunteers about the policies in orientation and training sessions.
   e. give volunteers a copy of the policies as part of their personnel manuals.
   f. make the policies specific to each volunteer by providing them an up-dated accurate, and measurable job description.

2. **Conduct an investigation or determination before firing a volunteer.**
   a. have a fair and objective investigator determine if policies were actually violated.
   b. never fire on the spot without conducting an investigation: use a suspension clause to allow time to examine the situation.
   c. make sure you have proof of the violation of the agency policies, either through testimony of others or regular evaluations of the volunteer's behavior that demonstrate unsatisfactory performance.
   d. also try to find out the volunteer's side of the story to determine if any extenuating circumstances exist.
   e. thoroughly document the investigation and its results.

3. **Apply the termination ruling fairly and equally.**
   a. establish a graduated punishment system: warnings for first offenses, or for minor transgressions, then more severe penalties.
   b. relate the degree of punishment to the level of offense.
   c. apply penalties even-handedly and without favoritism.
   d. allow for an appeals process.
   e. make use of a committee of peer volunteers to aid you.

SOURCE

101 Ideas for Volunteer Programs by Steve McCurley and Sue Vineyard, Heritage Arts Publishing, 1986.

There are no simple answers to these questions.

At Memorial Sloan-Kettering, we, in concert with the direct supervisors, often suggested that volunteers in high-stress positions take a leave of absence for a month or two. These decisions took into consideration other causes of stress in each volunteer's life as well as the personal support systems to which they had access. We also had a close enough relationship with volunteers that most would tell us about personal changes that were adding to their difficulties (such as the ones mentioned above), so that we could explore together whether a leave of absence would help. Our aim was to avoid losing a good volunteer who might temporarily be unreliable or irritable. We tried to be sensitive to the emotional needs of each volunteer. When the volunteers returned it was with more energy and a renewed commitment.

In all situations pertaining to volunteer performance or behavioral problems, take a look at the work environment. Do you and your co-workers model the behavior you want volunteers to exhibit? Have you tried to minimize the factors that may cause legitimate frustration in volunteers? Do you provide enough support for volunteers working in stressful situations? Are the work goals attainable so that volunteers feel they are accomplishing something?

You will find additional resources for dealing with difficult volunteers in Marilyn MacKenzie's book by that name (Heritage Arts Publishing, 1988) and in *Handling Problem Volunteers* by Steve McCurley and Sue Vineyard (Heritage Arts Publishing, 1998).

Can Volunteers Be Fired?

The short answer is, yes. Generally, terminating a volunteer is done by the coordinator of volunteers, but it usually is precipitated by those who have supervised the volunteer. Your organization must have a policy that specifies under what circumstances a volunteer's placement or contract can be terminated. Each organization must develop its own policy, and it ought to be similar to the organization's policy for terminating paid staff. A policy on firing needs to describe various grounds for termination and the process by which such action is taken: warnings, documentation, notice, appeals, etc. Volunteers, like employees, can bring suit for wrongful dismissal and/or defamation of character, so both the policy and the process must be developed properly.

If the safety of the client, other volunteers or the volunteer is at risk [personally], act immediately. In most situations, however, try to collect at least three examples of unacceptable behavior that you personally have seen....

Outline your observation and the result. Don't use long words, beat around the bush, or try to soften the blow with additional phrases. You may want to schedule an interview for Friday afternoon to allow the volunteer time to work and collect [his or] her thoughts. Don't apologize for your decision. It should not be a surprise if you've done the preparatory work. Your decision was the result of the volunteer's behavior. Rehearsal helps:

- "Mr. Jackson, I must terminate your volunteer activity here at the Centre."
- "Mrs. Wilson, you can no longer deliver Meals on Wheels for the Clappings Corner United Way."

...If possible, try to open doors to future volunteering opportunities. Can you in good conscience direct them to the Voluntary Action Centre? Could they come back after a period of treatment, or respite? Is there an opportunity to thank them for any aspect of their work?

SOURCE

Dealing with Difficult Volunteers by Marilyn MacKenzie, Heritage Arts, 1988.

FROM THE FIELD

Los Altos, CA — United Methodist Church

Removing a volunteer from a position in a church setting is challenging because the person is a member of the organization and is likely to remain one. In other settings you may be able to ask the volunteer to leave the organization if his or her performance as a volunteer is unsatisfactory but in a church one wouldn't do that. Even if the person feels that the work he or she is doing is a calling I intervene if the person is regularly causing discomfort to others or being completely ineffective. Sometimes this can be accomplished by offering another service opportunity to the person. Sometimes a personal talk in a friendly setting will help the person discover a new area to explore. Sometimes it is impossible to go the indirect route and you may simply have to inform the volunteer that a change in assignments is necessary. This is not the ideal way and you may lose a member if this is not done diplomatically.

We have also found it helps to set a three year limit on terms as committee chairs. This prevents members from feeling they "own" the position. Other members are automatically fed into leadership positions. Membership on our church committees rotate in much the same way: one third rotate off each year.

The best of all worlds is to properly match church members to the job according to their gifts, talents and availability. Members who have attended our "Discover the Gift of You" class have a real sense of where God is calling them to serve and are eager to work with me to find the best fit for them and for the church.

Nancy Roslund, Director of Lay Ministry, Los Altos United Methodist Church, Los Altos, CA

Terminate or Tolerate?

Probably every coordinator of volunteers reading this book has faced the difficult decision of whether or not to terminate a volunteer with a long record of effective service but who now, for any number of reasons, is causing a problem in the organization. Gratitude for past contributions wrestles with concern about the consequences of allowing the situation to continue and possibly worsen. Failing to act affects your reputation and the reputation of volunteers, and may put your organization at risk. Terminating the volunteer may also affect your reputation and may result in a bitter ending for a volunteer whose affiliation was valued by the organization and was, for the volunteer, a source of great pride. There are no easy answers and each circumstance will be different.

For example, you may have an elderly volunteer with many years of service to the organization whose mental or physical condition has declined to the point that the volunteer is not able to accomplish anything and may be a risk to him/herself or the organization. One option is to meet periodically with every older volunteer to assess how things are going. Together discuss the volunteer's health and well-being and, again together, determine whether s/he feels able to continue in the present assignment. If all volunteers know why you do this and feel this is a fair and rational process, they may be less defensive and may assess themselves with more objectivity. This might be combined with another option: create a "volunteer emeritus" category, which is what the Monterey Bay Aquarium did. On page 82 you will find additional information about this approach.

There are other examples of termination quandaries. One is when the volunteer is undergoing some sort of crisis (grief, divorce, physical illness, job insecurity) that seems to interfere with accomplishing formerly-excellent work. The issue here is how to tell if the performance change is temporary or long lasting. Would a short leave of absence or interim re-assignment to a project involving less risk solve your problem and still be supportive of the volunteer? Or will this crisis ultimately undermine the person's ability to bounce back and reassume the original responsibility?

Another challenge is when the problems concern a volunteer who also happens to be a major financial donor to the organization (or is related to one). This is connected to who may have referred this volunteer to the program in the first place, such as the president of the board of directors. Here, of course, the major issue is whether confronting the unacceptable volunteer behavior will affect that person's willingness to continue financial support. Even if you confer with your organization's executives and must act carefully, it is imperative that you protect the clients, staff, and other volunteers from the negative impact of any volunteer's poor conduct.

Sarah Jane Rehnborg, the Director of Volunteerism and Community Engagement at the University of Texas at Austin, shares the following fourteen factors affecting your decision about whether to fire a volunteer. Before concluding that a volunteer cannot remain with your organization, review these questions. Some are designed to help you evaluate your organization's performance so that you can better evaluate the volunteer's performance. Several questions will help you identify other factors that may also influence your decision.

1. Does the volunteer have a job description that is clear and current?

2. Has the job description been adequately explained? Has the volunteer's supervisor answered the volunteer's questions, and assisted the volunteer in understanding the scope of the position?

3. Does the organization have an orientation process in place?

4. Has the volunteer attended an orientation?

5. Could this situation be remedied by having the volunteer return to an orientation and/or training program?

6. Does the volunteer have a designated, accessible supervisor who knows how to supervise volunteers?

7. Have you previously documented the problem in writing, shared it with the volunteer and discussed ways to avoid this situation in the future? (This action would not be appropriate if the volunteer had done something extremely serious, such as threatening staff with a weapon).

8. As you have explored the nature of the problem you are now faced with, have you convened all of the parties involved in the situation at the same time so that all sides of the situation can be examined together?

9. Have you created an action plan to resolve the situation and has the responsible person met with the volunteer as specified in the action plan?

10. Have you involved the appropriate persons within your organization in this situation? For example, your executive director, legal counsel, or board chair may wish to be aware of a problem as it is developing and may be able to offer assistance in its management.

11. Have you explored the implications of terminating this volunteer in terms of:
    - the life situation of the individual?
    - the impact of this action on your program?

VOLUNTEER FOCUS GROUP QUOTES

Supervisors need to be open and honest with their volunteers. They need to keep an open line of communication. That's why you have to tell me about it when I do something wrong.

If you have to tell me about a mistake I've made, just do it. Don't get overly worried about my feelings. But please be diplomatic.

If I've made a mistake, don't just explain what I did wrong but give me suggestions about what to do the next time.

Usually if you've messed up you know it. So just talk to your supervisor, who helps it be a self-correcting, internalizing process.

If something is done wrong I would like to correct it.

If my supervisor had to reprimand me I sure hope she'd do it in private.

If I've made a mistake and you are trying to show me the right way ask, "Do you understand what I mean?"

I know I need to hear about mistakes I've made but if you could also say, "Don't worry," at least I'll know you understand I didn't do it on purpose.

— Volunteers

- the impact of inaction on this situation or your program?
- the impact of this action on your organization?
- the impact of this action on the recipients of service?
- the impact of inaction on the recipients of service?
- the ramifications of this action on the organization's public image?

12. Have you exhausted all the possibilities that would make this action unnecessary?

13. Have you taken steps to minimize or contain the damage that may result from this decision?

14. What organizational support, if any, do you need to implement this decision?

Rehnborg concludes by noting "once you have taken action and have assessed the consequences, you may also want to ask what you learned from this situation that will reduce the likelihood of a similar situation occurring in the future."

Examples for Discussion

We will end this chapter with six actual situations presented as discussion starters—all of them real and submitted by colleagues for this book (even though several of the contributors requested anonymity). Each describes a supervisory challenge involving one or more volunteers and how the organization handled the issue. You may or may not agree with the actions taken by these supervisors—we, and probably they, acknowledge that alternate scenarios can well be imagined.

No one can predict what situations will occur in your organization, but these discussion starters allow you to do some mental role play. You can consider these cases by yourself or perhaps find an opportunity for group discussion with other supervisors of volunteers and with volunteers themselves. For each situation, consider these questions:

- Can you diagnose what might have caused this situation to occur in the first place?
- What do you think of the way the supervisor and/or coordinator of volunteers handled this situation?
- Would you have acted the same way? What would you have done differently?
- What might have been the consequences of not addressing this problem or taking no action?
- What insight does this example give you into policies or practices you may need to put into place in your organization?

Following each example are additional specific questions for you to consider. There are no "correct answers" to any of these questions. Allow your instincts to guide your supervisory skills.

WRAP-UP TIPS:

It is much harder to keep a poor performer than it is to counsel and/or terminate one. —**Jill Friedman Fixler**

It is important to address a problem in an assertive manner without berating the volunteer. —**Susan Brown**

If there is one thing I have learned, it is to document any problems in writing. —**Terry Dunn**

Our starting point is always the volunteer job description. Supervisors use it as a tool to defuse the situation by depersonalizing it and looking at something that is written and objective. —**Lisa Taylor**

Many times volunteers don't want to complain, but if something is going wrong—especially in the beginning—it is essential to try to correct it. Depending on the problem, I either correct it myself or work with the volunteer's supervisor. —**Amy Hohn**

Before you characterize a volunteer as "unreliable" or "difficult," consider whether the person might just be unhappy. In my experience most unhappy volunteers are just in the wrong job. People measure their own success differently, subjectively. —**Nan Hawthorne**

Benny, a senior citizen, was a volunteer receptionist on one of the busiest floors of our twelve-story building which houses our clinics, recreational and support programs and a dining room. His job was to answer phones, take messages and greet clients. Benny was great on the phones and learned the job quickly. It was obvious that the clients loved him because one or more would often keep him company at the receptionist desk. Benny told his supervisor, Ron, he was glad to have this volunteer job because it reduced the loneliness and boredom he had felt since his retirement.

After a while, Benny began showing up earlier for his shifts and staying later, talking with clients. When Ron told him this was not necessary, Benny said that was okay since he didn't have anything else to do anyway. Ron let it go because it seemed harmless and the clients enjoyed Benny.

Then one day, Ron overheard one of the clients thanking Benny for taking him to a classical music concert over the weekend. Ron called the Volunteer Department and described the problem to the coordinator of volunteers, Ted. Ron and Ted met with Benny together. They thanked him for his good work but told him they had concerns about his staying on in his volunteer role because of his failure to follow agency procedures. Benny was surprised since he saw no harm in being friends with the clients, especially since they liked him and some of them were lonely, too.

Ron and Ted reminded Benny about his purpose in coming to the agency. They showed him his job description which outlined his specific duties and work hours. They also showed him the Volunteer Policies and Procedures Manual which governed relations between volunteers and clients. They reminded Benny that clients and volunteers had very distinct and separate roles in the agency. Benny's job as a volunteer was to provide services and the clients were there to access services. They sympathized with Benny's desire to find friends, but stated that their client pool was clearly not the place to do so and might, in fact, act as an impediment to someone trying to get services. They also said the agency could not take responsibility for what went on between Benny and the clients when they were outside the agency. Ron and Ted told Benny that if he wanted to continue volunteering, he would have to abide by the rules of the agency.

Benny stated that he saw the need for his compliance and said that he would be more careful about sticking to his volunteer role in the future. The supervisor thanked Benny and said he would check with him periodically to see how everything was going.

—Submitted by Thomas Weber, Coordinator of Volunteers for Client Programs, Gay Men's Health Crisis, New York, NY

- Can you diagnose what might have caused this situation to occur in the first place?

- What do you think of the way the supervisor and/or coordinator of volunteers handled this situation?

- Would you have acted the same way? What would you have done differently?

- What might have been the consequences of not addressing this problem or taking no action?

- What insight does this example give you into policies or practices you may need to put into place in your organization?

- In this scenario, the clients are not necessarily displeased with Benny (we aren't really told how they feel). How will you determine when a situation requires your intervention or when a volunteer and a client (or, for that matter, an employee) have the right to privacy or to decide for themselves how to act?

Our membership organization is located in a large city in the United States. Many of our 3,000 members are also volunteers for the organization.

One of the most popular benefits we offer our membership is the opportunity to get theater tickets at greatly reduced prices. Our theater desk, which is staffed five days a week by volunteers, solicits donated tickets from local theaters. The volunteers distribute these tickets to members, following a carefully developed procedure.

In May 1998 a volunteer who has worked the theater desk for many years and who has taken on the role of theater desk coordinator, approached his supervisor, the director of group service, to report that a member who wanted theater tickets had become verbally abusive when the volunteer had refused to provide tickets because the member did not have his membership card. The volunteer insisted that the member's theater desk privileges be suspended for a time. The supervisor of group service did not agree to this since this member had never before been troublesome. Instead, the supervisor said he or the executive director would speak to the member about etiquette when using the theater desk, and would warn him that a second infraction would lead to suspension of privileges. The supervisor's decision was shaped by other factors: he knew this volunteer was inclined to be argumentative, dismissive and rude, displaying an inflated sense of power as the "owner" of the theater desk and that his personality often provoked bad behavior in others. In fact, the supervisor had had problems with this volunteer before and had even suggested to the director of volunteers that the theater desk would be better off without this volunteer.

The volunteer was not satisfied with the decision and asked for a meeting with the executive director, who invited the supervisor of group service and the director of volunteers to attend. The volunteer expressed the view that by not taking action against the member, the staff was condoning the abuse of volunteers. The executive director restated his intention to speak to the member and to warn him about the consequences should there be further problems. The director of volunteers voiced her agreement with the executive director's decision. She, too, did not want the member's privileges suspended, in part because it was a first offense but also because the procedure did not clearly indicate that suspension would be the inevitable consequence of bad behavior. The director of volunteers was also influenced by having learned that just a month prior to the incident another member had cursed out the volunteer and that he had not asked for her suspension even though what she had said to the volunteer was far worse. Privately, however, the director of volunteers felt very sympathetic for the volunteer, sensing his pain at having been abused by a member and, in his eyes, betrayed by the organization.

Two weeks later the volunteer and the director of volunteers met. The volunteer stated how disappointed he was and announced that he was going to drastically reduce his hours at the theater desk, working only two days instead of five. He could not be dissuaded, even when he was told that the theater desk procedure would be changed to state that suspension of privileges would be an automatic consequence of abusive behavior and that the staff was also brainstorming ways to accommodate members who had forgotten their membership cards.

After this problem quieted down the organization developed a training program for volunteers about how to engage with members in a non-combative way. The volunteer continues to work two days a week at the desk.

— Submitted anonymously

- Can you diagnose what might have caused this situation to occur in the first place?
- What do you think of the way the supervisor and/or coordinator of volunteers handled this situation?
- Would you have acted the same way? What would you have done differently?
- What might have been the consequences of not addressing this problem or taking no action?
- What insight does this example give you into policies or practices you may need to put into place in your organization?your organization?

- How did this volunteer contribute to the conflict? Was the supervisor, who knew the volunteer was argumentative, also to blame?
- Does your organization have possible blurry lines between categories of constituents: volunteers, clients, members, donors, participants, etc.? How can you minimize conflict if a person falls into more than one category?
- Are you prepared for a volunteer to question a decision you make? How might you react if this happened?
- How can you judge when recurring problems overshadow the worth of the contributions made by a volunteer (or employee)?

I became the director of volunteer services at a large museum in the Midwest in 1993. When I started I was warned that my Thursday mornings would be ruined by Ms. X, an information desk volunteer since the museum opened in 1987, who was on medical leave.

Six months later Ms. X reappeared. She arrived at my office door a few minutes before her shift was to begin and announced that she wanted to get to know me. She made herself some tea at the station that I keep stocked for just such impromptu visits and settled into the extra chair in my office for a long chat. I called down to the information desk to let them know Ms. X would be late, figuring that it was important to have some "quality time" with her and that this chat would have to count as my daily visit to each shift of volunteers at the information desk.

The next Thursday morning Ms. X was back in my office for her tea and attention. Her visit was shorter, but only because I had to prepare for a meeting. This pattern continued for a few months, with her visits often lasting from thirty minutes to an hour. My supervisor noticed and commented negatively on Ms. X's visits. I began to dread Thursday mornings because I knew that very little work would be done in the middle of the morning. Something had to change.

The phrase from many old Western movies occurred to me: "Let's head `em off at the pass." My plan was to meet Ms. X each week when she arrived at the front door of the museum before she even had a chance to go to the fifth floor where my office—and my supervisor's—was located. I did this for four consecutive weeks, allowing five minutes to chat with her. Each week I asked about her husband, whose health was failing badly. I also told her one new thing that had happened in the museum since the previous week.

Giving those five minutes to Ms. X satisfied her need for my attention. She rarely came to my office after that unless there was something of great importance to discuss. Best of all, my attitude changed. I no longer saw Ms. X as a "problem" volunteer whom I resented because of her insatiable needs. Instead, because I had discovered a win-win solution, I was happy to give her the time she needed and deserved from me.

I am no longer at the museum but I keep in touch with my successor. Ms. X is still a "high needs" volunteer and my successor has maintained the practice of meeting her at the front door each week. It is a small price to pay for the time Ms. X gives so faithfully to the museum.

—Submitted anonymously

- Can you diagnose what might have caused this situation to occur in the first place?

- What do you think of the way the supervisor and/or coordinator of volunteers handled this situation?

- Would you have acted the same way? What would you have done differently?

- What might have been the consequences of not addressing this problem or taking no action?

- What insight does this example give you into policies or practices you may need to put into place in your organization?

- How does this story compare to Discussion Starter #2 which also involves a particularly demanding volunteer?

"Denny," a tall, somewhat scruffy-looking bearded college student, enrolled in the school's literacy volunteer initiative anxious to help young, low income, bilingual students gain proficiency in English and language arts. He attended the lengthy training as we requested and received a complete orientation to the policies governing the elementary school and its volunteer program, yet problems emerged almost immediately.

An over-grown kid in many ways himself, Denny enjoyed rough-housing with his students during recess, swinging the children and lifting them to his shoulders in spite of clear and strictly enforced rules to the contrary. We immediately and clearly advised him of the inappropriateness of his actions, but the situation recurred more than once. However, Denny was clearly concerned for the children and was reliable in attendance. He further went beyond the call of duty by organizing a "Bikes Bonanza" for the students, refurbishing 35 donated bikes for children without "wheels." Each bike was thoroughly re-constructed, a competitive writing contest (to support the goal of literacy and its real-life importance) was conducted to award the 35 bikes. Unfortunately, in the midst of all of these terrific accomplishments, Denny's poor judgement continued to hamper his performance. The final straw came on the day he arrived at school with a large and visible knife in his back pocket. The knife was intended for a classroom leather-cutting project, but the school was exceedingly clear about its weapons policy: go immediately to the main office and deposit the knife until the classroom session. Instead, Denny walked the building with the knife visible, setting a poor example to the children who idolized him.

Needless to say, after prior reprimands and multiple reviews of school policy and the problems with breaking these rules, everyone was out of patience with Denny. The principal, teacher, school volunteer manager and I discussed the situation and collectively reached the decision that this volunteer's behavior was risking the safety of the children and that outweighed other considerations. In the company of the principal and the volunteer manager, Denny was informed that it would not be possible for him to return to the school the following semester. He was extremely disappointed, but we felt that we had no choice after so many warnings.

—Submitted by Sarah Jane Rehnborg, Ph.D., CVA, Director, Volunteerism and Community Engagement, Charles A. Dana Center, University of Texas at Austin

---

- Can you diagnose what might have caused this situation to occur in the first place?

- What do you think of the way the supervisor and/or coordinator of volunteers handled this situation?

- Would you have acted the same way? What would you have done differently?

- What might have been the consequences of not addressing this problem or taking no action?

- What insight does this example give you into policies or practices you may need to put into place in your organization?

- How important was collaboration among the various staff members in this story? What circumstances in your organization might warrant cooperative action among several supervisors— and do you feel confident that you would be reasonably united in how you handle such situations?

Discussion Starter #5

Several times an older male volunteer whistled at me, a young female coordinator of volunteers. As I generally do when this occurs outside the work place, I shrugged it off and made no comment. He had been retired for some years so I figured he just didn't know that work place mores had changed.

A while later I received a report that this volunteer had been making some very inappropriate remarks and telling off-color stories to staff. This had offended one of the female workers. I spoke with the volunteer immediately. There were no further incidents and the volunteer continues to provide valuable service. I learned a lesson, too: it would have been so much better if I had explained to him after the very first incident that there is no place in today's work environment for such behavior.

—Submitted anonymously

- Can you diagnose what might have caused this situation to occur in the first place?
- What do you think of the way the supervisor and/or coordinator of volunteers handled this situation?
- Would you have acted the same way? What would you have done differently?
- What might have been the consequences of not addressing this problem or taking no action?
- What insight does this example give you into policies or practices you may need to put into place in your organization?
- Do you tend to wait until problems show a repetitive pattern before attempting to deal with them? How can you strike a balance between giving people a chance to make newcomer mistakes and allowing something to go too far?

Discussion Starter #6

In the spring of 1998 I became the site manager of a senior nutrition center funded by county government. Located in a densely populated suburban area in New England, the center is open five days a week and serves lunch to about 30 clients each day. In addition, we run programs and activities such as Bingo, ceramics and painting classes, and health screening. The center has five volunteers who work with our two paid staff members to prepare and serve meals and conduct our other activities. Most of these volunteers are also clients.

One of the first things I noticed about our little volunteer program (such as it was) was that it was very loosely run. No staff member was designated as our coordinator of volunteers. My predecessor evidently did not have any expectations of the volunteers. They could come in whenever they wanted and did not have set responsibilities. There was no application process nor was there a policy and procedure manual. I was also eager to recruit new volunteers. Being an organized person, I knew that these were areas I would want to work on.

But within a few days a far more serious problem came to my attention. The volunteers were stealing food! Evidently their view was that, as clients, all the food was purchased for them anyway, so if anything was left over at the end of a day, they believed they were entitled to take it home. In their minds this applied not just to leftovers but also to items in the refrigerator that had not been used that day, such as lettuce.

To make matters worse, the staff was aware of this and they knew the previous director knew. Although there was a County policy prohibiting theft of food, my predecessor had evidently looked the other way.

I was angry at the volunteers, angry at my predecessor and angry that I had to take action fast, even before the glow of my new position had worn off. Thinking calmly and rationally about what to do was one of the most difficult decisions I have ever made.

Here's what I did. After running my plans by my boss (the county nutrition program director) I had a confidential meeting with the paid staff on a Friday afternoon to tell them what I was going to do. The following week I called the volunteers together and told them that I intended to enforce the County rule: no food could be taken home by paid staff or volunteers. I emphasized I welcomed their willingness to volunteer but that they needed to understand that "volunteer" and "client" were two different roles and that volunteers were to be considered part of the staff and subject to the same rules that applied to staff. I asked each person present to think about whether s/he wanted to continue to be a volunteer and to let me know within one week what the decision was. I hinted that I had considered reporting this matter to the police but decided that I would first attempt to solve the problem by clarifying any misunderstanding that may have existed about the policy.

While I hoped the volunteers would eventually like me, it was more important at this point that they respect me and my authority and that the stealing stop immediately! So even though I had piles of work to do, I hung around the kitchen during meal preparation time and after meals were served. I acted far more menacing than I felt. Being new gave me an advantage: no one knew my real personality.

To my surprise, all of the volunteers decided to continue volunteering. Within three weeks I had developed a simple manual for them. One of the employees took responsibility for developing a schedule for the volunteers and also instituted a sign-in system. We got them name badges and aprons.

We not only have more food now; we also have a cohesive team of employees and volunteers who take pride in the service they provide for our clients. By the way, I've decided for the time being to keep my menacing persona!

—Submitted anonymously

- Can you diagnose what might have caused this situation to occur in the first place?

- What do you think of the way the supervisor and/or coordinator of volunteers handled this situation?

- Would you have acted the same way? What would you have done differently?

- What might have been the consequences of not addressing this problem or taking no action?

- What insight does this example give you into policies or practices you may need to put into place in your organization?

- Compare this story to Discussion Starter #2. How much difference does it make (should it make) if volunteers who are causing a problem are also participants or members?

- What situations in your organization may require "laying down the law" and who is likeliest to be the "menacing" supervisor to do it?

- Also compare this to Discussion Starter #5. Can you think of times in the past when you gathered your courage, spoke to someone about a concern, and discovered that the person accepted your point well? Why would volunteers be more or less likely to accept legitimate criticism?

Conducting Formal Evaluations

As a supervisor you should periodically evaluate all aspects of your program: your systems, your staff—paid and volunteer—your facilities, your training and continuing education programs, your own performance. Evaluation helps you and others identify what is going well—so that you can determine how to keep it that way—and identify areas that need improvement. Evaluation aids decision making; without evaluation you cannot set goals, plan how to reach those goals, or determine when you have met them.

Evaluation is a part of the training/supervision/feedback/recognition cycle that keeps everyone motivated and moving forward. As a supervisor, you evaluate your workers on an informal basis all the time. Assessing how things are going and how well someone is doing are integral to every supervisory exchange. Don't be silent about what you observe! Engage volunteers and employees in continuing discussions about how all of you feel about the effectiveness of your work. Schedule time to debrief or reflect about projects or situations when a benchmark of progress is reached or a crisis is over (some call this a "post mortem session").

Most people cringe at the thought of evaluation, both those who have to "do" them and those who have to "receive" them. Visions of school report cards haunt us through adulthood. Despite all the rhetoric about valuing constructive criticism, many of us feel the process is quite destructive. This is why organizations feel uncomfortable with the concept of evaluating volunteers.

Think of evaluation and performance assessment as "action planning": looking ahead rather than grading past work. Well-executed evaluation sessions emphasize people's strengths and the desire to make even good work better. The goal is not to lay blame if problems or weaknesses are identified. In fact, for volunteers—and employees—it is complimentary and

motivating when a supervisor assumes a team member can be capable of skillful performance if attention is paid to improvement. In their book, *Volunteer Management* (1996), Steve McCurley and Rick Lynch further note:

> *Failing to evaluate a volunteer sends a clear message that you don't care about the quality of the work being done, and that you don't care much about the volunteers. Both volunteers who know they are doing well and those who think they should be congratulated for good work will think less of the volunteer effort, and of you, if evaluations are not conducted.*

Approach evaluation as a two-way process. This is as much an opportunity to gain input from volunteers as to give them feedback.

Again, some evaluation can be done informally, by being observant and by continually asking for input from paid staff and volunteers. Some years back this was known as "management by walking around." That's certainly a good thing to do, but you may also decide to do formal evaluations. This chapter will provide information about five types of evaluations that pertain to the volunteers you supervise. We have included sample evaluation forms along with information about how they are used by the organizations that developed them.

If you want to implement one or more types of evaluation, first meet with your organization's coordinator of volunteers, who may have additional resources that will be helpful to you. He or she may also want to have some input in the process or the instruments you develop or may invite you to join with others in your organization who supervise volunteers to develop volunteer evaluation instruments you can all use. In fact, many of the survey form examples

If volunteers are responsible for results, they get the satisfaction of making progress toward a meaningful accomplishment. If, on the other hand, they are responsible only for the activities that may lead to some result, they are divorced from that satisfaction. The responsibility is often so fragmented that the volunteer loses sight of the result. As a direct consequence of this, results are poorly and inefficiently obtained and the volunteer gets bored.

Questions to ask yourself in giving responsibility for results include, "What do I want to happen because of the work the volunteer is doing?" and "What kind of change do I want to occur?"

[Another] critical element in good job design is to decide how to measure whether the results are being achieved. If people can't tell how well they are doing, if they can't tell if they are succeeding or failing, they tend to get bored with the activity. There is also no incentive to try a different course of action if you don't know that your present course is failing.

For some jobs the measure of performance is fairly obvious and easy to state. In other cases, measurement may be more difficult. In the case of the Girl Scout leader whose result is to have girls develop self-assurance, we need to do some hard work to determine how we should measure progress. We might ask such questions as:

"How will we know if girls have more self-assurance?"

"What will we see if they are or aren't self-assured?"

"What questions could we ask them to determine their degree of self-confidence?"

Many volunteer managers who do measure performance tend to measure the wrong things. They keep track of things like hours spent or miles driven or client contacts made. They are not really measures of whether the result is being achieved.

To determine how to measure a given result, involve the volunteers who do the job. Ask them these two questions:

"What information would tell us if you are succeeding in achieving results?"

"How could we collect this information?"

SOURCE

Essential Volunteer Management, Steve McCurley and Rick Lynch, Heritage Arts, 1996.

you'll read about in this chapter are probably most appropriately administered by the volunteer office, while you, as direct supervisor, deal with the responses and with more personal contact.

Also before proceeding, recognize that evaluation, done properly, will take time. So design the process in a manner that ensures the benefits will outweigh the costs. And try to remember what your own experiences have been as the subject of evaluations done by your present or previous supervisor(s) so that you can capture the best features and avoid those that should not be repeated.

The evaluation forms and processes described below fall into two broad categories: evaluation of volunteer performance (conducted by the supervisor and/or by the volunteer) and evaluation of the volunteer's experience (sometimes called satisfaction surveys).

Evaluation of Volunteer Performance

Some organizations evaluate volunteer performance after the volunteer has been with the organization for a few months. Annual evaluations are another option.

Be clear on exactly what you are evaluating. Linda Graff correctly distinguishes "between assessing an individual's *performance* and examining the *outcomes* of the project or program. Could it be that the

volunteer is doing well, but the job is not designed properly or extraneous factors have impeded success?" This is also Peter Drucker's distinction between "efficiency"—doing a job right—and "effectiveness"—doing the *right* job right.

An excellent manual on outcomes-based program evaluation, *Measuring the Difference Volunteers Make* (1997), is referenced in the bibliography. We will concern ourselves here mainly with performance standards.

Evaluation of New Volunteers

Conducting performance evaluations of new volunteers gives you an opportunity to note the progress the volunteer has made and to identify additional training needs before too much time has lapsed. It is particularly important to do formal evaluation if your organization has a trial or probation period for new volunteers. If performance is unsatisfactory you have the option of providing additional training and extending the trial period, with another review date following the second trial period. You and the volunteer may decide that additional training won't make a difference. In these situations, the organization's coordinator of volunteers will probably meet with the volunteer to work out another placement, assuming other options exist within your organization.

Here are some more tips on evaluating a volunteer:

- **There should be some system for regularly conducting a mutual review of the volunteer's performance.** How often you do so depends on the nature of the job and the individual volunteer. In the first few weeks of a volunteer's assignment, the supervisor and the volunteer may wish to meet weekly, not necessarily for a formal review but for a designated period, say 20 minutes or so, to talk about how things are going. "Checkpoint" is a good name for these shorter, more frequent reviews.

- **After the first few weeks, this discussion may occur monthly for the first six months, then yearly after that.** At the very least, the volunteer and his or her supervisor should meet for a mutual review once a year, or whenever the signed volunteer agreement expires.

- **Like all reviews, it should be an opportunity for two-way discussion on how things are going.** The supervisor discusses the volunteer's strengths and areas of improvement, and the volunteer discusses what kind of supervision and support he or she finds helpful, and how the YMCA and supervisor could better support him or her.

- **In the spirit of two-way communication, you might consider calling this discussion a "mutual review" or a "progress report."** Indeed the kind of two-way review described here is actually becoming popular in well-managed private businesses. More and more, employees are being asked to help evaluate their supervisors.

- **The review should include the chance for the volunteer to assess his or her own performance.** In fact, some organizations introduce the concept of reviews into their volunteer programs by beginning with a self-assessment process. If a longtime volunteer has never been reviewed before, he or she may find the process threatening. To overcome this, some organizations, in the first year of the review process, begin by asking the volunteers to assess themselves, the volunteer program, and the organization overall.

- **One way to conduct a review is for both the volunteer and the supervisor to fill out the same form,** asking the same set of questions. After discussion, the two may agree on a final version.

- **The review should also be a chance for the volunteer and the YMCA to renegotiate the job description,** adding new and different responsibilities, taking some away; in short, shaping the job description so that it continues to motivate and stimulate the volunteer while meeting a need of YMCA and the community it serves. **Remember, however, that all volunteers are different, and some may not want new or greater responsibilities.** It's important to ask the volunteer, "What can we do to keep you here—to keep you interested and motivated?" Just as you can't assume that all volunteers will be content with their same jobs for ever, you can't assume that all volunteers want to do something new or different each year.

- **As is with paid staff members, the review should be conducted by the volunteer's supervisor.** If the YMCA has a director of volunteer development or a coordinator of volunteer resources, that person can help the staff member prepare for the interview. However, that depends on the policies and procedures of the individual YMCA. In some cases, he or she can also help conduct the review.

- **Common sense dictates that the review take place in a quiet and private atmosphere,** free of interruptions from people or the telephone. The volunteer and the supervisor should be sitting face to face. The supervisor should not be behind his or her desk.

- **Let new volunteers know that there will be regular chances to discuss how things are going, from their perspective and yours.** The review process should be explained clearly to the volunteer from the start. It should be briefly outlined in the volunteer's job description. It's not fair to evaluate volunteers without giving them notice or without letting them know what they will be reviewed on....

SOURCE

The Seven R's of Volunteer Development by Celeste J. Wroblewski, YMCA of the USA, 1994.

At Arapahoe House, a drug and alcohol treatment program with 12 sites in Denver, Colorado, a "Volunteer/Student Performance Review" is used. It asks the supervisor to describe what "strengths, skills and accomplishments" the volunteer "brings to our program." Then the supervisor gives a rating of excellent, good, unsatisfactory, or not applicable in six performance areas, followed by "comments/areas of improvement" for each. The areas and Arapahoe House's definitions are:

- *communication skills*: written skills, ability to listen, professional language

- *staff relations*: relationship and communication with other staff, accepts supervision and feedback, interest in Arapahoe House
- *client relations*: resourcefulness, decision making, sensitivity and insight, problem solving, initiative, professional ethics, interest in agency
- *technical skills*: computer, filing, telephone, typing
- *record keeping*: charting protocol
- *personal attributes*: empathy, timely completion of tasks, accepts supervision, flexibility, stress management, self insight, initiative, attendance, punctuality, grooming neatness and appropriateness

There is also a section on the form for volunteer/student comments. When new volunteers have been with the agency for about three months, their supervisors complete the evaluation form and discuss it with each volunteer. The volunteer adds his or her comments, signs it and returns it to the coordinator of volunteers. The three month period was selected because by that time most volunteers will have worked at least 40 hours, which has proven to be a critical juncture point for most volunteers: most difficulties that a volunteer will experience will have occurred by then. Jill Friedman Fixler, most recently the coordinator of volunteers at Arapahoe House, reports that volunteers really appreciate the feedback. Nonetheless, she found it sometimes necessary to encourage supervisors to discuss problem areas with the volunteers. Fixler also monitored volunteer attendance closely because high absenteeism usually indicated a serious problem.

Annual Performance Evaluation

Assessing performance offers many benefits to volunteers. It gives you a chance to tell them—not for the first time, one hopes—the specific ways in which they have helped the organization so that you can praise and thank them. It also gives you the opportunity to assess areas of potential growth so that together you can decide what action to take. Arapahoe House uses the same form for both the three month and the annual reviews.

For the organization, performance assessments are a time to examine the effectiveness of training, identify new areas for in-service training, and possibly revise volunteer job descriptions. In fact, the whole issue of evaluation hinges upon having an accurate job description in the first place. If you and the volunteer have not agreed—at the start—about the work to be done, how can you later comment on its completion or effectiveness? This is also why volunteer job descriptions ought to include expectations about general qualities that make for any good worker: ability to relate to others; reliability; willingness to be a team player. So one of the key elements of volunteer performance reviews is to go back to the job description and see what was actually done in the period (and how well it was done), and then to determine if the work has changed or evolved enough to warrant revising the job description.

Some organizations that assess volunteers' performance ask the volunteers to do a self-assessment which they then discuss with their supervisor. This approach has two benefits: it conveys the organization's confidence in volunteers' ability to assess their own work and it is less time-consuming for the supervisor. It is also interesting to note that volunteers may evaluate themselves more critically than their supervisor might. On the next page Sarah Elliston shares some important comments on the benefits of self-evaluation and outlines a methodology for conducting it.

On pages 98 and 99, you will find two forms that are used annually by the Denver (CO) Museum of Natural History to evaluate volunteers who serve as exhibit interpreters or docent tour guides. Once the supervisor and the volunteer have completed their respective forms they meet so that the volunteer can review the form completed by the staff supervisor.

ARCHIVES

Although performance evaluation is an essential part of any well-managed volunteer program, it is a part that should be introduced sensitively and carefully into an existing program. Self-evaluation is probably the least threatening way to begin, especially if it is linked to program evaluation so that people see the purpose as growth and development rather than judgment or criticism. Peer evaluation is a logical second step, with a more objective evaluation instrument being introduced only after people have become comfortable with the process.

Introducing volunteer evaluations means that there must be a commitment on the part of those who manage the program to deal with the information generated. If volunteers are asked to provide input but do not perceive that they are heard, then evaluation becomes not just a useless but a negative process.

SOURCE

"Easy Does It: Initiating a Performance Evaluation Process in an Existing Volunteer Program" by Nancy A. Gaston, CVA, *The Journal of Volunteer Administration*, Fall 1989.

FROM THE FIELD

Current thinking in the management field is that self-evaluation is the key to continuous improvement. (Glasser, Deming) In order to want to change, we have to be given the opportunity to personally identify what needs to change and how to make that change. We change what we're doing when we finally realize that what we are doing isn't getting us what we want and when we can identify something new that might help. (Glasser, 1998)

This process of self-evaluation has to take place in an atmosphere of trust, where we feel listened to and not attacked. Change only occurs when we feel accepted (Gordon, 1970). We don't defend against self-evaluation because it is our own view of ourselves. If the process is done in an atmosphere of safety, where the threat of criticism isn't present, the self-view can be insightful, honest and useful. The mantra becomes, "I like being trusted to evaluate myself. What can I do to help out more, here?"

Three questions developed by Mame Porter who trained teachers in Texas years ago, are simple yet incredibly effective in a self-evaluation process. Mame's first question is "What did you like about what you did?" It invites us to self-evaluate by looking at the positive first. A colleague of mine added the question to her performance reviews of volunteers, asking them to describe what they had enjoyed about their work and of what they were most proud. Looking at the positive first built an atmosphere of trust and safety for the volunteer and invited them to identify pride in their work and skills, thus building self-esteem.

In keeping with setting a tone of respect and safety, Mame's second question asks, "If you had the opportunity to do this again, what might you do differently?" We often know what has gone wrong and why, if a situation was tense, if the work wasn't done correctly, or if some system or part broke down. Given the invitation to reflect without anticipating punishment, we can describe the error and the solution. The opportunity to trust our perceptions instead of having another tell us, is another important self-esteem developer.

My colleague found that this question allowed the volunteers to articulate what hadn't been successful and why. They knew when they had made mistakes and were very honest about their motivation. They told her what they would do differently, or if they didn't want to do it again, which led to discussion of what other work they might like to do. This question allowed the volunteers to take responsibility for themselves by identifying their faults and how to correct them as well as telling their supervisor what work they wish to do in the future.

Based on an understanding that there is a built-in resistance to unsolicited advice, Mame's third question invites us to request advice. By asking "What help do you need from me?", my colleague gave permission to the volunteers to request specific help with tasks and resources. As she listened to their requests, she discovered that she had a renewed interest in assisting the volunteers do their jobs. She was eager to help them get the training and resources they needed. Discussion of their responses to this question led to a renewed interest on the part of the volunteer also, because he or she could see that the help would be forthcoming. Since the ability to ask for help is a characteristic of high self-esteem, this question is another building block of self-esteem.

An unexpected benefit of using these questions in the review process was that my colleague found both she and the volunteers had a good idea of their goals for the next year by the end of the conversation. Identifying target dates for certain work to be done, they were able to cut their planning time in half and each felt good about it. My colleague was stunned at how quickly the performance reviews went—and on what a positive note they ended.

As more of our work is done in teams with flattened management systems, the ability to self-evaluate becomes paramount to success. An individual can use Mame Porter's Three Questions, alone or with a colleague, to reflect on completed work at any time. In this case, the questions become "What do I like about what have done?", "What would I do differently next time?", and "What help do I need and whom do I need to ask?"

Mame Porter's Three Questions are a deceptively simple tool with an immense impact on the volunteer program, the volunteer, the supervisor, and ultimately on the service to the clients. Volunteers come away from the asking of the questions feeling pride in their work, the challenge of really being able to reflect on what worked and didn't work, and a willingness to get help. All three questions allow the supervisor the opportunity to share expertise without having to give negative criticism. What better way of conducting a performance review than to build self-esteem, correct mistakes, and have all involved come away feeling that everyone has won?

References: William Glasser, *Choice Theory*, 1998; Thomas Gordon, *Parent Effectiveness Training*, 1970; Bill Scherkenback, foreword to *Deming's Road to Continual Improvement*, 1991.

—*Sarah H. Elliston, Professional Development Associate, United Way Volunteer Resource Center, Cincinnati, OH*

Denver Museum of Natural History
TOUR GUIDE SELF-EVALUATION

The purpose of this Self-Evaluation form is to give the volunteer a tool to assess themselves in preparation for a performance review. It is for the use of the volunteer and does not need to be shared with anyone.

ATTENDANCE:

1. Do I attend required meetings and training? _____ Yes _____No
2. Do I arrive at least 15 minutes ahead of time for my shift? _____ Yes _____No
3. Do I finish my shift on time? _____ Yes _____No
4. Do I give sufficient notice so a substitute can be found for my shift? _____ Yes _____No
5. Do I check the schedule on my shift to see if there are any tours that day? _____ Yes _____No

PRESENTATION:

1. Am I warm and friendly as I greet visitors? _____ Yes _____No
2. When giving a tour, do I wait for the group to assemble before I speak, then face the group and continue when everyone can see and hear? _____ Yes _____No
3. Am I relaxed as well as assured in my speaking approach? _____ Yes _____No
4. Is my presentation appropriate to the ages of the visitors?
   Attention Span _____ Yes _____No
   Vocabulary Level _____ Yes _____No
   Physical Needs _____ Yes _____No
   Knowledge _____ Yes _____No
5. Am I flexible? Do I respond graciously to unexpected events when with a group of visitors? (crowded areas, distractions from other people, etc.) _____ Yes _____No
6. Do I help visitors relate exhibit information to familiar experiences? _____ Yes _____No
7. Do I give clear transitional statements between areas of the exhibit? _____ Yes _____No
8. Do I vary the pace to make the tour more interesting? _____ Yes _____No
9. Do I reinforce good answers? _____ Yes _____No

CONTENT:

1. Are the goals of my tour clear to me and my group? _____ Yes _____No
2. Do I develop concrete ideas which visitors can grasp? _____ Yes _____No
3. Do I give visitors ideas of what to look for in the exhibit? _____ Yes _____No
4. Do my tours have an introduction, a body, and a summary? _____ Yes _____No
5. Do I make clear the difference between fact and opinion? _____ Yes _____No
6. Do I revise my presentation to keep them fresh? _____ Yes _____No
7. Have I learned more about the collections/exhibit carts this year? _____ Yes _____No
8. Do I have complete knowledge and familiarity of the exhibit? _____ Yes _____No
9. Do I keep abreast of changes in the exhibit? _____ Yes _____No

GENERAL:

How can my team leader be more supportive?

How can the staff be more helpful?

What further training and assistance would I benefit from?

Denver Museum of Natural History, 1996.

Denver Museum of Natural History
Short Evaluation

NAME: _____ DATE: _____

DEPARTMENT: _____

EVALUATED BY: _____

TOTAL NUMBER OF HOURS WORKED: _____

RATINGS: 1= EXCELLENT (Clearly exceeds job requirements)
                  2= SATISFACTORY (Meets all job requirements)
                  3= UNSATISFACTORY (Needs additional instruction)

PERSONAL FACTORS	RATINGS	STAFF COMMENTS
Attendance and punctuality		
Shows initiative: Handles unexpected situations/problems		
Quality of work: Understanding of job, accuracy		
Completed training, attended orientation		
Positive attitude		
Maintains effective working relationships with staff and volunteers		
Personal appearance		
Accepts supervision and creative criticism		
Potential leader: Inspires interest and enthusiasm in others		
Additional Comments:		

6/98

Paula Meadows, the manager of volunteer services, indicates that staff and volunteers like their respective forms and have reacted positively to the evaluation process. When supervisors have serious concerns about a volunteer's performance they meet with Meadows to discuss various options: additional training, reassignment, termination.

Regardless of who completes the assessment form, regardless of whether you have one form or two, a meeting between you and each volunteer to discuss the evaluation is a necessity. In this meeting you need to affirm the volunteer's strengths; acknowledge the specific ways in which your unit has benefitted over the year from the volunteer's presence; and discuss areas of potential growth. Together you can then explore how to facilitate that growth, whether through additional responsibilities, training, networking, or reading. In order to outline the volunteer's strengths and enumerate the specific ways he or she has contributed to your unit you will either have to have a phenomenal memory or an effective system for documenting such things throughout the year. Clearly, formal evaluation of this kind is time-consuming and should only be done if it is going to be done well.

If you conduct evaluations for the purpose of looking ahead rather than back, the process should be motivating to each volunteer. It is an opportunity for you to praise accomplishments on an individual basis and to demonstrate interest in the volunteer's ongoing skill development. So a "good" performance assessment is wonderful recognition.

But what if a volunteer is not doing well? Or if the evaluation process uncovers problems not previously uncovered? Unless you are willing to tackle such potentially negative outcomes, don't bother evaluating. As we said in the previous chapter on performance problems, you owe it to the volunteer who has the problem, and to every other volunteer performing well, to address the issue.

Situations may arise when your assessment of a volunteer's performance differs sharply from a volunteer's. Anticipate how you will handle this. This is especially important if the outcome of the assessment may involve removing the volunteer from your area. Your organization's grievance procedure should provide direction. The coordinator of volunteers may be able to serve as a mediator or may ask someone else in your organization who supervises volunteers to serve in this capacity. The important thing is that you must be fair and objective.

Never use the annual assessment as an opportunity to tell the volunteer about all the things he or she has been doing wrong for a whole year. And, of course, you should not wait for this occasion to say a kind word. If you have been an effective supervisor all along, there will be few surprises when the annual assessment is done.

Volunteer Satisfaction Surveys

Volunteer satisfaction surveys are also important. They are typically conducted shortly after a new volunteer starts with the organization, then annually, and when a volunteer leaves the organization.

New Volunteer Satisfaction Survey

After a volunteer has been a part of your unit for four to eight weeks, you may want to give him or her a simple questionnaire that focuses primarily on the volunteer's experience. This gives you an opportunity to learn about any problems or difficulties the volunteers is experiencing that may impede good performance or cause him or her to resign. You will need to develop a system for tracking the starting date of new volunteers so that the questionnaire can be mailed or given to the volunteer at the appropriate interval. Providing a stamped, return address envelope will increase the likelihood of a reply. It will also help if, during your first face-to-face meeting with each new volunteer, you mention when the questionnaire will be provided, emphasize how it helps you, and strongly encourage each volunteer to return it. In addition to tracking the start date and the date when the questionnaire should be given out or mailed, you will also have to track returns. If the percentage of returns is very low you may need to take some action to increase the response, but a low response may, in itself, indicate some problems. You will also need to decide whether to do a second (and third) mailing.

If you can, meet with each new volunteer after you have read his or her questionnaire. If you cannot meet face to face, contact the volunteer by phone. Make notes on the questionnaire about points you want to discuss. Be sure to use this opportunity to provide specific praise, to thank the volunteer and to decide together what steps may need to be taken to remedy problems or obstacles the volunteer has identified. State what action, if any, you can take and be sure to honor your commitment.

A three month evaluation form is used by OMNI Youth Services, a non-profit organization in Buffalo Grove, Illinois that serves troubled teens by matching them with a volunteer mentor. Approximately six new volunteers are matched each month. The questions on the evaluation form are as follows:

1. Are you comfortable with your relationship with your youth?

2. Is the relationship progressing according to your expectations? Please explain.

3. Are you clear about the next steps you will take in your relationship with your match?

4. How successfully have your goals for your match been addressed/met? Please describe any changes in your goals for the match.

5. Are you satisfied with the level of contact you have with your supervisor? (i.e., would you like more, less, or the same amount of contact?)

6. Do you have any questions about OMNI's programs and services?

7. What, if anything, could have been done differently with regard to:

   a. ...your initial meeting with your youth?

   b. ...training content or format?

8. Would you like a follow-up call from Lu regarding anything on this evaluation?

9. Please provide any comments/suggestions.

Three months later they receive the evaluation form by mail. The initial return rate is approximately 50%. OMNI staff call those who don't return the form; these calls bring the return rate up to 60%. A second call is made to those who didn't respond, but in this contact the caller conducts the evaluation by phone. Thus there is feedback from every new volunteer.

OMNI staff are committed to getting this feedback because they know by experience that the first three months are the most difficult for new volunteers. By learning about the concerns or problems expressed by the new volunteers, the staff can intervene. Lu Salisbury, OMNI's director of volunteers, notes that the most common request by new volunteers is for more contact from their supervisor. This contact is by phone as OMNI's volunteers work in the field and only come to the office occasionally for support group meetings, which are described elsewhere in this book. Retention of new volunteers has significantly improved since OMNI instituted the three month evaluation process two years ago.

The Glaucoma Research Foundation in San Francisco also surveys new volunteers. Their form is on the next page. Note that, in addition to a numerical response, volunteers are invited to write comments. According to Lisa Perreault, volunteer program assistant, the forms are given to new volunteers after they have been with the organization for three weeks. Once the forms have been turned in either she, or John Bergeron, the volunteer program manager, or the volunteer's direct supervisor meet with each volunteer personally to discuss anything that has surfaced in the written survey. Perreault observes that this two-part approach is especially effective because some volunteers are inclined to put more in writing while others would rather talk about their observations. Also, by giving volunteers the form before the interview, they have time to give careful thought to their answers.

The Foundation gives the same survey to volunteers periodically during their time with the organization. The formal evaluation process is supplemented by regularly asking volunteers for informal feedback to ensure that their concerns have been addressed. The evaluation process has also helped the Foundation learn what aspects of their work the volunteers find to be the most enjoyable and meaningful. The aim of their evaluation process is to make the volunteer's experience as interesting and rewarding as possible.

New volunteers at Memorial Sloan-Kettering received a simple two-page questionnaire after six weeks. Mailing these and tracking the responses were handled by the Department of Volunteer Resources. Copies of the questionnaires were given to each volunteer's supervisor, and we took the initiative to discuss with the supervisors any significant issues that were mentioned in the questionnaires. We also contacted volunteers who expressed major dissatisfaction with their placement or who were experiencing difficulty with the work. Our intent was to intervene, either directly or in partnership with the supervisor, and try to prevent the volunteer from resigning or just fading away. We had few problems with volunteer retention largely because we closely monitored new volunteers.

Here's one final tip from Linda Graff. Be sure to ask the simple question: "Do you think you're doing a good job?" This can be quite a discussion starter.

Annual Satisfaction Survey

You can also learn the volunteers' perspective by asking all your volunteers to complete annual evaluations of their experience. You may want to consult with volunteers and paid staff when designing your form.

It is important to ask about a variety of issues that have a bearing on a volunteer's effectiveness: how challenging the work is; the volunteer's understanding of your unit's goals and how he/she fits in; volunteer-paid staff relations; continuing education; access to supplies and equipment; the physical environment; support and feedback; appreciation/recognition. You may get some very helpful comments if you give volunteers the opportunity to comment on various aspects of your unit's way of operating. The anecdote which Terry Dunn shares on page 103 illustrates that often volunteers see things that paid staff don't see simply because paid staff are so used to the way things arc. In addition, volunteers may be more willing than paid staff to be honest. The fear of loss of a paycheck may keep some paid staff from telling the emperor that he is wearing no clothes, so to speak.

While annually evaluating all aspects of the volunteer's experience is important, be sure that you remain focused on the purpose: to learn what you are doing right (or could be doing better) that affects volunteers' effectiveness and their commitment to your organization. If some volunteers use the questionnaire

Volunteer Self-Evaluation

Please circle from 1–5, 5 being the highest

1. Has your volunteer experience here been a positive one?

    1   2   3   4   5

What would you like to be different?

2. Are you satisfied with the work you are given to do?

    1   2   3   4   5

3. What type of work would you like to do?

4. Is your workspace a good match for you?

    1   2   3   4   5

5. What can be done to make it better?

6. Do you feel that your skills and talents are being utilized?

    1   2   3   4   5

7. What skills and talents are not being used?

8. Are there any skills that you would like to acquire?

9. If you could change anything about your work assignments, what would you change?

10. Are you satisfied with the amount of work you are being given to do?

    1   2   3   4   5

11. Does your supervisor communicate his/her expectations effectively with you?

    1   2   3   4   5

12. Do you feel that you have input over the assignments that you are given?

    1   2   3   4   5

13. Do you feel that you have been appreciated for the work that you do?

    1   2   3   4   5

14. How do you like to be recognized for your work? Party? Card? Certificate? Etc.

15. Do you feel that you have been appropriately trained for the kind of assignments that you receive?

    1   2   3   4   5

16. What keeps you coming back time after time to the Foundation?

Source: John D. Bergeron, Volunteer Program Manager, Glaucoma Research Foundation, San Francisco, CA

Evaluation is a big part of our program. The volunteers who are in training are given two evaluations to fill out, one at the midpoint and one at the end of training. Their evaluation includes the actual components of training as well as their assessments of the training staff, some of whom are also volunteers. Six months after volunteers complete training and are working for the organization, we give them a follow-up evaluation. All volunteers also do an annual evaluation; they rate their supervisors (some of whom are also volunteers), other paid staff, the facilities, resources, and their total experience as a volunteer. All evaluations are done anonymously. Everyone is made aware of what their numerical rating is and any comments made by the evaluators.

An evaluation process is indispensable. The information we receive is invaluable in learning about problems and concerns that we would never have known about otherwise. For example, in 1997 many volunteers expressed dismay at the drab appearance of the phone room. As staff who work here every day, we didn't realize how bad it had gotten. So we took action. The atmosphere has changed significantly and everyone — including the paid staff — has been positively affected.

Even when we can't take immediate action we respond to each suggestion. "We liked the idea about changing computer software to make it easier to access the Internet. Right now what's getting in the way of implementing that change is...."

So while we may not always be able to move on volunteers' suggestions or complaints, at least they know we are always listening, thinking about and considering their issues.

Thus for the volunteers a major benefit of the evaluation process is a sense of empowerment. They get to vent concerns and suggestions; they are heard and action is taken. Their opinion counts and has an impact on the agency. The camaraderie and sense of belonging that seems so important to the smooth running of our phone room is enhanced.

The benefit to paid staff is less burnout and turnover among volunteers, fewer personnel problems, more contented volunteers. Sometimes a volunteer is having problems getting along with others. When several people bring it up, it gives us back-up when we address the situation with the volunteer in question. The feedback is seen as coming more from the peer group rather from the "authorities."

The results of our general evaluations are put in the Volunteer Daily Log for everyone to read. We leave out all personal comments and scores. They are put in the individual's private folder, which each individual has access to and can then choose whether to share them with the others.

— Terry Dunn, Volunteer/Training Coordinator, Florida HIV/AIDS Hotline, Tallahassee, FL

to highlight personal needs without regard to the purpose of their affiliation with your organization, don't get sidetracked into believing that you must meet those needs.

As with the survey of new volunteers, you should aim to meet with each experienced volunteer once you have reviewed his or her annual satisfaction survey. Consider whether this could be done in small groups.

Exit Surveys/Forms

Eventually all volunteers will leave your organization. Some will leave for reasons beyond an organization's control. Perhaps the volunteer is ill or is moving. But some will leave because the affiliation has become meaningless or too difficult. Exit interviews explore these factors.

Even if your organization's coordinator of volunteers conducts exit interviews, you may also want to

do them with the volunteers who are leaving your unit (some of whom may be leaving to work in another area of the organization). Exit interviews seek the volunteer's perspective on the whole organization. The assumption is that volunteers at this point may be more candid about the organization's weaknesses and problems than they were while they were still working in the organization. Your ability to hear these comments openly and then assess them objectively will be beneficial to the whole organization.

On page 105 you will find a copy of the exit survey used by the Fire Department of Chesterfield, Virginia. Note that it is a simple self-mailer.

While exit surveys/forms are important, they do not eliminate the need to do similar surveys early on in the volunteer's affiliation with your organization, especially if your primary purpose is to remedy problems that may be interfering with a volunteer's effectiveness or feelings of belonging.

Putting It All Together

Once you have determined which method(s) you will use, assess whether you can quantify some of the data you have collected. If, for example, a large percentage of your new volunteers are listing the same deficiencies in the orientation process, you certainly have guidance about what to examine more carefully. If your organization has a quality assessment program, you may be able to incorporate your volunteer assessment measures into that program. Investigate whether there is software that will easily allow you to capture numerical responses on the assessment documents you develop.

Be sure to report any results of annual evaluations to all program participants: volunteers, paid staff, perhaps other department heads. The coordinator of volunteers may want to collate all unit evaluations into an annual report on overall volunteer contributions to the organization. The point of evaluation is not to reminisce about the past year; it's to plan for the coming year. So specify what actions you will take as a result of the process. In that way, the time and effort you put into the evaluation processes you choose will ultimately add to your effectiveness and motivate your team to meet the goals of your unit.

WRAP-UP TIPS:

Evaluation/feedback is a volunteer benefit. **—Jill Friedman Fixler**

A systematic evaluation process is crucial for any volunteer program. Sitting down for just a few minutes with your volunteers and asking them some very basic questions increases volunteer morale, improves volunteer retention rates, allows you a chance to clearly voice your expectations, and lets you find out more about a volunteer's skills and potential. **—John Bergeron**

It may take some research to uncover the true reason a volunteer is leaving, however an exit interview should be conducted or an exit evaluation form be completed to determine the reasons. **—Ohio Society of Directors of Volunteer Services**

Exit Survey

Upon leaving this agency, we request your assistance in helping future volunteers have the best experience possible. The information from this survey will be compiled with responses from other former volunteers to assist in the retention program of the volunteer rescue squads and fire companies in Chesterfield County. All responses are anonymous. (Please check all that apply)

Agency _____

Member Number _____

Membership Type
- ☐ Administrative
- ☐ Auxiliary
- ☐ Active (includes Associate & Junior)
- ☐ Life

Check those things you liked about your volunteer experience with this agency

- ☐ Action / Excitement
- ☐ Teamwork / Camaraderie
- ☐ Pride / Recognition
- ☐ Make friends
- ☐ Commitment to Agency
- ☐ Training / Achievement
- ☐ Other _____
- ☐ Service to community
- ☐ Helping people
- ☐ Get to know the community
- ☐ Self-satisfaction / Fulfillment
- ☐ Fringe benefits (i.e. tax benefits, etc.)

Check those things you did not like about your volunteer experience with this agency

- ☐ Internal Agency conflict
- ☐ Time commitment / Hours
- ☐ Lack of support
- ☐ Financial strain
- ☐ Other _____
- ☐ Training requirements
- ☐ Stress level
- ☐ Lack of recognition
- ☐ Type of calls

Why are you leaving the organization?

- ☐ Job transfer
- ☐ Health
- ☐ Family commitments/changes
- ☐ Change in job requirements
- ☐ Other _____
- ☐ Age
- ☐ Lost interest
- ☐ Dissatisfaction
- ☐ Disciplinary action

Did you reach your desired level of training? ☐ Yes ☐ No

Were you provided with proper equipment and facilities to do your job well? ☐ Yes ☐ No

Were you provided enough training to do your job well? ☐ Yes ☐ No

What certifications did you obtain while a volunteer? (Check)

Firefighter ☐	① ② ③	
State Fire Programs Instructor ☐	① ② ③	
Officer ☐	① ② ③ ④	
ICS ☐	① ② ③	
Hazardous Materials ☐	① ② ③ ④	Instructor
Vertical Rescue ☐	① ② ③ ④	Instructor
Vehicle Extrication ☐	① ②	Instructor
MPO ☐		
EVOC ☐		Instructor
Confined Space Rescue ☐		
Trench Rescue ☐		
Water Rescue ☐		Instructor
CPR ☐		Instructor
EMT ☐		Instructor
Shock Trauma ☐		
Cardiac Tech ☐		
Paramedic ☐		
Nurse ☐	LPN RN	Practitioner

Other Certifications (list) _____

Would you be interested in joining another volunteer emergency services organization? ☐ Yes ☐ No

If yes, what type: ☐ Rescue ☐ Police ☐ Fire

Did being a volunteer in this organization help you in your everyday life and/or the work force? ☐ Yes ☐ No

Do you think your volunteer work made a positive difference in
- the community ☐ Yes ☐ No
- the organization ☐ Yes ☐ No
- your life ☐ Yes ☐ No

Would you recommend your volunteer position to someone else?
☐ Yes ☐ No
Why? _____

E:\Wamsley\PM4\Young\VRS-Exit.PM4

Other Comments

_____
_____
_____
_____
_____
_____
_____
_____
_____

Dear Volunteer,

Thanks!

from the bottom
of
our heart ...

Thank You !

(Above) Front of Exit Survey.
(Left) Back of Exit Survey Card.

Submitted by Lisa M. Garey, Volunteer Coordinator, Chesterfield Fire Department, Chesterfield, VA.

8
Adjusting Your Supervisory Style to the Individual or Group

Throughout this book I have emphasized that supervision involves a relationship between the supervisor and the individual being supervised. It goes without saying that each of those relationships is unique. You are unique. There has never been another person in the world exactly like you nor, despite the prospects of cloning, will there ever be another person exactly like you. So it is with each volunteer you work with: each is a unique individual. Working with volunteers will be, over time, like reading a book: new facts, sometimes startling surprises, will be revealed page after page. It is to your credit if that fact delights rather than annoys you!

In this chapter we will provide guidelines to help you to make appropriate adjustments in your supervisory style to fit the "type" of individual with whom you are working. Please bear in mind that these are simply guidelines; they will point you in the right direction but not eliminate the need for you to use your own judgment about each person you are working with. As Marlene Wilson (1976) says: "The manager who manages everyone alike is in deep trouble."

We will also touch on variations in your supervisory style necessitated by the population your volunteers are working with. Reflect for a moment on the many topics you have already read about in this book: defining expectations, orienting and training, coaching and supporting, providing continuing education, praising and thanking. The way you do these things and the amount of time you devote to each will in large measure depend on the kind of work your volunteers are doing. Volunteers working with rape victims will need more support than those working in a museum. You will need to think more about risk management if your volunteers are doing emergency rescue work than you would if they work in a library.

Susan Ellis, this series' editor, has outlined nineteen different types of situations commonly encountered in volunteer supervision, with some general insights and brief suggestions to get you thinking about how you might adapt your methods in each case. Then we have noted issues unique to specific settings, fields, or assignments. We have organized the tips, stories and other material provided by colleagues in the field at the end of the narrative section, under the appropriate categories. Their wealth of experience will be useful to you. Even if none of the situations described by our contributors exactly fits your situation, their comments will undoubtedly spark a new idea you can adapt.

In addition, your coordinator of volunteers may have books or other resources that will help you, or you can call the Volunteer Center in your community through which you can connect with others in your area whose work is similar to yours. Also check the annotated bibliography at the end of this book. If you have specific questions or difficulties, try posting it on CyberVPM, the field's excellent electronic listserv (see page 146).

Perhaps the best way to determine what adjustments might be necessary in your supervisory style is simply to ask your volunteers for their input. You may do this informally, through focus groups or by creating an advisory body that you meet with periodically.

One of the wonderful challenges of the position you are in is the opportunity for you to grow professionally. Your ability to adapt the principles of good supervision to the uniqueness of each individual and each situation is what distinguishes a great supervisor from a mediocre supervisor. Give your volunteers the best you can be!

Special Situations

1. Older Volunteers/Aging in Place

Older volunteers are a tremendous asset and potential talent pool. First, recognize that today's "senior" needs to be approached by level of activity, not just date of birth:

- Young seniors are often very active and fully capable of helping in any volunteer role. In fact, they can apply all sorts of formerly job-connected skills and devote lots of time to your organization. Female seniors in this age range may well have workplace credentials as well as homemaker talents.

- Middle seniors may still be very competent, but may also have health, sight or hearing problems. They may limit their driving. They may also be resistant to things like electronic technology (though don't assume this—many seniors love the Internet).

- Older seniors are the fastest growing age category in our society. Everyone ages differently, but many of these volunteers may have limited physical capacity.

A related, but sometimes more problematic category, is the volunteer who is "aging in place." This is someone who joined you when s/he was younger and fit, but has grown older and now has diminished capacity. The quandary, of course, is that you feel loyalty to a volunteer who has contributed many hours of devoted service and it is awkward to have to confront the changes in ability that age may bring. But for the sake of your service recipients and the volunteer personally, you must find ways to balance the best interests of everyone.

Supervision tips:
1. Know the volunteer's sight and hearing limits and give written material or oral instructions with this in mind.

2. Pay attention to physical fatigue and talk with the volunteer about his/her strength and endurance.

3. When possible, buddy them up with younger volunteers. This technique is especially good for volunteers "aging in place," who know the job but could benefit from some support and perhaps oversight.

4. Insist on a rotation policy for everyone so that no volunteer becomes so entrenched in one assignment that it's impossible to make a change. Offer an "aging in place" volunteer an alternate assignment that makes use of long-time service, such as helping with new volunteer orientation—but only if s/he would be good at it!

5. Don't ignore a deteriorating situation. Sometimes starting a concerned (but caring) conversation gives the volunteer the opening to admit to feeling insecure and less able to do the work s/he formerly considered a breeze.

6. Only when appropriate, consider involving the volunteer's grown children in approaching their parent about changing abilities, or even the family physician.

2. Youth as Volunteers

This is a very large category and can be defined in various ways. Depending on the number and diversity of volunteers in your organization, you may need to distinguish between children, teenagers, college-age students, and perhaps even young adults. And, of course, each young person's maturity level must be assessed. Some ten-year-olds are capable of handling responsible tasks, while some twenty-year-olds shouldn't be left alone!

Perhaps the major challenge is to distinguish between prejudice and truth. Because they are young, teenagers may be immature or at least less experienced. But don't assume this in all cases. Not all young people insist on working with loud music playing on the radio. Test your assumptions.

The point is not to place young people into the same assignments as adult volunteers in all cases (though sometimes this works fine, especially if the work is done in groups). The challenge is either to adapt existing work to meet the skill level of the younger volunteers or to create assignments that tap the unique abilities young people offer. This is an area in which the coordinator of volunteers can be helpful to you. Also, there should be organization-wide policies in place to cover parental permission forms and adult behavior around underage volunteers.

Supervision tips:
1. Remember that young people rarely have much experience with adults who are not a parent or a teacher. Expect to demonstrate how a leader of a project interrelates with those who are doing it.

2. Try to avoid isolation. Even if working on a project independently, it's comforting to a youngster to see other people around.

3. Recognize differing attention spans. Provide some alternate work to break any monotony. Explain when and how to take breaks. Be sure there's something available to drink other than coffee!

4. Adults make some assumptions that young people do not. So you'll have to specifically give permission to: use the phone, use the staff restroom, ask for supplies, etc. Anticipate some of these needs before they arise. Also set boundaries, as in: "You are welcome to use the phone as necessary for local calls, but not for personal calls longer than a few minutes."

5. You may need to recruit adult volunteers (or older teens) who like the assignment of team leader for young volunteers. That way you do not have to supervise every youth personally or daily, but you have provided necessary oversight.

3. Service-Learning Students

Service-learning is an even more specialized situation beyond the general category of "youth." This refers to curriculum-based community service that has learning objectives, monitoring by a teacher or professor, and time for reflection on the experience. Students generally receive academic credit and a grade for their service-learning. Some students are required to perform a certain number of hours of community service in order to pass a class or even graduate (see "Mandated Service" below). But many students elect to take courses with this opportunity to test classroom theory in the real world.

Recognize that some students may not be doing volunteer work with you totally out of a desire to be there. Ideally they will like the work, but the academic requirement may be their prime motivator. Also, the faculty may be unrealistic as to what the student can/should learn in a brief period of time. Finally, the student may have "semester messiah" syndrome—feeling that one or two courses give him/her the ability to whip things into shape. On the positive side, students can be extremely helpful because they can read and write well (one hopes!), don't mind doing research as well as hands-on work, and can give a focussed amount of time.

Supervision tips:
1. Make it clear you are not the professor. Yes, you will be evaluating work, but not for a grade. Your goal is to get work done as effectively as possible. Assignments should be discussed as they are worked on. Students sometimes approach agency assignments like a term paper: they go away and work alone and then tremulously "hand it in" for a grade. In the real world, if something about the assignment is a problem, you need to talk about it and that's a good thing.

2. Know in advance what the learning goals are and try to add conversations about these subjects into your supervisory meetings. Be sure the student understands the context of his/her work.

FROM THE FIELD

The key to a good volunteer program involving teens is good planning, training, communication and monitoring. Following orientation each youth volunteer at our facility receives two one-on-one trainings with an experienced and specially trained youth peer trainer. The trainer leads the new volunteer through each of the tasks assigned on a step-by-step basis. After this training the new volunteer works with another volunteer as s/he gains experience.

All positions for youth volunteers are quite structured so that both the volunteer and the staff know the expectations. The structure keeps the volunteer busy through the shift.

We are also careful to provide a safe and secure experience. We anticipate potential hazards and develop and implement plans to avoid them. This is not only good risk management; it is also reassuring to the parents, whose confidence we carefully cultivate.

Communication with the parents/guardians is essential. We send them a letter when their teen begins volunteering, with information regarding the position and schedule. We assure them that they will be working in an environment with caring and concerned employees. Because this may be the teen's first experience working in an adult world, we encourage the parents to call us if issues about the experience come up at home. We also notify parents promptly if any changes are made with the teens' schedule or assignment.

Beverly Robinson, Manager, Volunteer Services, Minnesota Masonic Home, Bloomington, MN

---

3. Clarify the role of the classroom teacher. Will s/he be visiting on site? Asking for a journal or other written observations? If there is a problem, should you call him or her about it?

4. Do not allow "observation" to take precedence over learning-by-doing. Your organization is not a learning lab for the student to "visit." It's a real-life work environment with a service purpose. The student's learning should derive from helpful participation.

4. Mandated Service

The concept of "mandated volunteering" is, to many, an oxymoron. That's why most of the programs described below use vocabulary such as "community service" to focus on the activity rather than the motivation. Obviously both the supervisor and the "volun-

Welfare reform workers can include: 1) "able-bodied" individuals who are receiving food stamps and are now required to perform community service hours weekly in order to continue receiving this assistance; or 2) individuals who are transitioning off public assistance into full employment, and are assigned to a community work experience slot for a few months. Some tips to supervisors:

- Ask the caseworker how the situation has been explained to the participants. Has it been labeled "employment," "working for free," or "volunteering"? This will tell you whether you need to provide more explanation of how they fit into your organization and may also affect their attitudes.

- These individuals may need to move through several types of assignments in order to develop their skills at a steady rate. Keep offering new and more complex types of tasks. The more experience they can gain and the more skills they can learn, the easier it will be for them to find work.

- When evaluating their work performance, pay attention to work habits such as coming to work regularly and on time, following directions, and getting along well with fellow workers. Let them know these qualities are appreciated and valued by employers and offer as much positive reinforcement as possible.

- Encourage individuals to keep a daily log of the type of tasks they work on. This will give them a sense of accomplishment, and come in handy when putting together their first resume or job application.

- Assist your co-workers in understanding why these individuals are placed with you and how they can make the experience a win-win situation. Allow individual relationships to develop according to personality preferences and styles. Learning how to be part of office teamwork is valuable.

- Include these workers in staff meetings and other office functions as much as possible. Each one can be a learning opportunity.

- If your community service workers are actively looking for work, discuss the following:
  - Do they have access to the daily want ads, or can staff bring them from home?
  - Do they want help compiling a resume? Completing applications?
  - Are there job openings in other organizations you can tell them about?
  - Is there a way your human resources staff can be of assistance?

- Hold some type of celebration when one of these workers "graduates" successfully from the placement or finds employment. This type of milestone is critically important for self-esteem and self-confidence, and deserves recognition from the organization. Offer to be a continuing resource for the individual in the future.

Katherine Noyes Campbell, Executive Director, Association for Volunteer Administration, Richmond, VA

teer" may have trouble accepting the "voluntary" nature of the work. Even more interesting, some traditional volunteers may object to being categorized in the same way as someone being made to work by a government authority.

The point in this book is not to explain, justify, defend or criticize mandated programs. Whether or not you want to label these people "volunteers," they offer your organization new sources of help. Even if someone must give hours, they can still be caring and have talents to share. The issue is not how volunteers come to an organization initially—it's why they stay.

Think about the goals as: first, to serve your clients (as always); second, to give this volunteer a chance to make the most of the opportunity; and third, to encourage this person to be pleased enough with the work that he or she chooses to remain on with your organization for a time past the mandated number of hours. Quite a number of people do.

For all the categories below, a useful piece of advice is: don't assume! Someone may be in a situation unwillingly and yet be able to make the most of it. Also, someone's past record may not indicate overlooked talents or skills. Practice positive self-fulfilling prophecy. If you design work to challenge all volunteers, and then deal with people as individuals with something of value to share, you will more often be pleased than disappointed.

Special issues/supervision tips:

- Court-ordered programs

  Court-ordered service, or alternative sentencing, can be used for many different crimes. You'll be surprised that you can't tell what someone was accused of! Working with offenders is a matter of developing trust and minimizing concern for risk. The more you express expectations at the

An important point stressed by many of the programs surveyed is the need to adhere to your stated policies and expectations. Make them clear to everyone and then follow through—without guilt! Consider reiterating the rules in writing to any individuals who need it. There may be a legitimate reason why the offender has erratic attendance—even the best of volunteers have occasional emergencies—so your emphasis should be on the need to keep in touch with you should this happen. Keep your tone professional, not punitive.

Here are some additional comments regarding supervision:

"...When I feel they are really slacking off I set up a system whereby they are given a set number of hours for the completion of a project. For instance, if I know a job shouldn't take more than 3 hours to finish, I assign the task with that understanding. But this happens rarely."

"I would like to emphasize that prompt and reliable feedback from agencies is essential to the success of community service programs. If a probationer fails to report when expected or takes an extended leave of absence, the probation officer has no way of knowing this unless he or she is advised by the agency."

....It is important to share recordkeeping expectations when you are making initial agreements with a referral source, thus avoiding surprises later on. Volunteer programs that are loosely structured without much formal recordkeeping may need to spend a little more time on this task in order to comply with the court's need for documentation....

"Court-referred volunteers are responsible for recording their own hours, just like other volunteers; but they must have them verified by a staff member who initials each day's entry of hours."

SOURCE

Opportunity or Dilemma: Court-Referred Community Service Workers, by Katherine H. Noyes, Virginia Department of Volunteerism, 1985.

start, the easier it will be to set and enforce standards. The court cannot order you or your agency to do anything! If the situation is not working out, say so.

Maintain confidentiality. While you have the right to know the court status of a volunteer, it is not anyone else's business unless the person chooses to share the information on his/her own. In the manual, *Opportunity or Dilemma: Court-Referred Community Service Workers* (1985), Katie Noyes Campbell addresses the question of labelling court-referred workers as different from other volunteers:

> ...A few programs also use a different term (such as "service worker") to refer to the court-ordered individuals in all contexts, contending that both staff and "regular" volunteers feel more comfortable distinguishing these people as a different type of worker. Again, this is a practice which relates to the overall philosophy about how these workers should be incorporated. While such labelling may seem to make things easier in the beginning, it does verge on being a violation of privacy and may in fact contribute to a negative attitude on the part of the offender. Decisions about definitions and terminology—both on paper for recordkeeping purposes and in practice—must be made carefully and with sensitivity.

Depending on the crime committed, don't place the person into a volunteer situation that has temptations. Use a buddy system if you can.

- Welfare to work

  Welfare reform is still a largely undefined area. However, in many states, community service is one option for people who need to maintain their public assistance benefits. Such volunteer program participants may resent that their service is tied to a welfare check. Some participants will have literacy problems and may not have developed world-of-work skill habits. Some may feel out of place, including concern over what to wear. As a supervisor, be alert to these issues which can interfere with good intentions.

  For some excellent suggestions on working with workers resulting from welfare reform, see the contribution from Katie Noyes Campbell on the previous page.

- Student graduation requirement

  This is similar to service-learning already discussed, but not all graduation requirements are curriculum based. In other words, students can be told to do hours on their own and bring back some sort of proof—with no faculty member doing any reflection/debriefing academically. Here the importance is helping the student to see that his or her service is making a difference.

Be aware that many requirements are for only a token number of hours of service. If you need more participation to warrant your supervisory time, you may have to insist on more hours than the minimum number set by the school. If this expectation is expressed at the start, students unwilling to give extra time will not apply to work in your agency.

- For all mandated workers, remember:

  - How the assignment is designed is key.

  - Don't assume the absence or presence of skills/talents. Seek these out.

  - You will probably need to pay extra attention to attendance and time records, as the duration of the service is imposed by a third party. You may also have to submit performance reports to the outside authority.

  - Clarify the role of any outside liaison (probation officer, teacher, etc.).

  - Maintain confidentiality about personal issues and background.

5. Families Volunteering Together

Family volunteering has intrigued people for a long time, but there are still few organizations that actively seek out this pool of volunteers. The word "family" should be defined loosely. Sometimes all members of a family will indeed commit to an assignment together. So you might involve both parents and all children. More common is a mix-and-match approach: one parent and one or more children; extended family members of any age; grandparents and grandchildren. Many ages can be represented.

Family members might focus on the same assignment or client, truly volunteering as a unit. Another option is that everyone comes in together but then scatters to do individual work.

Family volunteering has great potential but also some pitfalls. What's good: a group of people sharing responsibility for one assignment assures that it will be done; they form their own support group; it's a way to gain input from youngsters without having to find non-related adults to supervise. What can be a problem: some members of the family may be there unwillingly (usually adolescents dragged into service); parents may speak for everyone without group discussion; family conflicts can surface during volunteering.

Supervision tips:
1. Get to know all the volunteers and don't fall into the trap of dealing only with the adults. On the other hand, ask the family to designate their main contact person so that you can communicate consistently with one person, especially for things like schedule changes.

2. Help the family to organize their assignment so that all members are doing tasks they enjoy and are good at.

3. You can suggest that one or more family members break away to do a special assignment whenever you sense tension or see that someone wants to do more.

4. Find ways to recognize each individual for his or her contribution as well as thanking the family as a unit.

6. People Exploring Careers

As the work world shifts madly, more people are seeking mid-life career changes in addition to young people just starting to build their resumes. Usually this motivation for volunteering is not a problem, but occasionally the volunteer might start "auditioning" for a paid job, ask to observe or participate in things beyond the scope of the assignment, or ask for a reference prematurely.

Supervision tip:
As with other volunteers, it is helpful if you know the agenda. It's generous to help the volunteer explore your career—and it's a nice way to "give back" to your profession. But there are freedoms to volunteering that may be limited if the person is trying to win favor as a future job applicant. For example, volunteers criticize more freely and can take greater risks. Try to shift the focus to exploring the career field, rather than on getting a job with your organization.

7. Experts Giving Technical Assistance

A wide range of experts can be tapped as volunteers to assist in countless ways. These skilled volunteers may be university faculty, business executives, community leaders, or other VIPs. The point is that the volunteer—by virtue of the assignment—is going to be more qualified than employees in a particular subject. While the expertise may be needed, it may be hard for the "supervisor" to accept the volunteer's credentials. On the other side of the coin, the expert volunteer may mistakenly assume a complete lack of knowledge by the staff and so be patronizing.

Supervision tips:

1. Even experts need orientation to the agency and how it does things. Don't confuse knowing a specialty skill with knowing how to apply it to your setting. That's the partnership: you bring the understanding of your organization and its needs.

2. This is more of a "consultancy" model than a "supervisory" relationship. You delineate the needs to be met and decide if they have been met, while the volunteer provides the know-how and correct approach to doing the job. It's not hierarchical; it's two equal partners.

3. Because of the above, set goals for how you will know when the work is done and what intermediate benchmarks will tell you both you're on the right track.

4. Even though the volunteer is skilled, you don't have to accept all advice given. Raise questions and feel free to suggest ideas based on your knowledge of the situation in this case.

5. If the volunteer is a business/corporate person, be prepared to have to explain how things work in a nonprofit or government agency. For example: how decisions are made (often needing board action); how the budget may be restricted or limited; etc.

6. While this is an excellent procedure to follow with any volunteer, be prepared to use time efficiently and productively with an expert volunteer. This means scheduling meetings and sticking to an agenda, having materials prepared in advance, and responding to requests promptly.

7. Despite the differences, never lose sight of the fact that this is still a volunteer. Thank you's are always appropriate! As are party invitations, recognition gifts, or anything else any other volunteer would receive.

8. Corporate Volunteers

Please note that, just because many volunteers are coincidentally employed somewhere, they are not "corporate volunteers." This term refers to volunteers who come to your organization through some company-based initiative—either a full-fledged employee volunteer program or at least recruited through some company communication mechanism. So they have some sort of tie to their employer, much like students or court-ordered workers are connected to their placement sponsor.

Supervision tips:

1. Read the tips recommended for both "technical assistance volunteers" above and "organizational group volunteers" below.

2. If employees volunteer together, be sure to encourage teamwork and good morale (that's what the company wants from the effort).

9. People in Transition

The concept of the "transitional volunteer" was developed to identify those volunteers who are moving from one phase of life to another. This can include such life stage factors as: coping with grief or illness; the first year of retirement; sudden unemployment or any job change; marriage or divorce. It can also include the period needed to resume a normal life after a period of institutionalization, addiction, or incarceration.

Eva Schindler-Rainman first delineated the concept of transitional volunteering in 1981 and outlined the issues involved (see Archive on page 114).

Supervision Tips:

1. It is important to know if a volunteer is in transition—but without prying into personal information that tells more than you need to know.

Volunteering can play a major role in helping people through the changes in their lives, but it requires considerable sensitivity from those of us who are in charge of volunteer programs to realize their full significance.

Individuals who are involved in a transition are in a position of some weakness. They are venturing (willingly or not); they may be uncertain, hesitating between the uncomfortable and the unknown, or between the known and the new; they may have been forced into a difficult position and be looking for new ways to escape or alleviate it. They may be learning about things they have not faced up to before. We have to be sensitive to the position that they are in, to their feelings with that, and to the ways they react or cope with it.

SOURCE

Transitioning: Strategies for the Volunteer World by Eva Schindler-Rainman, Voluntary Action Resource Centre, Vancouver, Canada, 1981.

2. Allow the volunteer to move at his or her own pace in wanting to interact with others or in accepting increased responsibility.

3. Provide short-term, goal-oriented tasks for which the volunteer can feel a sense of accomplishment and worth.

4. Help transitioners to experiment with new activities. Creativity and innovation can be very healing.

5. Be patient and expect some back tracking. Few people progress in a straight line. It may be one step forward and one step back for a while.

Not all volunteers undergoing personal transitions will need hand-holding, but most will appreciate sensitivity from you. Observe the volunteer's mood and behavior (is s/he crying? gazing distractedly?) and offer a friendly ear if necessary. It has often proven true that people coping with major change will plunge into volunteer work with energy and genuine commitment—if you give them the chance.

10. Mental Health Issues

There is a world of difference between the volunteer who comes to the organization for therapeutic reasons and the volunteer who, once on board, manifests emotional disturbance. The latter may require professional intervention. The former can be wonderful as long as you, as supervisor, do not get put into the role of "therapist."

The spectrum of mental health problems is broad, ranging from depression to schizophrenia. There are also gradations of mentally-challenged youth and adults, who are not mentally ill but have varying degrees of developmental disabilities. Obviously each diagnosis will require different tactics.

When a condition is known from the start of the volunteer's service, it is possible to select the best assignment and supervise as needed. Many mental health issues are controllable with medication or do not interfere with the ability to do productive work. If a condition manifests itself unexpectedly, it presents a different supervisory challenge that might require the intervention of a mental health professional.

Supervision tips:
1. Clarify—with the referring physician or teacher—the potential and limits of the volunteer. Are there any situations that should be avoided (such as missing medication times or fear of enclosed spaces)?

2. Be welcoming and accessible so the volunteer can admit any discomfort as it develops.

3. Keep the person occupied and knowing what is expected each day or shift.

11. Volunteers with Physical Disabilities

People with physical disabilities are a huge category of prospective volunteers, because the term covers many different capabilities and limitations. Of course, the Americans with Disabilities Act (ADA) has made it clear that your agency must be accessible to employees and volunteers (and clients) with physical challenges. The main issue will be wondering about the volunteer's ability to do the work—and possible need for adaptation.

Supervision tips:
1. Once you have determined that the candidate is qualified for the volunteer position, talk openly about his or her possible adaptation needs. Remember, it isn't a surprise to them that you noticed they are in a wheelchair, or blind, or whatever! They already know this! This makes them the best judges of what they can or can't do. If you have a concern, raise it and see what you can work through. If necessary, experiment for a while and then assess the results.

FROM THE FIELD

The Visiting Nurse Service (VNS) provides home health care and community based health services to 22,000 patients each week in the New York metropolitan region. In 1995, the Young Adult Institute (YAI) of the National Institute for People with Disabilities offered their participants to VNS as volunteers. Most are 20+ years old and are developmentally delayed or have other disabilities including emotional problems. Most are able to read and write, many travel on their own, but all are able to communicate and are willing and able workers.

The supervisor from YAI and the volunteer field coordinator met to discuss the capabilities of the volunteers. This enabled us to design appropriate jobs based on our needs and their skills. Most of the jobs we assigned to them can be done in groups. They collate new patient intake materials and package supply kits for the nurses' visits. They receive a short orientation about the agency and the importance of their specific jobs with an opportunity provided to ask questions and discuss what they learned. Their supervisor is shown the work by the coordinator of volunteers and he/she explains it to the volunteers and oversees their work. There are daily informal meetings with the YAI supervisor, where any changes in the work routine are discussed. Providing space for the volunteers has proven to be the biggest problem encountered.

The higher-functioning volunteers from the center assist with telephone surveys of agency clients, asking prescribed questions and noting responses. Since they follow instructions without wavering, they do not get caught up in trying to solve problems or in idle conversation. They are polite, direct and able to complete more surveys than some of our other volunteers. Training for this activity is conducted by the coordinator of volunteers with the assistance of the YAI supervisor. A great deal of time is spent at role play on the telephone, teaching them how to introduce themselves and use the appropriate tone of voice and helping them to become familiar with the questions. If someone is not working out, they are assigned to a different job. Those who become frustrated by no answers are also moved to another position. The coordinator is very adept at not making this seem like a demotion. The reward is actually being able to call a "real person." Each caller is closely monitored by the volunteer field coordinator for the first week and by the YAI supervisor after that.

Although the volunteer field coordinator has a very strong commitment to this population, she would not have been able to make it work if the staff had indicated any negative feelings. They are generally compassionate and sensitive, but when it comes to getting the work out, they want to know that the volunteers will complete it on time and without constant checking on their part. This is not any different from working with a non-challenged population. Having the appropriate jobs at the skill level that the volunteers can handle seems to be a crucial factor in the success of this program.

Some problems related to self-control and noise level have arisen. When the volunteers call across to each other, speak too loudly or carry on conversations where others are working, the supervisor or coordinator will approach them and quietly remind them that they are at work and need to follow the rules of courtesy. This strategy is usually effective.

Praise for a job well done is ongoing as is a big, "hello, happy to see you" each time they arrive and a "thank you" at the end of the day. The coordinator was quick to point out that these volunteers are not treated differently than any other volunteers who come into our office to work. She knows they are special but they don't.

We find that it is important that work be ready for these volunteers when they arrive and that they are placed in areas where things are relatively calm. They need to feel they are a part of the agency. When one of the volunteers heard that nurses were trying to obtain food for patients in need, she obtained approval to coordinate a canned food drive at her center and in our office. The volunteers made posters and collected and boxed food to give to the nurses for their patient visits. They also made holiday gift bags and sold them to staff to raise money to buy more canned goods.

Staff is invited to our holiday party for the volunteers, which gives them the opportunity to say thank you. The staff is sensitive to these young adults and the atmosphere of mutual respect and caring is clear to anyone that comes into the office.

Rhoda White, Director of Volunteer Services, Visiting Nurse Service of New York, New York, NY

FROM THE FIELD

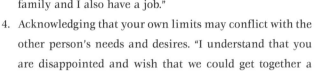

Testing a person's limits or boundaries is a common occurrence in the development of any relationship. Volunteers who work as buddies with clients who are mentally ill may find that their client has unrealistic expectations of the volunteer. If the volunteer does not set limits, burnout is a likely consequence.

The goal of setting limits is to create a healthy, effective relationship between the volunteer and the client. To set limits, volunteers must think through their own expectations, what they are willing and not willing to do and how much they are willing to compromise. Steps to effective limit setting are:

1. Knowing your boundaries. How frequently will you meet with your client? Where are you willing to go with your client? Will you give your client your office telephone number?

2. Stating your limits. Be gentle but firm. "Generally our visits will be once a week for about two hours."

3. Explaining the reasons for this limit. "I would like to spend more time with you but I have obligations to my family and I also have a job."

4. Acknowledging that your own limits may conflict with the other person's needs and desires. "I understand that you are disappointed and wish that we could get together a couple of times a week."

5. Proposing a compromise. "Let me suggest something. When your birthday comes, let's do something special. I also think we could occasionally plan a longer day together."

6. Eliciting feedback regarding the compromise by engaging the client in discussion. "I value your opinion. So that we can maximize our relationship tell me what you are feeling." Whenever possible avoid asking questions that elicit a yes/no answer.

Bernice Skirboll, CVA, Executive Director and President, COMPEER, Inc., Rochester, NY

FROM THE FIELD

Here are some tips on supervising volunteers with a history of severe mental illness or currently in treatment:

- Meet the volunteer with a mental illness as you would any other.

  Cover his/her interests and talents, describe your needs and tasks, then together decide where to start. These volunteers have time and commitment as well as talents. Expect as much diversity as you would from the general population in education, past experience, etc. They may serve on the Board or chair a committee. They may have computer experience or they may take responsibility for leading a group. They may prefer to work alone, or with others.

- Plan for success.

  Any volunteer, but particularly a volunteer with a mental illness, needs to have meaningful work and experience success rather than failure. A volunteer with a mental illness may react more strongly to stress and become very discouraged. Performance may be greatly affected. An honest relationship will allow open communication about signs of stress.

- Build flexibility into the task.

  Offer flexible hours, flexible days, sharing the task. Expect variations in performance as the illness cycles, encouraging

treatment evaluation if indicated. Be assertive in letting the volunteer know that this is OK. Be assertive in giving emotional support. Remind them that flexibility is built into the task for more difficult periods.

- Establish a personal relationship.

  Ensure that there can be trust and the possibility of discussing work needs related to treatment or medication if the volunteer so desires. Follow the lead of the volunteer in this. Persons with a mental illness can "read the illness" in their particular situation.

- Give support as you would for any other volunteer.

  Offer materials, training, evaluation, commendation. Give special attention to emotional support and open communication.

- Appreciate the uniqueness of the individual and the task he/she is performing.

  Persons with a mental illness do remember the dreams they had before the illness developed and they do have a passion to perform and contribute. As they help your organization you help them continue dreaming.

Kay Rittenhouse, Volunteer Services Director, NAMI of St. Louis, MO

2. If it would be helpful in training, assign an able-bodied volunteer to buddy with the new volunteer—or assign an experienced person with a similar physical challenge. If the volunteer will need ongoing assistance (such as someone to read out loud or to move objects), assign a permanent partner and design the project to be done by two.

12. Participant-Volunteers

The term "participant-volunteer" refers to volunteers who are themselves currently clients or recipients of your services. The most common examples are: seniors who are members of a senior center helping with meals or parties; people with AIDS being buddies to others with AIDS; all self-help groups such as Alcoholics Anonymous. A closely-related variation is family members of clients, such as parents of students in that classroom, grandparents of a child with a specific disease who raise money for research, etc. Another variation is when "members" of an association, faith community, or other organized group offer to take on specific "volunteer" roles.

The challenge is the balancing act: how to encourage the best participation without extending status privileges over other volunteers or participants/members, and without compromising standards of performance because you feel you can't ask this volunteer to leave (they still have the right to be program participants or members).

A possible variation on this theme is when employees offer to volunteer in your organization on their own time. This is generally frowned upon under the Fair Labor Standards Act, unless the volunteer assignment is totally different from the employee's paid job.

For any type of participant-volunteer, the supervisory question is: Will the supervisor feel free to correct work done by this volunteer "insider"?

Supervision tips:
1. A written volunteer job description is vital here! It must clearly state what it means to be a "volunteer" as separate and apart from being a client, member etc. This should be reinforced in all orientation and training. And supervisory sessions ought to deal with anything that might blur the lines (as in: "What will you do if your daughter becomes bored with this activity but the other children want to continue playing?").
2. Sometimes a uniform, smock, or identifying button helps to separate when the person is a participant and when "on duty" as a volunteer.

FROM THE FIELD

Each blind person has different visual acuity; some have enough vision to travel independently, others may need assistance. Be sure that the blind volunteer's skills and experience fit the volunteer position s/he will fill. Supervisors should also remember to:

1) Speak directly to the person with vision loss, not through another person;
2) Give clear and precise directions. Do not say "over there" or "down the street." Instead say, "to your right" or "four blocks straight ahead."
3) Ask questions. Open communication helps understanding.
4) Do not change your vocabulary. It is OK to use words such as look, see or watch.
5) Identify yourself to a blind person.
6) Maintain your usual level of voice.
7) Let a blind person know when you are leaving an area.
8) Do not leave half-way open doors or other obstacles in the path of a blind person.
9) When guiding someone with a visual impairment, let that person take your arm; do not take his/her arm and push the person ahead of you.
10) Remember that a blind or visually impaired person is just like you, except for a loss of vision.

Mike Cataruzolo, CVA, Supervisor, Volunteer Services, Perkins School for the Blind, Watertown, MA

---

13. External, Self-Organized Groups

Volunteers often work in groups and/or come to their assignments because they are members of an external association that has made a group commitment to your organization. If individually-recruited volunteers engage in a group project, or you have formed a committee of any sort, you may well continue supervising on a one-to-one basis. Or you may begin to interact with the group collectively, with perhaps some private sessions with the designated leader.

Special supervisory issues arise when the group is already affiliated and comes to you *as* a group. The possibilities are many: civic and service clubs; faith community projects; corporate employee teams; youth clubs/troops; student associations; etc. First define the parameters:
- Does your organization know all the group members as individuals, or is the relationship with the group's leader(s) who, in turn, work with the members?

On CyberVPM, in response to posts about dealing with disabilities, Nan Hawthorne added some personal thoughts:

...I think what I appreciate about these comments is that they bring the discussion into the world of the real impact of bias. You can call me "differently abled," "blind," "low vision," or whatever you want and it has little impact on whether or not I can do your volunteer job. But if you say I have to drive when I really didn't have to, I can't. That's what happened with Big Sisters—-I was turned down on the basis that a Big Sister MUST have a car. (No, it wasn't a rural area.)...What I recommend to folks is that you are DEAD SURE the car or the lifting is, in fact, an integral part of the job. Not just a desirable one. Let me give you two examples I've experienced firsthand.

Don't assume an employee or volunteer must have a car just because you aren't familiar with alternatives or just have a "bad attitude" towards public transportation. For requiring a car or driver's license to be defensible under the law driving must be a primary responsibility, not a means to achieving other responsibilities. For instance, I applied for a volunteer program manager job with a nonprofit. I was a strong candidate in all ways—very positive interview, everything great, UNTIL I had to take my magnifier out to read something. The room temperature dropped about 20 degrees. The director said, "I'm sorry, you must drive a car. I can't have my staff spending hours on the bus going to meetings." This is an entirely indefensible reason to require driving. Transit is available. Work can be done while riding on buses. Driving is only a means, not an integral part of the job. (No, I didn't sue because they covered their infraction too skillfully.) They lost

a crack VPM to bias. What you could say in a job description is, "If driving, must have a valid in-state driver's license."

Another example, also from a job hunt story. I was told by a very nice, intelligent woman that I respect that a job would require being able to lift 40 lbs. The job was, again, VPM. The lifting was training materials. No, sorry, again not an integral part of the job. Simply supplying a twenty dollar luggage cart would have solved the problem. This, again, is not a defensible physical requirement.

It is true that "disabled people" covers an incredibly diverse group! Sometimes the needs and concerns of the different segments can be diametrically opposed. Even cultures can be amazingly different, as, in my observation, the cultures that develop in groups of visually impaired people as opposed to hearing impaired people.

I do occasionally say "I don't see well" because I don't "look" blind unless you are really observant. And using the term sometimes provokes outright disbelief in my "claim." (Which is, of course, the most difficult issue to deal with of them all!) But I also, in practical terms, find saying "I don't see well" can result in people thinking I just need new glasses or whatever. That somehow I should take some steps to see better. Not that I have a legitimate request for accommodation. So I've abandoned that terminology for the most part as impractical. Now I usually say I'm "visually impaired" or "partially sighted."

Nan Hawthorne, Managing Director, Sound Volunteer Management, Seattle, WA

- Is the group accepting responsibility for all aspects of, say, a shift (as in handling Monday evening in the gift shop) or a project (filming a video tour of the facility)? Or are you in charge and the group comes in mainly as a set of participants for that assignment?

- Does everyone in the group work at the same time, in the same place, on the same project? Or on the same project but in shifts throughout the week or month (one at a time)? Or on the same shift, but then disperse to work on different assignments until it's time to go home together?

Supervision tips all center around the answers to the above questions. But regardless, it is useful to develop a specialized form of job description, maybe

called "Group Project Description," defining the overall agreement about the project, who does what, etc. It may then be necessary to have individual job descriptions within the group project, or possibly instruction sheets that everyone gets on site. Also, clarify who deals with problems. You or the group leader? How?

In one of the earliest books in the field on volunteer management, *Leadership for Volunteering* (1976), Harriet Naylor said:

> We have also learned that group placements double commitment to serve, by adding peer pressure. A volunteer serving with a group has to answer to his peers as well as to the "volunteers" and the paid staff involved. Even if the volunteer works one-to-one with a client or on his own, his identity as a group member for

Approach people [in an all-volunteer organization] as much as possible in terms of what they have to give, what they want to do rather than what you think they ought to want to do. The worst thing you can do here is what we usually do with new members—"hit" them right off with a list of things we old-timers have decided need doing. Instead, ask them what they would like to do, would like to learn, and would not want to do...You'll find that ultimately you get as many of your needs met that way, maybe more of them, while at the same time conveying a respectful, welcoming non-intimidating attitude to the prospective volunteer...

One day Bob (I'll call him) showed me six goals the neighborhood organization had set last year. I asked him how we did and he said, pretty well, we achieved three of the six goals.

I congratulated him and then suggested we should talk about the three goals we failed to achieve. "What three goals?" said Bob. "Wait a minute," said I. "You can't ignore missed goals if you want to do better next year" etc., etc. "No," said Bob, "We didn't fail to achieve those three goals. We made a mistake calling them goals, because IN A VOLUNTEER GROUP LIKE OURS, WHAT VOLUNTEERS WON'T DO CAN'T BE A GOAL!" a little tricky, perhaps, but a solid point underneath. In an all-volunteer group, what volunteers won't do, ultimately won't get done. The program is literally the product of the people. Therefore, set goals in the first place on the basis of what volunteers are willing to do. More than just "willing," if possible.

SOURCE

When Everyone's a Volunteer by Ivan H. Scheier, Energize, Inc., 1992

feedback or social purposes will insure his performance for the honor of the group as well as for the sake of the service.

14. All-Volunteer Organizations (AVOs)

A special type of group is the organization that is entirely composed of volunteers. You may have an auxiliary or friends group that supports your work, or you may collaborate with any type of membership association ranging from a tenant council to a PTA to a soccer league.

Ivan Scheier, in his book *When Everyone's a Volunteer* (1992), highlighted one of the most important challenges of all-volunteer (or "non-staffed") groups this way:

You might be able to hold together a staffed organization by paying people to do some meaningless things or things they are not helped to see as meaningful. Your ability to do this in an all-volunteer group is strictly limited because, once you run out of grudging obligation as a motivation, volunteers will ultimately and consistently do only that which they perceive as meaningful.

15. One-time vs. Ongoing Service

Over the course of a year, you will spend most of your supervisory time on volunteers who accept ongoing assignments with you. However, you may also benefit from volunteers in short-term, intensive assignments (some technical assistance projects fall into this category), with episodic schedules (perhaps

handling work arising only once a quarter), or even one-time volunteers. If you have many special events, whether for fundraising or to complete specific work deadlines, you will be responsible for making the most of efforts offered by volunteers one day at a time.

Clearly, you will spend less time supervising the one-time volunteer than the ongoing one. However, you still need to assure yourself that the one-day-only volunteer is doing the job. Here's where instruction sheets, checklists, buddy systems, and all the other techniques we've been describing are invaluable.

16. When Volunteers Supervise Other Volunteers

Often volunteers take on leadership roles that put them in the position of supervising other volunteers. Naturally this is the norm in all-volunteer groups, but there are all sorts of administrative assignments in agencies that require experienced or skilled volunteers to help others. Don't assume people intuitively know how to work with one another as volunteers! In fact, few volunteers have ever received training about volunteering as a subject unto itself. They may bring the same stereotypes and negative attitudes to their supervisory role that some employees demonstrate.

Complicating the volunteer-to-volunteer relationship is the desire to be liked. Paid supervisors also want to be liked, but accept that their jobs may require the unpleasant tasks of criticizing, negatively evaluating, and even firing those who report to them. Remember that volunteers happily contribute their time and talents to a cause but, in return, want to feel good about their efforts. If facing a problem with another volun-

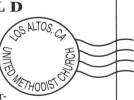
teer may result in bad feelings or ongoing disputes, some volunteers will avoid any form of confrontation.

Supervision tips:

1. Train volunteers who will supervise others in how to be a supervisor and what the special issues are when supervising other volunteers. (Give them this book to read!)

2. Clarify the scope of authority being delegated: how much and any limits.

3. Encourage the supervisory volunteer to share his or her feelings about the role. Acknowledge that being a leader of peers is sometimes uncomfortable, but stress the importance of their efforts to the organization and the product at hand.

4. Make sure all volunteers know who has been given supervisory authority and that you will support—and expect—collegial relationships.

17. Off-Site Volunteers

We have already provided you with many suggestions for working with volunteers in the field. Always keep in mind that when people do not see, touch, and experience daily activities as they occur in your organization, it becomes an intellectual exercise to feel connected. Anything you do to demonstrate that off-site volunteers are a welcome part of the whole team will be very appreciated. Pay special attention to the communication ideas in Chapter 4.

18. Virtual Volunteering

Virtual volunteering is the first truly new way of contributing one's talent to emerge in a very long time and obviously required the invention of the Internet to evolve. Please note that the term is not "virtual *volunteers*." The people are indeed real! It's their volunteering that takes place online, via a computer and modem. Virtual volunteering is a variation on the theme of off-site workers and is connected to the modern employment trend of telecommuting. Every principle and technique that we have stressed in this book for face-to-face supervision also applies to virtual supervising; it's just that some elements require extra emphasis.

The types of virtual assignments already in place are quite diverse and will undoubtedly continue to expand as we all become more practiced at electronic interaction. The Virtual Volunteering Project initiated by Impact Online studied the ways that volunteers are active in cyberspace and how organizations are managing them. For more detailed information, visit the Web site: www.serviceleader.org/vv.

Some virtual volunteering is done entirely online and, despite your role as supervisor, you may never meet the volunteer in person. But other forms of virtual volunteering are integrated into real-world activities, such as keeping in touch with a one-to-one client by e-mail in between personal visits, representing your organization on special listservs, or doing Web research of any kind.

Refer back to the discussion of electronic communication in Chapter 4 to help you work with volunteers on line. In addition, the "From the Field" by Jayne Cravens on page 121 gives excellent pointers about netiquette. She also advises:

Management via the Internet comes naturally to some people; for others, there is a significant learning curve...For many virtual assignments, particularly working with technical assistance volunteers, you can manage by results rather than by process. One company describes it as not managing the way elementary school teachers do, by attendance and citizenship, but, rather, managing as college professors do, by results. Another example:

managers may have to shift from a "steamroller" approach in which employees are told how to do work, to a "snowplow" approach in which the manager becomes the facilitator and enabler of work. It's a shift from being a supervisor who controls the work being performed to a facilitator who provides help, assistance, and planning through electronic media.

Some of the tips below also come from the experiences of the Virtual Volunteering project.

Supervision tips:
1. Regular online reporting is one way to connect with remote volunteers, to make up for seldom or never seeing each other face-to-face. Provide clear and concise guidelines to volunteers concerning the expected frequency of communications, what types of communications are expected and when (such as a list of actions completed weekly, monthly, or quarterly), and the desired format and content. Reply to these progress reports as soon as possible to acknowledge receipt. If the volunteer doesn't report in as agreed, e-mail him or her to check in on progress.

2. If you feel you must meet all volunteers in person (and have good reasons for doing so), then by all means require a face-to-face interview, training, and other on-site interaction. Of course, this will limit your potential pool of volunteers to those living in geographic proximity, but if your comfort level demands this, it's o.k.

3. Don't forget the telephone! Even though you will communicate most of the time by e-mail, an occasional phone call has many benefits. Perhaps most important, you and the volunteer can hear the tone and emphasis of your voices, giving many clues as to how you both feel about

FROM THE FIELD

Working with those we don't see on a daily basis takes some getting used to, but in many ways, the usual management principles still apply. With the advent of new communications tools such as the fax machine and e-mail, it also has become easier than ever. More and more employees are working from home, so why not volunteers? At the national office of the American Lung Association, we work with volunteers from all over the country. One volunteer recently completed a project for us from her home in Seattle and she and the staff member who coordinated this project never met!

There are many benefits to developing these off-site relationships: they eliminate concerns about having adequate work space for a volunteer, or an extra phone, or computer; you can offer opportunities for those who can't help during traditional business hours or have difficulties getting around because of a disability.

Some things to keep in mind to make these relationships work:

- You need to rethink your application process. It's one thing to recruit volunteers who live in your community and can meet with you in person, but it's another to recruit volunteers from outside your region. Do you have offices or volunteers in other cities than can help you? Depending on the volunteer project, you may be able to just conduct a phone interview (and don't forget to check references).

- You need to feel comfortable delegating a project and letting go of the reins. Give volunteers the freedom to make decisions but make sure that you keep in regular contact.

- Put it in writing. Detailed position descriptions, written instructions, follow-up memos, and project outlines leave little room for misunderstanding.

- Regular, ongoing communication is key. Ask for reports—by phone, a quick note or e-mail, a standard form that can be faxed—to make sure that things are progressing as you would like. Establish a time each week, every other week, or monthly that is convenient for you both to catch up on project progress. Write these "appointments" on your calendar as you would other meetings.

- Return calls, faxes, e-mails on a timely basis. Let volunteers know the best time of day to reach you. Have a back up system in place in case you are unavailable. Make sure you know the best method to communicate with each other.

- Don't forget recognition! Send thank you cards or leave "hope things are going well" messages on answering machines or voice mail. Be creative—send Starbucks coupons and treat volunteers to a coffee break.

- You want to try to make this relationship as personal as possible. Exchange pictures if this would be helpful. Spend some time getting to know each other, even if it's by phone. If there is a time when you both will be in the same area, try to meet for coffee or lunch.

The key to successful off-site relationships is to make sure these volunteers truly feel a part of your organization and that their time and efforts are valued and appreciated—which is really no different than what any volunteers expect.

Sheri Wilensky, Director of Volunteer Outreach, American Lung Association, New York, NY

lots of things. This emotional sense will make your e-mail messages more meaningful, because you will be able to "hear" the words as they are meant, rather than as they read. The telephone also allows you to discuss issues in more depth than brief e-mails ever can.

4. To make them feel included, treat online volunteers with the same respect and recognition as on-site volunteers. Keep off-site volunteers informed of team, project, and organization information. Make sure that all pertinent office memos or newsletters are regularly distributed via e-mail or snail mail to remote volunteers. Online volunteers should receive the same invitations, information and thank you's sent to on-site volunteers.

5. Celebrate the successes. Honor online volunteers both off-line and online! Again, online volunteers should receive whatever forms of "thank you" are given to on-site volunteers. You can also develop a Web page to honor volunteers—both those you see on site and those you don't. If volunteers are geographically too remote to attend on-site celebrations, try to come up with a way for such volunteers to participate via technology such as a teleconference or a live chat.

19. National or State Offices and Local Volunteers

Simply by virtue of distance and perspective, the relationship between organizational headquarters or state/regional offices and local chapters or groups is fraught with inherent difficulties. Communication can

122 SUPERVISING VOLUNTEERS • ENERGIZE, INC

Local chapters rarely function as the national level expects them to. Often local chapters do their best and are not intentionally doing things differently from national policy. But they focus their activities on the primary mission of the organization—what it was established to do for the community. Local chapters may not have much interest in national concerns such as producing standard financial reports, fundraising to support the national office staff, or even recruiting new members if there is no immediate local shortage. The perspective—and priorities—at the local level is rarely the same as at the national level. Requests from or campaigns developed by the national office are postponed or forgotten.

Then there are also those local chapters that just want to do their work differently. They develop different solutions from those suggested by the national level. They may not even open the mail from the national office. Cynics say that within ten miles of the drive home from the national meeting such members have already invented ways of dodging the supposedly agreed-upon policies...

Most organizations do try to have regular written and oral contact with members of local boards, especially chairpeople, secretaries and treasurers. But research indicates that a lot of the mail coming from the national level (by some guesses, as high as 20%) is opened too late or not at all...National volunteers and staff have many stories to tell about the impossibility of getting in touch with someone at the local level. There are stunning examples of local chapters never returning telephone messages, not wanting to use answering devices, endlessly postponing meetings with representatives from the local level, and the lack of communication with the national office about membership and officer name and address changes. So if the local treasurer is new, the local chapter knows but no one tells national administration...

The concept of management is based upon clear relations between someone who is the manager and others who are managed. Such a relationship between national headquarters and local chapters simply cannot be clarified, even with attempts at written contracts. It is too easy for local chapters to dodge such agreements on the basis that they outline intent, not rules. [So what to do? Here are a few suggestions:]

- A national board must work continuously to keep the organization simple. National policies must be uncomplicated and limited to important issues that relate to the primary processes of the organization...

- Local chapters must have trust in the national board and paid staff and in the internal democratic procedures that lead to a decision. To gain such acceptance, the national board must visibly represent the mission and core practices of the organization. Trust can be created by developing quasi-personal contact between the national and local levels. For example, organizations can establish a "visit national headquarters" program for local volunteers...

- Instead of intervening and laying down the "law" about what the national organization wants, the national office can foster compliant local chapter behavior by providing needed and wanted support. Such support can be given through ready-to-use materials, consultations from experts, workshops, training, and all kinds of resources. Using such support materials to implement policies and practices requires a good sense of timing and the right approach. The wrong way to do it is to send materials to local groups and insist that these resources be used. Instead, offer the materials, explaining that the local chapters may use them if helpful—and then make sure the materials are of excellent quality. The trick is to balance insistence with suggestion.

SOURCE

From the original manuscript by Lucas C.P.M. Meijs, Erasmus University, Rotterdam. Later published as "Management Is Not Always the Right Word!" in *The Journal of Volunteer Administration*, Spring 1996.

break down, both in clarity and tone. Distance tends to distance people!

Supervision tips:

1. Try not to act like you're "at the top" and they're "down" at the local level (although they may act like this in reverse, in which case you must call them on it).

2. Decide which *rules* are necessary to insist upon system-wide and which are *guidelines* that can be adapted more flexibly for local needs. Clarify each set.

3. Err on the side of too much communication rather than too little. But this does not mean drowning the field in tons of paper! Short, concise reports are more effective than multi-page tomes. Color coding can help, too. Follow all the tips we've given for working with any volunteers "in the field."

4. Encourage local volunteers to visit headquarters as often as possible. In fact, set up appointments for this, not just "whenever you're in town." Research shows that the more people see for themselves, the more positive they are.

5. Make telephone contact once in a while as well as by letter or e-mail. The personal touch is the only way to assess tone.

6. Respond to questions promptly, and explain why you can't do something if your answer has to be no.

7. Cross-fertilize. Use your position to put local people in touch with one another as well as with you. This is recognition to those you identify as doing something as a model for others, and also demonstrates that you all have good ideas, not just those of you "on top."

8. Recognize that a local volunteer may feel disengaged or lonely. That's why communicating with more information than specifically needed demonstrates that s/he is part of a bigger team.

Setting-Specific Issues

Apart from having to adapt to the various volunteers you supervise, it is worthwhile to note that there are variables posed by the setting in which you work. Some are obvious:

- *Size:* The larger your facility, the more complex the interrelationships among people and work units. Ideally, you can counteract the impersonality of a large organization by making sure your work unit feels welcoming. Size also affects how many layers of administration might come between a volunteer and decision-making about suggestions made. You may have

to explain the chain of command and be an advocate for the point of view of the volunteers you supervise.

- *Professional vs. lay expertise:* Many organizations have a paid staff composed of highly-trained people in professional fields. Whether this means doctors, social workers, curators, or any other area of expertise, adding volunteers to the mix requires a clear understanding of roles. Sometimes you will be recruiting volunteers with the same professional skills, in which case you must be alert to threats posed by fuzzy boundaries. In many situations, you will purposely be recruiting volunteers precisely because they bring skills quite different from the core paid staff. Then the concern becomes one of mutual respect.

- *Physical environment:* If you are lucky enough to work in a setting with a lot of space, extra offices or work areas, and other environmental perks, it will be easier to integrate volunteers into the work day. On the other hand, if your staff already works in tight quarters with little room to spare and little privacy, recognize that adding more bodies to the mix may cause consternation. It is not irrelevant to ask: can we physically accommodate volunteers? Scheduling more people than you have chairs on a given shift is going to hamper effectiveness!

- *Available resources:* Connected to physical environment, where will volunteers actually work? Will they have adequate desk surface space to be efficient? Do they have access to key tools such as computers, copiers, and other equipment—when these are needed? The point is not that volunteers need all sorts of luxuries. As a supervisor, you must assure that resources necessary to successful completion of an assignment are provided or that you help volunteers find alternate ways of doing their work.

Some variables are more subtle:

- *Degree of formality:* What is the tone of your organization? Do people tend to dress conservatively or casually? How will volunteers be expected to dress? Formality is also evidenced in such things as the use of first or last names (or professional titles), face-to-face chats versus written memoranda, many rules and forms to complete. Volunteers can fit in anywhere, but they need you to prepare them for what type of look and behavior will be most acceptable.

- *Diversity:* If volunteers and employees are indistinguishable from one another, that may be fine. But if the volunteer corps is visibly older or younger than paid staff, or on a different educational or income level, or from a different social class, such differences must be managed. The ideal is to celebrate the diversity and find ways to blend these many perspectives and differing talents into all-around better service. As supervisor, however, you must consciously work to make this happen. Pay attention, too, to the possible differences between volunteers and the people you serve.

More than anything else, these variables require you to be a diagnostician. The better you are at recognizing and identifying the things that can affect the work of both employees and volunteers, the more likely you will be to maximize the positives and find solutions for the negatives.

Field-Specific Issues

As I said earlier, you will also have to adjust your supervision to the work your volunteers are doing and to the populations with which they are working. Return to the essence of supervision: empowering volunteers to be successful in their work. What could you do to equip volunteers to be successful in your unique environment? What follows are just a few suggestions and generalizations. Although your specific situation may not be covered, I hope this section will cause you to think carefully about your environment. Talk with the coordinator of volunteers and with other supervisors of volunteers in your organization about how you might address some of the issues this section raises for you. And, of course, speak with your volunteers about their ideas and needs.

Lingo and the Insider-Outsider Culture

All organizations develop a special language to shortcut communication. I recently encountered this at a bank when a teller told me she needed a word to process my transaction. Puzzled, I asked what she was saying. It turns out that the phrase, "I need a word," means "I need authorization from my supervisor." What special language—lingo—does your organization have? You may have trouble answering this question because your own use of that lingo is second nature to you! Help new volunteers feel like insiders by giving them a glossary of your lingo. You may also need to provide definitions of technical or legal terms they are likely to hear. Even if it is not essential that they understand these terms, providing them is a courtesy and will help volunteers feel that they have not suddenly been transported to a foreign land.

You will also need to help volunteers integrate into organizations that have strong insider-outsider cultures. Law enforcement agencies have these characteristics but so do many clubs and other membership organizations, where the unwritten rule seems to be, "you're not one of us until you've been here 20 years" or some variation thereof. Needless to say, no volunteer who feels like a outsider is likely to stay long. The subtle message is: "You don't belong. Go away." Assess the culture of your organization by recalling how you felt and what you experienced during your first days of employment. Work with paid staff to provide an orientation for volunteers in which the reasons behind the insider-outsider culture are honestly explored. It may also be helpful to have experienced volunteers tell new volunteers how they acclimated to your culture. They may have some funny stories to share!

Feelings and Lack of Control

What is the real problem that brings clients to your organization? To what extent can you, your paid staff or volunteers "fix" the real problem? As I read about the emergency rescue work of volunteers and paid staff following the crash of the Swissair flight in the summer of 1998, I thought about how difficult it must have been for them as they talked with and comforted relatives of the victims. Don't you suppose that they all—at least at an unconscious level—wished they could bring the victims back to life? Do workers in hospitals wish they could cure all disease? Do counselors of children who have been sexually abused wish they could erase the child's past and create a whole new set of pain-free experiences?

When confronted with our lack of control over the very problems or causes that drew us in the first place to an organization, we may experience feelings of helplessness, hopelessness, frustration, and anger. If you do not help volunteers cope with these feelings and develop more realistic expectations they will burn out and leave. Worse, they will stay and create problems. The realities of your organization and the expectations of prospective volunteers should be carefully explored during the interview. Orientation and training can also help volunteers assess and modify their expectations. Provide ongoing support groups so that volunteers and staff can together express their feelings, grieve and support one another. A trained facilitator is essential for this process. You should have processes for supporting your volunteers if they work in/with: sick children, abused or neglected children, domestic violence, emergency work, crisis intervention, the terminally ill, people with severe disabilities, or animals that have been abused or neglected.

The Physical Environment

Even though it was 25 years ago, I vividly recall my one-and-only visit to Trenton State Prison to attend a meeting with the prison's coordinator of volunteers. My purse and briefcase were searched and I had to walk through a metal detector. Then there was the constant jangling of huge rings of big keys, the slamming of barred doors, the visible presence of uniforms, the eyes and ears that were continually scrutinizing my every move and the environment around me. And I was only going to an office area of the prison!

When a new volunteer starts in your unit, what will s/he see, hear, smell? The more it differs from a "normal" environment, the more attention you will have to give to explaining it, assessing volunteers' reactions, and giving them time to adjust. Perhaps an analogy to consider is the process many swimmers use when standing at the edge of a pool or at the ocean when the water is cold. Put a toe or foot in; when that begins to feel comfortable, expose a little more skin to the alien environment!

You may be so acclimated to your setting that you no longer notice the characteristics that may be frightening or make people uncomfortable. Can you look at it with new eyes? Of course, one thing you can do is to ask new volunteers to tell you about their first impressions. A focus group might be a good way to do this. Also ask them to offer suggestions about what might have been done to help them adjust. Here are some other issues to consider:

- Do your clients have severe disabilities or do they look or act in ways that may be confusing, scary or unpleasant? How can you help new volunteers feel comfortable and safe?

- Are there unpleasant odors? They may come from clients, from the physical plant, or from chemicals, medicine or disinfectants. How might this affect volunteers?

- What unusual sounds might be characteristic of your environment? For example, if you work in an animal shelter and one continually hears the sound of whining dogs behind closed doors, what might a new volunteer think of that? Equipment or machinery that makes unusual noises may be frightening. Slamming bar doors, heavy sliding doors, alarm bells, coded loud speaker announcements, raised voices—all these may need to be experienced slowly and explained.

- Does the physical environment have unusual characteristics? The first time I approached a sally port I didn't even know what it was, to say nothing of where I was to stand to enter and exit it. If you feel foolish because you don't know what a sally port is, you have just experienced discomfort.[1] Maybe your new volunteers have similar feelings in your environment. Look at your doors, windows, the configuration of your building. Do signs help newcomers find their way around? Do staff seem approachable or do they simply walk by those who are lost or confused? Do many people in your organization wear uniforms? If so, what do the various colors or styles mean? Do clients wear leg irons? handcuffs? restraints? helmets? braces? What can you do to help volunteers understand why?

By paying attention to lingo and the culture of an insider-outsider organization, to the feelings brought on by lack of control, and to the physical environment, you can be proactive in providing the orientation, training and support that your volunteers will need to be successful in your unique setting. If you don't take the time to do this, you are likely to be faced with high turnover and performance problems.

This is where we need to direct you to the Energize Web site. As Susan said in the Foreword (page iii), we received more contributions from colleagues in the field than we could reasonably publish in book form. Many of these submissions were so useful that we hated the thought of simply cutting them out. So we have created a virtual appendix to this book on the Energize Web site. Go to http://www.energizeinc.com/supervising.html and you will find real-life examples of how to supervise volunteers working in special settings or in special assignments. There are particularly excellent items regarding mental health care and justice programs. And, please, add your own examples so we can—collectively—add to the knowledge of our field.

---

[1] In case you'd like to know, a "sally port" is a special security entrance with two locked doors, one of which opens while the other remains secured, something like a waterway lock.

The Role of the Coordinator of Volunteers

In a decentralized volunteer program, the coordinator of volunteers generally maintains responsibility for: setting policy; volunteer recruitment; interviewing, screening, and placement; organization-wide volunteer recognition activities; establishing and maintaining volunteer records; and overall program evaluation. The coordinator of volunteers also serves as an internal consultant to staff who supervise volunteers, by providing training on how to supervise volunteers, and offering advice and suggestions on their supervisory role. Some volunteers will work directly with the coordinator of volunteers in managing the volunteer program itself. For volunteers placed in other units throughout the organization, the coordinator of volunteers is a liaison and functions much like a personnel or human resources department relates to employees once they have been hired.

The coordinator of volunteers should meet regularly with those who supervise volunteers to determine together the things that would strengthen the involvement of volunteers in the supervisor's unit. They may discuss job descriptions, training programs for volunteers, whether volunteers need additional training or support, scheduling issues, volunteer-staff relations, and communication with volunteers, especially those who are off-site or who work when the supervisor is not available.

At Memorial Sloan-Kettering this team approach to assessing volunteer involvement throughout the Center was highly organized and effective. My two assistants and I each had our own caseload of departments where volunteers worked; each of us served as the primary liaison between the Department of Volunteer Resources and the supervisors in our respective areas. Each of us met periodically with each supervisor in our areas and had regular telephone contact with them. The frequency of meetings was determined in part by the number of volunteers and the level of difficulty of their work.

For example, the assistant director of volunteer resources who was the liaison with the staff in the pediatric playroom met at least monthly with the director and also met frequently with all four employees in the playroom. At these meetings they hammered out stricter requirements for who could be a pediatric playroom volunteer, developed an orientation class for new playroom volunteers, and wrote a handbook for the volunteers. In addition, this assistant usually attended the regular support meetings that the playroom staff held for their volunteers.

With other areas we met with supervisors only a few times a year, but all of them knew that they could call their liaison in the Department of Volunteer Resources anytime they had a question or an idea, and certainly when they had a complaint! The statistics we kept on volunteer coverage as part of our quality assessment program were regularly shared with the supervisors. We also notified the supervisors of volunteers' birthdays and any other personal news in which we expected them to be interested.

This collaboration proved invaluable when supervisors faced complex problems. When a twenty-year, much loved volunteer in the gift shop developed a serious health problem that interfered with her performance, the manager and I had several discussions before deciding together how to handle the situation. And because of these close relationships, if a volunteer came to us with a complaint about a supervisor (which was rare), we knew enough about the person and the work unit to know what to do with the complaint, too.

As National Volunteer Week approached each year, we gave staff supervisors ideas about a wide

"*Supervisors should keep the line of communication with the volunteer coordinator open at all times.*

It's important that the supervisor and the volunteer coordinator be aware of how each volunteer is doing.

If a supervisor is having any problems with a volunteer, s/he should let the volunteer coordinator know about them."

— *Volunteers*

FROM THE FIELD

DENVER, CO — TRAINING BY DESIGN

In each organization where I have worked, I have developed a volunteer supervisors' manual that explains the responsibilities and logistics of supervising volunteer personnel. I make it a point to meet with each new manager to explain how volunteer personnel can be an asset to his/her ability to meet departmental goals and objectives. Many volunteer supervisors (such as housekeeping, food service and clerical staff) do not have other supervisory responsibilities in the organization and therefore lack any skills in this area. I have found that most employees are thrilled to have support and mentoring in this facet of their job performance. Because I know the supervisory style of the staff, it is much easier to match volunteers to the style of the supervisors. This internal consultation has helped to build the credibility of the volunteer programs. It has taken me out of the role of "doer" and into the role of manager of volunteer programs.

Jill Friedman Fixler, President, Training By Design, Denver, CO

FROM THE FIELD

NEW YORK, NY — VICTIM SERVICES, INC.

We have approximately 70 programs in about 60 locations through the five boroughs of New York City. I must maintain an active relationship with the volunteer supervisors in the field. I use e-mail to transmit memos and other tidbits to keep the lines of communication open At least once every two weeks I telephone every supervisor. I never miss an opportunity to encourage and support the supervisors.

Kim A. Payne, Volunteer Resources Coordinator, Victim Services, Inc., New York, NY

range of activities they could undertake—some very simple, some more elaborate—to acknowledge their volunteers. In addition to planning their departmental activities, most supervisors also attended our Center-wide volunteer recognition ceremony and many helped by serving as ushers, greeters or hosts.

We conducted workshops for staff who supervised volunteers. Just as we expected them, as supervisors, to empower their volunteers to be successful in their work, we in the Department of Volunteer Resources were committed to empowering supervisors to be successful. As some of them had no experience supervising paid staff, they appreciated the opportunity to learn something new. Some of the learning came from listening to others in the workshops share tips on volunteer supervision. We also provided a packet of reading material.

It is important to delineate the division of responsibilities between the coordinator of volunteers or the volunteer services office and the various units in which volunteers work. On the next page you will find an excellent outline of expected interrelationships from the American Red Cross.

Direct vs. Liaison Supervision

In a decentralized volunteer program, the coordinator of volunteers is the supervisor only for those volunteers carrying assignments directly for the volunteer program itself. But most volunteers are deployed throughout the organization, working in partnership with paid staff in other departments or work units. Therefore, the day-to-day supervision of most volunteers is the responsibility of an employee in each area, possibly the department head, or perhaps another volunteer. In a decentralized system, it is especially important that the coordinator of volunteers and those who directly supervise volunteers clarify key issues:

1. The process that will be used to make changes in volunteers' job descriptions.

2. The supervisor's responsibility for providing orientation, training, and continuing education/support for volunteers within his or her unit.

3. The supervisor's responsibility for evaluating performance.

American Red Cross

SHARED RESPONSIBILITIES FOR VOLUNTEER ADMINISTRATION

RESPONSIBILITIES OF EACH SERVICE OR DEPARTMENT*

The service or department—
1. Defines volunteer job functions and assists in writing job descriptions in consultation with the Office of Volunteers.
2. Determines both the immediate and long-range need for volunteers.
3. Provides input into the planning of and participates as needed in the implementation of a coordinated recruitment process.
4. Interviews referrals from the Office of Volunteers and accepts volunteers for placement or refers them back to that office for a different assignment.
5. Refers volunteers who are recruited by the service or department to the Office of Volunteers for processing.
6. Provides orientation to the service or department, assigns tasks, and schedules the volunteers.
7. Starts volunteers on the job with an appropriate job induction and provides on-the-job training and planned growth experiences.
8. Reports appropriate volunteer activity and personnel information to the Office of Volunteers.
9. Provides an early follow-up on all new volunteers to ensure proper placement and job satisfaction.
10. Provides supervision and appropriate support.
11. Participates in planning ongoing recognition by the service or department for volunteers.
12. Promotes volunteers within the service or department or recommends the volunteer for broader experience outside the service or department.
13. Refers volunteers back to the Office of Volunteers with a recommendation for reassignment or referral to another agency.
14. Refers volunteers to the Office of Volunteers for exit interviews.

RESPONSIBILITIES OF THE OFFICE OF VOLUNTEERS

The Office of Volunteers—
1. Provides overall coordination for volunteer management functions.
2. Develops volunteer personnel policies.
3. Provides consultation and technical advice, and develops volunteer job descriptions in collaboration with departments or services.
4. Gathers, compiles, and keeps updated information regarding skills, positions, and the number of volunteers needed.
5. Coordinates the planning and implementation of a recruitment process.
6. Interviews potential volunteers and refers them for placement.
7. Processes volunteers recruited by an individual service or department.
8. Provides basic Red Cross orientation.
9. Consults with services and departments regarding job induction, planned growth experiences, and volunteer career development.
10. Follows up with volunteers and the services or departments to ensure proper placement and job satisfaction.
11. Provides consultation regarding paid and volunteer staff relationships.
12. Ensures formal recognition for all volunteers.
13. Confers with services or departments regarding the leadership potential of volunteers for positions of greater responsibility in the Red Cross.
14. Provides a mechanism for reassignment or for referring volunteers to other agencies.
15. Provides exit interviews and a transfer record for volunteers leaving the community or the unit.
16. Manages volunteer grievance system.

*Note: Refers to all Red Cross units: Regions; field service teams; Blood Services regions; state service councils; chapters; service to the Armed Forces stations; and national headquarters.   ARC 2360

Nancy and Luke were volunteer team leaders on Buddy Team #17. They supervised ten other volunteers who did buddy work or provided ongoing one-on-one emotional and practical assistance, off-site, to clients with AIDS. In order to make client assignments to the volunteers on their team, Nancy and Luke counted on the Buddy Program staff to provide them with up-to-date, accurate information regarding client needs.

The last few client assignments made to their team had outdated or wrong information. Twice Nancy and Luke spoke to the Buddy Program Coordinator, Hank, who assured them this wouldn't happen again. Two weeks later a new client was assigned to Bob, a volunteer on their team. When Bob called the client, the client said although he was a client of the agency, he had no desire to receive buddy services. He asked Bob how he had gotten his information, putting Bob in an awkward position.

Nancy angrily called Hank and called him "incompetent." Then she and Luke asked the Volunteer Department to intercede on their behalf. Rhonda, the Volunteer Coordinator, called Hank and requested a meeting in which she would mediate between both sides.

At the meeting, Nancy and Luke chronicled the string of client matches made on their team which had faulty information, culminating in the story of Bob's last assignment. They were still angry and wondered why this was still going on.

Hank explained systems problems which made getting up-to-date information to the volunteers difficult. When the program was started, people requested buddy service at the time they became clients and underwent an extensive psychosocial interview detailing their needs and situation. However, over the years, more requests for buddy services were coming from people who had been clients of the agency for over a year or two. In many instances, the information in their client intake was no longer accurate. Also, because the emphasis was on getting people into services as quickly as possible, clients were not re-contacted after being referred to the Buddy Program until they were called by their volunteer. A third problem was that the Buddy Program didn't have sufficient staff to make prior phone connections in a timely way. A combination of these factors resulted in Luke's and Nancy's experience. Hank also took offense at the way Nancy had spoken to him in their last phone conversation.

Rhonda stressed the need to always address each other professionally and to have patience with each other no matter what was going on. Obviously, the bad matches weren't happening on purpose, but were the result of mistakes. She emphasized how everyone was on the same side in the fight against AIDS. Nancy apologized to Hank for her disrespectful remark, but again expressed how frustrated she's felt. Hank took responsibility for the bad information that had been passed along to them. Rhonda suggested addressing the problem by having volunteers supplement the Buddy Program staff. In that way clients could always be contacted before referrals were made to the buddy team. Hank thought this might be a good option and wanted to explore it more. He assured Nancy and Luke that no more assignments would be made to their team that hadn't been contacted beforehand by his office.

Thomas Weber, Coordinator of Volunteers for Client Programs, Gay Men's Health Crisis, New York, NY

4. The extent of the supervisor's responsibility for handling and documenting performance problems and at what point the coordinator of volunteers gets involved.

5. Whether the supervisor has the authority to terminate a volunteer from his or her position in the supervisor's unit and/or in the organization.

6. What, if any, responsibilities a unit supervisor may have in relation to the volunteer program as a whole (such as staff meetings, adhering to policies, attending recognition events, etc.).

What you want to avoid is what Carol Robins, Director of Volunteer Resources at The Lighthouse, Inc. in New York describes:

> It isn't uncommon for staff to think that volunteers are gathered in a "pool" somewhere in the Volunteer Resources Department, to be fished out when a need arises. In order to give the volunteers their due, and empower them to serve the agency to the maximum, an appreciation of the process involved in incorporating volunteers into the lifestream of the agency is imperative.

Clarifying these and other points helps the supervisor to work with volunteers more effectively, and helps the coordinator of volunteers be a supportive liaison for both volunteers and employees.

What does staff need to know to be successful working with volunteers?

Training programs are generally designed to affect one or more of the following types of learning: knowledge, skills and attitudes.

Knowledge: Staff who work with volunteers may need knowledge in the following areas:

- trends impacting volunteering
- policies and procedures for the volunteer program (e.g., dismissal, risk management, performance review)
- information about significant groups of volunteers working at the agency (e.g., seniors, youth, corporate)
- roles and responsibilities of staff in the volunteer program

Skills: Staff who work with volunteers generally need skills in:

- delegation
- interviewing
- recognition
- supervision
- job design
- conflict resolution
- communications
- motivation
- performance reviews

Attitudes: It is important for staff to examine their attitudes regarding:

- the value of volunteers
- importance of management functions such as performance reviews, risk management
- willingness to delegate
- confidentiality
- cultural differences

What do staff already know?

Some staff are managers who have the basic skills of personnel management and mainly need to transfer these skills, with some adaptations, to the management of volunteers. Other staff may have no formal education or experience in management and therefore need some basic skill development to work effectively with volunteers. Thus you may need to design several adaptations of the training.

Occasions to Provide Volunteer Management Education to Staff

Each organization will have different opportunities that are particularly suited to its focus, structure, and size. Listed below are a few times when volunteer management training might be considered:

- When staff is newly hired
- When a new volunteer program is initiated
- During agency re-organizing
- At the first meeting of a committee or task force
- During staff meetings: Ask to provide in-service training at several meetings during the year or ask for a regular brief time to provide information and education on effective volunteer utilization at each meeting.

SOURCE

Training Busy Staff to Succeed with Volunteers by Betty Stallings, Building Better Skills, 1996.

Moreover, it helps volunteers, especially those who are new, know which questions or ideas to discuss with their direct supervisor and which to discuss with the coordinator of volunteers.

Another important topic that the coordinator of volunteers must discuss with those who supervise volunteers is who is responsible for scheduling volunteers and following up on unexpected absences. At Memorial Sloan-Kettering, the Department of Volunteer Resources was responsible for all scheduling. We knew what volunteer coverage the departments needed and it was our job to provide that. Volunteers notified us—nearly always well in advance—of upcoming absences and, of course, called in when they were sick. It was our responsibility to find, if at all possible, a qualified substitute and then to notify the supervisor. We worked hard to maintain the required coverage, which helped promote the notion that volunteers are reliable.

Whether it's the coordinator of volunteers, the volunteer supervisor, or a volunteer captain or liaison in your organization who does the scheduling and arranges for substitutes, there must be an efficient system and method for documenting coverage. Volunteers must know who they are to call when they will be absent (or perhaps there is a simple form they complete when they know in advance about a vacation or business trip).

It is equally important that someone be designated to call a volunteer who is unexpectedly absent. To fail to make that call conveys loud and clear to the volunteer that he or she wasn't missed either personally or for what the volunteer was to do that day. The call needs to be pleasant, of course. Perhaps the volunteer was absent because his wife unexpectedly went into labor and it simply slipped his mind to let you know. Or perhaps the volunteer did tell you he would be out and you forgot!

Preparing Volunteers to Be Supervised

The meaning and purpose of supervision should be raised during the initial interview with each prospective volunteer. Whether or not a volunteer will be a successful worker in an organization depends not just on ability but also on the relationship that develops with the volunteer's supervisor. Prospective volunteers need to know how they will be supervised and what your organization sees as the purpose of supervision.

Generally it is the coordinator of volunteers who conducts this initial interview. S/he may then refer the prospective volunteer to you for a second interview, may schedule the prospective volunteer for formal training before finalizing a placement, or may be authorized to place the prospective volunteer in a position in your organization directly, without a second interview. Jill Friedman Fixler shares the model she used at Arapaho House:

If the volunteer interview and screening process is effective, supervision is a relatively easy process. An initial screening interview should determine what the volunteer's expectations and skills are. This interview is helpful in determining with what supervisory style the volunteer will work best. Each supervisor should have the opportunity to do a second interview after which he/she decides if the volunteer is placed. This gives the supervisor more ownership in his/her team as opposed to viewing volunteers as the sole responsibility of the Volunteer Manager. As a result of utilizing this management style, I have rarely had to terminate volunteers or reassign them for conflicts with their supervisor.

Everyone's comfort level, the structure of the organization, and the time available for interviewing are the three guiding factors in who does screening and placing of new volunteers.

If you interview prospective volunteers you may find the statements and questions that follow will help you explore various issues pertaining to supervision. This interview also presents an opportunity to discuss your supervisory style so that you and the prospective volunteer can separately or together explore your compatibility.

Try opening with comments such as:

Let's talk a little about supervision. Our organization sees supervision as a benefit to volun-teers as well as a way to assure the best service to our clients. The job of those who supervise volunteers is to provide training, information, feedback, praise and, when necessary, comments on performance or behavioral problems. Without supervision our volunteers would feel like they were working in a vacuum. We want volunteers to feel connected, supported and accountable. As part of the placement process here we talk about supervision so that we can determine together what kind of supervisor you would work with the best. I have some questions and, if you have any, I'll try to answer them.

Then choose the questions you like from the list below:

- Tell me about some of the supervisors you have had in the past. What did you like about the relationship you had with them? What did you dislike?

- How would you describe the ideal supervisor?

- How do you react to criticism about your work?

- In what ways can supervisors help the people they supervise do a really good job?

- Do you believe that volunteers should be held accountable for the quality of their work? Please explain.

- If your supervisor was having a bad day and was, let's say, impatient with you or forgot to say "thank you," how would you feel? How would you react?

- How would you tell your supervisor about a mistake you had made?

- What would you want your supervisor to do if you were in a conflict with a paid staff person?

- From time to time our agency has had to fire volunteers. What do you think about that?

- What kind of supervisor do you think you would work best with?

- Perhaps you are or have been a supervisor yourself. If not, try to use your imagination. What does a supervisor want from the people s/he supervises?

- If a supervisor sees that a volunteer is having difficulty with the work, what should the supervisor do?

- In what ways should a supervisor treat volunteers differently from the way s/he treats paid staff? Please explain your answer.

The strategic plan developed in 1996 by The Lighthouse, Inc. forecasts a continually growing need for volunteer participation in both traditional and innovative ways. The ability of staff throughout the organization to know how to involve volunteers and to supervise them were determined to be the two critical elements that would foster growth in our volunteer program.

With the support of the senior vice president of human resources, to whom I report, I developed volunteer management training seminars. Since 1997 the assistant director of volunteer resources and I have presented these annually to all staff of every department, regardless of whether volunteers work in their departments. Using an interactive format designed to promote sharing and encourage creative thinking about volunteer roles, the agenda includes information about the role of the Department of Volunteer Resources as well as a discussion about the responsibilities of the staff in departments where volunteers work. We cover how to greet, train, monitor, evaluate and recognize volunteers.

The workshop lasts from 30 minutes to an hour, depending on how many participants there are and how many questions they have. We begin by requesting a volunteer, giving no details whatsoever as to what the volunteer is needed for. The completely predictable response is a resounding silence. After a few moments, someone usually takes pity on us and offers to volunteer, but does so by asking, "to do what?" This is the perfect opportunity to explore, through group discussion, the notion that people need to know what they are being asked to do before they will volunteer. This clearly demonstrates the importance of carefully developing volunteer jobs. During the remainder of the workshop we outline the responsibilities of the Department of Volunteer Resources, emphasizing that we provide ongoing support to staff who supervise volunteers. We distribute some of the forms we use and describe how we recruit, interview and match volunteers.

By interacting in this way with staff from throughout the organization, I have learned about the group dynamics and communication styles of each department, factors I take into consideration when making placements. I want to match volunteers not only with a job description, but also with the whole style of a department.

Response to the seminars has been unanimously positive. Departments that did not have volunteers working in them began to wonder if volunteer assistance might enable them to fulfill dreams about work they wanted to undertake. Departments that already had volunteer involvement were able to focus on ways to improve their supervisory skills and the relationship between volunteers and paid staff. All staff now have a better understanding of the role of the Department of Volunteer Resources staff and they often call on us for consultation. And they know to involve us in the resolution of any serious problem with a volunteer. In short, the seminars have really empowered paid staff to be effective supervisors of volunteers.

Carol Robins, Director, Volunteer Resources, The Lighthouse, Inc., New York, NY

Training Staff to Supervise Volunteers

In her contribution above, Carol Robins emphasizes the importance of training those who supervise volunteers. It is not enough to place volunteers with staff who are willing to supervise; employees need support and guidance on how to be good supervisors. This is too important to be left to chance. My observation over the years is that the one thing supervisors most need to know is to start with high expectations of volunteers. Once they understand that, they eagerly embrace all the other aspects of volunteer supervision and do it with enthusiasm.

In addition to workshops, the coordinator of volunteers can provide supervisors with handbooks and other print material on supervising volunteers. On page 134 you will see portions of a handbook developed by Linda Johnson, Director of Volunteer Services at Palo Pinto General Hospital, for volunteer supervisors there.

Janice Allan, director of volunteers at the Boulder County Justice System, meets informally with employees who are new to supervising volunteers, not only to get acquainted but also to let them know what her responsibilities are and to outline what their working relationship will be like. Each supervisor receives a copy of the volunteer flow-chart (see page 135), a handy summary of that working relationship. At the end of this chapter is the "Supervision Walk-Through Analysis" Susan Ellis developed to guide supervisors through a consideration of the sequence of activities volunteers will do, the pitfalls they might expect, and what can be done to be supportive.

The Middle Management Factor

Good communication between frontline supervisors of volunteers and the coordinator of volunteers may overlook an important constituency: middle managers. First, it is important for volunteers to be assigned throughout the organization, at many levels. If volunteers can be found working only with the lowest level of workers and rarely with administrators, the message is sent that: if you get promoted high enough you will no longer have to deal with volunteers. The more people who have the chance to interact personally with volunteers, the greater the support the program will have.

Problems can occur if middle managers see volunteers as "taking the time" of the employees in their department without recognizing the benefits of the effort. Make sure middle managers sign off on volunteer assignments developed within their areas and participate in discussions about training and recognition, for example. Volunteer activity and accomplishment reports should be shared routinely with department heads and other administrators, too.

On the other side of the coin, some middle managers expect successful volunteer involvement without understanding that supervision does take time. The more everyone appreciates the art and science of supporting volunteers, the less friction there will be.

Help middle managers find tangible ways to recognize the hard work their employees have put into assisting the volunteers they, in turn, supervise. Suggest that achievements in this area be made part of the employee's annual performance review and be used as one of the criteria for promotion. After all, volunteer supervision is invaluable training in how to supervise anyone.

The Role of the Volunteer Program Secretary

One person plays a vital role in supporting volunteers but is often overlooked in a discussion of program management: the secretary in the volunteer services office. Of course, you may not have a full-time secretary but, if you do, recognize how important s/he is in setting the tone of the entire office. The way the telephone is answered, messages taken, information dispensed—all project an image. Is it the image you want? Does it establish expectations of friendliness and efficiency?

Train any employees or volunteers who work in the volunteer office to fulfill their role well. Emphasize the importance of:

- Welcoming prospective volunteers on the phone and in person.

- Making callers/visitors feel that someone has listened, heard and understood their question, request or concern. It isn't necessary to have all the answers on the spot—just to assure callers/visitors that someone will help them soon.

- Dealing efficiently with details: volunteer profile data, schedules, requests for volunteer assistance, etc.

- Distinguishing between critical problems and the need of some volunteers (and employees) to vent.

BOULDER COUNTY JUSTICE SYSTEM VOLUNTEER PROGRAM
VOLUNTEER FLOW - CHART

Boulder County

RECRUITMENT, SCREENING, INTERVIEWING

The JSVP conducts recruitment. Prospective volunteers are screened for minimum qualifications and must fill out an application form. The JSVP conducts record and reference checks. Director interviews volunteers for 45 - 60 minutes to determine if there is an appropriate match between the volunteer and the program.

↑

Director of Volunteer Services meets with staff to discuss their volunteer needs and assist in formulating job descriptions. A job description must be on file with the JSVP before recruitment can begin.

↑

Staff requests volunteers from the JSVP. Request must be for a position which helps the department reach its stated goals in a way that expands or enhances a service and does not replace paid staff.

REVIEW PROCESS

The JSVP recommends that supervisors establish a 4-6 week probationary period for volunteers. This enables the supervisor and the volunteer to review the placement and make any necessary adjustments. Either the volunteer or supervisor may terminate the placement at this time.

↑

TRAINING

Volunteers attend a JSVP orientation session prior to, or shortly after, starting volunteer work. Supervisor provides on-the-job training. Volun-teers are encourage to attend JSVP special topics workshops and any departmental training sessions.

↑

PLACEMENT

Volunteers are referred to program supervisor(s). Copies of the application and director's interview notes are forwarded to supervisor. Volunteer interviews with potential supervisor(s) to assess suitability for program. If supervisor uses a placement contract, it is reviewed with volunteer at this meeting. Volunteers who are not accepted are referred back to the JSVP. Once a volunteer is placed, the JSVP keeps monthly records of his/her hours.

COMPLETION OF ASSIGNMENT

When the volunteer has completed the original time commitment she/he may renew, transfer to another position, or leave the Justice Center. When volunteers leave, we recommend that supervisors do an exit interview. The JSVP sends a thank-you card and an exit evaluation form to every departing volunteer. Copies of return evaluations are forwarded to supervisors. Volunteers are given letters of reference upon request.

↑

EVALUATION

Three to six months after placement, it is recommended that the supervisor and volunteer meet for a formal evaluation session. This is an opportunity for both parties to mutually discuss job satisfaction and performance. A written evaluation, signed by supervisor and volunteer, will assist in providing direction for new goals or job assignments.

↑

RECOGNITION

As a way of thanking volunteers, the JSVP coordinates formal recognition events in the spring, during National Volunteer Week, and around the holidays. Staff are encouraged to recognize their volunteers on an ongoing basis and include them in any departmental events.

FROM THE FIELD

The Volunteer Services Department of the Medical Center at Princeton (400 beds, plus a psychiatric unit and a long term care unit) is staffed by four full-time and two part-time employees. My secretarial title was upgraded to office coordinator in 1990 to reflect more accurately what I do, thanks to the Director of Volunteer Services, Susan Kozo, who met with our executive vice president to pursue this upgrade.

I play a unique role in relating to ongoing volunteers because of my constant presence in the office from Monday through Friday. I greet everyone by name, know the department where they volunteer, show care and concern in the case of illness, loss of job, family problems, etc. and share in their happy times. I know what information about the volunteers Susan wants me to also pass along to her.

I believe volunteers think of me as warm, friendly, caring, sensitive, trustworthy and professional. I truly care about each and every volunteer. I plan well and am focused, good with details and I work hard to maintain a quality program.

I always exhibit good phone etiquette. When prospective volunteers call I give them concise information about the application process and invite them to an upcoming information session at which attendance is required prior to scheduling an interview.

When I greet a new volunteer on his or her first day, I explain the sign-in/out process, provide a training packet and name tag. I then escort the volunteer to the department or nursing unit for introductions to the staff, who have previously been notified about the volunteer's time of arrival. When new volunteers return to sign out, I ask about their first day's experience, thank them for their commitment and tell them how much we look forward to seeing them on a regular basis. I bring all positive comments as well as concerns or dissatisfactions to Susan's attention.

I am Susan's essential ally by holding interruptions to a minimum when she is busy; interceding for and protecting her if she is distressed; scheduling and confirming appointments and screening calls; listing all correspondence and messages taken in her absence for her review upon return; trusting my inner senses when making decisions in Susan's absence; encouraging and allowing her to trust and confide in me; and always having mutual respect for one another.

Susan has continually nurtured, supported and empowered me over the years we have worked together and I consider it a privilege to be a part of the wonderful team in the Volunteer Services Department.

Louise Menapace, Office Coordinator, Volunteer Services Dept., The Medical Center at Princeton, Princeton, NJ

- Maintaining confidentiality and limiting gossip.
- Keeping an ear out for issues that the coordinator of volunteers ought to address.

The secretary may also be a supervisor of volunteers. Volunteers providing clerical assistance in the office, entering data into the computer, or doing other on-site projects ought to be coordinated by the secretary, as s/he is the person directly connected with this work. So your secretary may need training in how to supervise volunteers, too. Be alert, also, as to whether other secretaries throughout the organization are supervising volunteers and don't overlook them when you schedule workshops or meetings.

WRAP-UP TIPS:

I encourage staff to become conscious of creating a welcoming environment, incorporating new volunteers into the team, and explaining the history of the particular library branch and its staff, patrons, and community culture…Volunteers and staff need to know they can always come to the Volunteer Services Department with any problems, questions or need for changes. —**Kay Keenze**

Development of the supervisor's management skills is absolutely vital to the success of the day-to-day working relationship with volunteers as is empowerment of the supervisor to handle routine problems. —**Carol Robins**

We find that our biggest challenge is convincing staff that volunteers not only need feedback, but that most of them want it! Consequently, we spend a fair amount of time talking about coaching strategies. —**Lisa Taylor**

I give supervisors copies of relevant articles from The Journal of Volunteer Administration. —**Rhoda White**

I often arrange my work hours to fluctuate so as to see all volunteers. I make a special point to visit with those who work in groups, especially in the busy areas…. —**Lucy McGowan**

Working to continually improve the relationship between paid and volunteer staff is a two-way street. We need to shift our focus from providing services for the public to providing services with the public.

—**Christopher Dinnan in Department of Corrections Manual, Waterbury, VT**

Guiding Supervisors to Developing a Supervision Plan

This worksheet can be used to help a supervisor do a "mental walk-through" of what happens in his or her work area over a period of time. Because experienced workers have long ago internalized the work flow, it is necessary to step back and examine it from the perspective of a newcomer. The more a supervisor can clarify the sequential steps to accomplishing the work, the better he or she will be in training new volunteers (and employees), in anticipating possible problem areas, and in taking steps to avoid or minimize problems.

Supervision Walk-Through Analysis

These are the stages of the work to be done:	These are the potential pitfalls of each stage:	These are the things I can do to help at each stage:

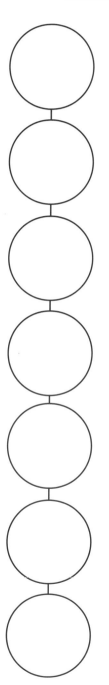

And when the work is done, here is how I can make everyone feel good about it (and maybe want to help again):

Source: Energize, Inc., handout 1990.

10

Assessing Your Own Skills

Think for a moment about your own boss—either the one you have now or one you had in the past. Perhaps you will be able to identify attributes and behaviors that make him or her a great boss. Or perhaps you will see attributes and behaviors which cause you to think of him or her as a poor boss. Perhaps you have even found yourself wishing you were in your boss's shoes, saying to yourself, "If I were the boss around here, I sure would do things differently." Imagine all the things you would do better than your boss does!

As a supervisor of volunteers and quite possibly of paid staff, too, you are the boss. In this chapter you will have the opportunity to apply to yourself some of the standards and expectations you have or have had of your own bosses. How will you measure up?

Another way to assess your performance and attitudes as a supervisor of volunteers is to reflect on your own experience as a volunteer. Perhaps you are currently volunteering somewhere or have volunteered in the past. Think about those who supervised you. In what ways were they model supervisors? What did they do—or neglect to do—that made your volunteer work less meaningful or successful than it might have been?

A Self-Assessment Survey for Supervisors of Volunteers

The previous nine chapters have provided a framework you can use to develop your own supervisory skills and style. Now look at the Self-assessment Survey that begins on page 141. Thanks goes to Ivan Scheier for the format, which is modeled after one he designed to help organizations assess volunteer-staff relations (in *Building Staff/Volunteer Relations*, Energize, 1993). I have clustered the questions to match the content of the nine chapters in this book (and each chapter is noted for reference).

I encourage you to photocopy and do the self-assessment survey now. When you are finished you will be able to identify some areas that you will want to work on. Set some specific goals and a target date. Start small and be realistic about what you can accomplish. When you have accomplished these goals, you can set more.

Consider discussing your tentative goals with your organization's coordinator of volunteers and/or with some—or all—of the volunteers you supervise. No doubt they will offer practical suggestions as well as encouragement. You may even want to designate someone as an accountability partner—someone you authorize to hold your feet to the fire, so to speak, regarding your goals and deadlines. Choose an accountability partner who will not easily let you make excuses!

You may also want to select some questions from this survey and ask some or all of your volunteers to evaluate you. This could be done anonymously or you may want to invite a small group of volunteers to meet with you to review the statements together.

You will notice that, although you will be "scoring" yourself on each item, there is not a "grand total" line at the end. This is because the value of the self-assessment does not lie in your aggregate total score. Rather, examine the *pattern* of your responses. Do you rank high on certain types of behavior and lower on others? Which scores do you feel might be improved, and how? The survey is a tool for you to use in analyzing your approach to many aspects of supervising volunteers and employees. Don't look for a final grade—concentrate on the learning process.

I would also suggest that you take the self-assessment survey again a year or so from now. I hope you will find that your performance has improved and that you are closer to being the kind of supervisor you want to be—the supervisor you know you can be.

Putting It All Together

Earlier in this book I said that, in large measure, the effectiveness of volunteers is dependent on the quality of supervision they receive. Even if you have only skimmed this book you probably agree with my statement that working with volunteers takes time. To ensure that volunteers are effective you will certainly have to do many things:

- design the job properly

- use your organization's interview and placement process to match the right volunteer with the job

- provide an orientation to your work unit

- provide initial training, and then continuing education and support

- build a relationship with each volunteer that is characterized by mutual trust, mutual respect, and mutual recognition of each other's competency and professionalism

- build positive relationships between the volunteers and paid staff you supervise

- communicate, communicate, communicate

- give feedback, especially positive feedback, to volunteers about their work and their value to you as individuals

- treat each volunteer as a unique person by remembering his/her name, birthday and facts of personal significance

- say thank you often

- seek the opinions of volunteers

- deal with performance problems professionally, promptly, and honestly

- create meaningful mechanisms to assess volunteers' performance

- maintain an effective relationship with your organization's coordinator of volunteers

Do you have the time to do all of this well? If you have other responsibilities besides supervising volunteers, you may be very pressed for time. You may be inclined to conclude you can't be a good supervisor of volunteers. And yet, you may be eager—even desperate—to involve volunteers in your work unit. Does your situation feel like a Catch-22?

Take courage! With the help of this book and the many other resources we have mentioned, you can be an effective supervisor of volunteers. But it is essential that, if you feel you are faced with a choice of quality (the quality of your work as a supervisor) versus quantity (the number of volunteers you wish you had working with you), by all means choose quality! Even if you have time to involve only a small number of volunteers, most of them will stay if you are doing things right. This is far better than continually facing high turnover, high absenteeism, and poor performance that will certainly characterize volunteer involvement if good supervisory systems are not in place.

My hope for you is that every volunteer (and employee) you supervise will say: "You help me be the best!"

A SELF-ASSESSMENT SURVEY FOR SUPERVISORS OF VOLUNTEERS

Listed below are 50 statements that describe the attitudes and actions of effective supervisors of volunteers. If you find a few statements that are not relevant to your program or unit we encourage you to substitute statements of your own.

Please rate yourself on each of the statements using the following scale:

4 = always
3 = frequently
2 = occasionally
1 = rarely or never

My Attitudes and Beliefs (Introduction)

1. I endorse our organization's philosophy of volunteerism (the reason our organization involves volunteers). _____

2. I think of volunteers as real staff. _____

3. I recognize that even though my organization does not pay a salary to volunteers, they are not "free" in that I, and others, must invest time and effort in training, supervision, evaluation, recognition, etc. _____

4. I am committed to being an effective supervisor of volunteers. _____

Aspects of the Supervisory Relationship (Chapter 1)

5. I express my passion for the mission of my organization and the goals of my work unit. _____

6. I demonstrate competency in my field/position. _____

7. I reflect a caring attitude toward the volunteers I supervise, individually as well as collectively. _____

8. I am accessible to the volunteers I supervise. _____

9. The volunteers I supervise would describe me as approachable. _____

10. I develop written descriptions for each new volunteer position in my work unit. _____

11. I give each volunteer feedback—simple and frequent comments on his or her work. _____

12. I systematically share appropriate information with volunteers. _____

13. My relationship with each volunteer is characterized by mutual trust, mutual respect, and mutual recognition of competency and professionalism. _____

Defining Expectations (Chapter 2)

14. The volunteers I supervise would say they know exactly what I expect of them. _____

15. Volunteer position descriptions are reviewed annually and revised as necessary. _____

16. I act with awareness that a volunteer's time should never be wasted. _____

17. Each volunteer in my unit is given a well-organized orientation. _____

Training and Providing Support (Chapter 3)

18. Each new volunteer in my unit receives appropriate training. _____

19. I provide continuing education for the volunteers in my unit. _____

20. Volunteers in my unit who are at risk for burnout have access to adequate and ongoing support. _____

21. I remove obstacles to productivity. _____

22. If there are obstacles I cannot remove I explain that to the volunteers who are affected. _____

23. I maintain good communication and an effective relationship with volunteers who are in the field. _____

24. I help each volunteer become familiar with the goals of my work unit and see the connection between his or her work and these goals. _____

25. I remember the name of each volunteer I supervise. _____

26. I learn at least a few things of interest (family, hobbies, history) about each new volunteer. _____

27. I am a good listener. _____

28. The volunteers I supervise would describe me as trustworthy. _____

29. I seek suggestions from volunteers not only about the work they are doing but about the work unit as a whole. _____

30. I build collaborative relationships between the volunteers and the paid staff in my unit. _____

Communicating Effectively (Chapter 4)

31. I respond promptly to all written, telephoned and electronic messages from volunteers. _____

32. I notify volunteers of important changes or developments that would affect them or would interest them. _____

33. Volunteers understand the purpose of the reports they complete and they receive follow-up information on their reports. _____

34. My directory of volunteers' names, addresses and telephone numbers is up-to-date. _____

Coaching and Encouraging Your Team (Chapter 5)

35. I express my appreciation to each volunteer I supervise. _____

36. During National Volunteer Week (and/or on other appropriate occasions) I organize at least one volunteer recognition activity in my unit. _____

37. I participate in the formal, all-agency volunteer recognition events that my organization sponsors. _____

Solving Performance Problems (Chapter 6)

38. When orienting new volunteers I tell each one about my approach to dealing with performance problems. _____

39. My approach to dealing with volunteers' performance problems is fair, professional, and effective. _____

40. I deal promptly and directly with concerns about volunteer performance -when they arise. _____

41. I document performance problems in accordance with the system of my organization. _____

42. When assessing how to handle complex or chronic performance problems, I consult with my organization's coordinator of volunteers. _____

Conducting Formal Evaluations (Chapter 7)

43. I measure volunteer retention against the standard I have set for my unit and then make appropriate changes in the supervision of volunteers in my unit. _____

44. I evaluate the performance and assess the satisfaction of new volunteers. _____

45. I evaluate the performance and assess the satisfaction of all volunteers at least annually. _____

46. I conduct exit interviews (in person or in writing) with all volunteers who leave my unit. _____

Adjusting Your Supervisory Style to the Individual or Group (Chapter 8)

47. I know the special needs of the various types of volunteers in my unit. _____

48. I adapt my supervisory style to the various types of volunteers in my unit. _____

The Role of the Coordinator of Volunteers (Chapter 9)

49. My organization's coordinator of volunteers and I have an open, ongoing relationship. _____

50. My organization's coordinator of volunteers and I collaboratively develop and implement methods for evaluating various aspects of the organization's volunteer program, including my own performance as a supervisor. _____

Annotated Bibliography and Resources

Books available from Energize, Inc. are marked with an asterisk (*). For your free copy of the latest annual "Volunteer Energy Resource Catalog," call 1-800-395-9800 or fax 215-438-0434. Or, visit our Web site and browse the Online Bookstore: www.energizeinc.com.

Volunteer Management Books with Sections on Supervision

Ellis, Susan J. *From the Top Down: The Executive Role in Volunteer Program Success,* revised edition. Philadelphia, PA: Energize, 1996. *

Although the subtitle suggests that only executive directors should read this book, it is, in fact, a "must-read" for coordinators of volunteers and those who supervise volunteers. Organizations that truly study— and discuss—this book will have a clear vision for why they want to involve volunteers and how to do so effectively.

Eystad, Melissa, ed. *Measuring the Difference Volunteers Make: A Guide to Outcome Evaluation for Volunteer Program Managers.* St. Paul, MN: Minnesota Department of Human Services, 1997.*

A concise, to-the-point guidebook that simplifies outcomes-based evaluation. Describes what it is, how to collect what types of data, and how to present evaluation findings.

Graff, Linda. *Beyond Police Checks: The Definitive Volunteer and Employee Screening Guidebook.* Ontario: Graff & Associates, 1998. *

Provides the rationale for initial screening and ongoing credential checks, models for developing screening processes, and a variety of screening tools to raise the reader's comfort level with this sensitive and vital subject.

Graff, Linda. *By Definition: Policies for Volunteer Programs,* 2nd ed. Ontario: Graff & Associates, 1997.*

Defines and explains policy-making for and about volunteers. Applicable to any type of setting, this book provides proactical examples of general and specific policies.

MacKensie, Marilyn. *Dealing with Difficult Volunteers.* Downers Grove, IL: Heritage Arts Publishing, 1988.

Concise, on-target advice for how to work with volunteers that pose supervision problems.

McCurley, Steve and Rick Lynch. *Volunteer Management: Mobilizing All the Resources of the Community.* Downers Grove, IL: Heritage Arts Publishing, 1996. *

This book covers all the essentials of developing and maintaining a good volunteer program. Particularly helpful to supervisors are the seven chapters that cover orientation and training; supervision; evaluation, corrective action and termination; retention and recognition; and volunteer-staff relations. There is an extensive appendix on further reading and a large collection of sample forms.

McCurley, Steve and Sue Vineyard. *Handling Problem Volunteers.* Downers Grove, IL: Heritage Arts Publishing, 1998.*

This short book offers numerous practical tips for supervising numerous types of "problem" volunteers including the prima donna, the resentful former peer, the liar and the organizational terrorist. Also helpful are descriptions of the three steps to correcting actions and how to give and receive feedback.

Scheier, Ivan H. *Building Staff/Volunteer Relations.* Philadelphia, PA: Energize, Inc., 1993. *

This book will be invaluable to anyone who supervises volunteers. Particularly important are the staff and volunteers teamwork checklist, the perspectives on volunteers checklist and an appendix that lists topics for policy formation about volunteers. The book includes the classic letter from Frank Miller in which he voices his serious concerns about the professionalism of volunteers.

Scheier, Ivan H. *When Everyone's a Volunteer: The Effective Functioning of All-Volunteer Groups.* Philadelphia, PA: Energize, Inc., 1992.*

Most volunteer management literature focuses on the agency-based volunteer program. This book helps those groups that are entirely volunteer run. Challenges common wisdom on boards of directors, ways to share work equitably, and resource development. The reader will find many useful suggestions on how volunteers can lead other volunteers towards mutual goals.

Stallings, Betty B. *Training Busy Staff to Succeed with Volunteers: Building Commitment and Competence in Staff/Volunteer Teams.* Pleasanton, CA: Building Better Skills, 1996. *

This book emphasizes the new paradigm—the shift that has occurred in the role of the volunteer coordinator—from do-er of all aspects of an organization's volunteer program to in-house consultant, trainer and catalyst. It provides the theoretical and practical framework for Stallings' 55 minute expandable training series—training modules (which come with a computer disk) that coordinators of volunteers can use for in-service training.

General Audience Books on Management and Supervision

Blanchard, Kenneth and Spencer Johnson. *The One Minute Manager.* New York: Berkeley Publishing Group, 1983. (Check this. Originally published in 1982 by William Morrow and Company, Inc.)

The essence of this popular little book is that goals begin behaviors—consequences maintain behaviors. One minute goals, one minute praisings and one minute reprimands are the methods prescribed by the authors for all who want to be effective supervisors.

Covey, Stephen R. *The 7 Habits of Highly Effective People: Restoring the Character Ethic.* New York: Simon and Schuster, 1989.

The seven habits advocated by Covey in this important book deal with personal management and interpersonal leadership. Developing these habits will create lasting personal and professional change.

DePree, Max. *Leadership is an Art.* New York: Dell Publishing, 1989.

Although written for the business community, this easy-to-read, thought provoking book will inspire all coordinators of volunteers and supervisors of volunteers to assess their beliefs about leadership and their attitudes about those they lead.

Hirsh, Sandra Krebs. *Work It Out: Clues for Solving People Problems at Work.* CA: Davies-Black Publishing, 1996.

The numerous practical ideas presented in this book on fostering teamwork are based on differences in personality types, as categorized by the Myers-Briggs Type Indicator (MBTI). Although the inventory is not included in the book, the 16 personality types are described in detail.

Kruger, Richard A. *Focus Groups: A Practical Guide for Applied Research.* Newbury Park, CA: SAGE Publications, Inc., 1988.

Focus groups provide a forum for participants to state preferences, to provide information about why they think or feel the way they do. Leaders who want feedback on proposed actions can use this book to learn how to conduct a focus group.

Laborde, Genie Z. *Influencing with Integrity: Management Skills for Communication and Negotiation.* Palo Alto, CA: Syntony Publishing, 1983.

The subject of this book is summed up in this statement which appears on the last page: "The meaning of communication is the response you get. If you are not getting the response you want, change what you are doing." Supervisors who want to change their communication skills will be able to do so by a careful reading of this book.

Maslach, Christina and Michael P. Leiter. *The Truth about Burnout: How Organizations Cause Personal Stress and What to Do About It.* San Francisco: Jossey-Bass, Inc. Publishers, 1997.

The authors identify six sources of burnout—work overload, lack of control, insufficient reward, unfairness, breakdown of community and value conflict—and describe the emotional and physical consequences. Their recommendations for organizational change will help responsible supervisors and leaders make their organizations healthier for all.

Nelson, Bob. *1001 Ways to Energize Employees.* New York: Workman Publishing, 1997.

Nelson, Bob. *1001 Ways to Reward Employees.* New York: Workman Publishing, 1994.

These two books have very little text. Instead, they are a collection of hundreds of practical ideas currently in practice at dozens of American companies of all sizes. Numerous tips and pithy quotes from CEOs and management experts are included. Supervisors will find most of the principles apply equally to volunteers.

Roberts, Wess. *Leadership Secrets of Attila the Hun.* New York: Warner Books, Inc., 1985.

Practical tips for effective leaders are cleverly interwoven with accounts of the life of Attila, the mighty leader of the Huns. Supervisors will especially benefit from the 90 "Attilaisms" that end the book, for example: "If you tell a Hun he is doing a good job when he isn't, he will not listen long and, worse, will not believe praise when it is justified."

Schaef, Anne Wilson and Diane Fassel. *The Addictive Organization: Why We Overwork, Cover Up, Pick Up the Pieces, Please the Boss and Perpetuate Sick Organizations.* San Francisco: Harper, 1988.

This landmark book explores the origins and characteristics of addictive organizations: isolated leaders, a striving for power and control, confusion and crisis orientation, judgmentalism and perfectionism, denial and dishonesty. The high personal cost of working in such an organization is outlined.

Schwarz, Roger M. *The Skilled Facilitator: Practical Wisdom for Developing Effective Groups.* San Francisco: Jossey-Bass, Inc. Publishers, 1994.

This book includes sample ground rules for governing group interaction, how to keep meetings and other group processes on track, handling negative emotions that hamper a group's effectiveness and a diagnostic approach for helping groups identify and solve problems that could undermine the group process.

Vineyard, Sue. *The Great Trainer's Guide: How to Train (Almost) Anyone to Do (Almost) Anything!* Downers Grove, IL: Heritage Arts Publishing, 1990.

This easy-to-read book provides information about adult learning principles, formats and methods for training, and how to prepare and use training tools like flipcharts, overheads and transparencies. It includes numerous ice-breakers, sample evaluation forms and dozens of practical tips for trainers (the best: wear comfortable shoes).

Special Situation Books

Ellis, Susan J., Anne Weisbord and Katherine H. Noyes. *Children as Volunteers: Preparing for Community Service, rev. ed.* Philadelphia, PA: Energize, Inc., 1991.*

This book is based on the belief that "volunteering is the perfect way for children to be welcomed as productive, active members of a community." Helpful to organizations involving children as volunteers, it will also aid youth group leaders and teachers wanting to develop volunteer service opportunities for youth under age 14. Included are numerous accounts of children as volunteers, concrete guidelines, sample parental consent forms, and an important chapter on legalities and liabilities.

Kiely, Arlene Barry. *Volunteers in Child Health: Management, Selection, Training and Supervision.* Bethesda, MD: The Association for the Care of Children's Health, 1992.

The lengthy section that deals with supervision will be helpful to anyone who supervises volunteers regardless of the setting. The section on helping volunteers develop realistic expectations is especially important for those who work with volunteers in a child health setting.

Kuyper, Joan with Ellen Hirzy and Kathleen Huftalen. *Volunteer Program Administration: A Handbook for Museums and Other Cultural Institutions.* New York: American Council for the Arts, 1993.*

This comprehensive manual provides practical information as well as sample forms, profiles of actual volunteer programs in cultural organizations and tips from volunteer administrators. The book includes an extensive resource and networking guide.

Mitchell, Jeff and Grady Bray. *Emergency Services Stress: Guidelines for Preserving the Health and Careers of Emergency Services Personnel.* Englewood Cliffs, NJ: Prentice-Hall, Inc., 1990.

This guidebook provides an overview of the causes and effects of the stress experienced by emergency service providers and practical information on how to prevent, alleviate and recover from it. Supervisors will find particularly helpful the sections on stress reduction policies and the development of critical incident stress debriefing teams.

Rehnborg, Sarah Jane. *The Starter Kit for Mobilizing Ministry.* Tyler, TX: Leadership Network, 1994.

Published in a handy looseleaf format, this manual outlines the seven steps for building a lay ministry program with a Biblical foundation. Step Six involves developing systems for supervision, which is defined as offering support, affirmation, feedback and evaluation. The book includes numerous sample forms and a large appendix of additional resources and references.

Seidman, Anna and John Patterson. *Kidding Around? Be Serious! A Commitment to Safe Service Opportunities for Young People.* Washington, DC: Nonprofit Risk Management Center, 1996.

The authors of this informative text state that virtually all accidents are preventable, and then provide numerous risk management strategies designed for organizations that involve volunteers under age 18. The book also contains more than a dozen thought-provoking hypothetical case studies, with suggested solutions.

Weaver, John D. *An Untapped Resource: Working with Volunteers who are Mentally Ill.* Walla Walla, WA: MBA Publishing, 1993.

This booklet describes the signs of mental illness and offers detailed advice about how to interview someone who has or has had a severe mental illness. It does not cover issues of supervision.

Weems, Jr. Lovett H. *Church Leadership: Vision, Team, Culture and Integrity.* Nashville: Abingdon Press, 1993.

Churches seeking to involve members as volunteers will benefit from the insightful analysis this book offers on the role of leadership in creating an open organization. Especially helpful are the exercises at the end of each chapter.

Electronic Resources

CyberVPM Web site and listserv: http://www.cybervpm.com

Includes an online introductory course for volunteer management (the "Volunteerism Mini-University"), training and other resources. A real-time chat room is available. Regardless of your level of experience, take advantage of site developer Nan Hawthorne's outstanding listserv, "CyberVPM" (Cyberspace Volunteer Program Management). This free, active electronic bulletin board brings questions and answers from volunteer management colleagues around the world directly to your e-mailbox.
To subscribe, send an e-mail to: LISTSERV@CHARITYCHANNEL.COM with the message: SUBSCRIBE CYBERVPM < your first name last name >

Energize, Inc. Web site: http://www.energizeinc.com

Focused exclusively on information needed by leaders of volunteer efforts, offers free access to a library of articles and book excerpts, quotations and parables about volunteering, recognition ideas, a directory of DOVIAs and state associations, a volunteer management job bank, a calendar of conferences and training events, and up-to-date contact information for—and hyper links to—a wide range of international volunteerism resources. The site also has a full Online Bookstore with over 75 books and videos for sale. Every month the site features a new "Hot Topic" essay by Susan Ellis and visitors are encouraged to post responses.

Points of Light Foundation:
http://www.pointsoflight.org
   This site provides a directory of all Volunteer Centers in the United States, and information on National Volunteer Week, the National Community Service Conference, and other POLF-coordinated activities.

Association for Volunteer Administration:
http://www.avaintl.org
   The site of the major professional association for volunteer program managers. Find information on the International Conference for Volunteer Administration, The Journal of Volunteer Administration, ethics and standards in the field.

Volunteer Today "Electronic Gazette":
http://bigjohn.bmi.net/mba
   Another site providing volunteer management information, links, and resources, plus up-to-the-minute "news" items of interest to the field, compiled by trainer/author Nancy Macduff.

Virtual Volunteering: http://www.serviceleader.org/vv
   Learn all about how to start and manage the new service category of virtual volunteering. This site contains everything you need to know about what virtual volunteering is and how to apply the principles of real-world volunteer management to cyberspace.

Contributor Credits

Archive Resources

All of the pre-published materials below have been reprinted in this book with permission of their publishers. When requested by the publisher, you will find additional contact information with the reference. Following each reference is the chapter(s) in which quotes appear.

American Management Association. "Ten Commandments of Good Communication," in *AMA Executive Communication Course.* New York: AMA, 1955. (Chapter 4) http://www.amanet.org

American Red Cross. "Shared Responsibilities for Volunteer Administration," in *Volunteer Personnel Administration Handbook.* Washington, DC: American Red Cross, 1993.(Chapter 9)

Beach, Lisa. *A Nuts & Bolts Guide to Non-Profit Newsletters.* Oviedo, FL:*Non-Profit Nuts & Bolts* Newsletter, 1998. (Chapter 4) 4623 Tiffany Woods Circle, Oviedo, FL 32765; phone: 407-677-6564, fax: 407-677-5645, http://www.nutsbolts.com

Bramhall, Martha. "How to Prevent Volunteer Burnout," interviewed by Donna Hill. *Voluntary Action Leadership,** Winter, 1985, pp. 20-23. (Chapter 6)

Brown, Kathleen. "Thoughts on the Supervision of Volunteers," *Voluntary Action Leadership,** Spring, 1984, pp. 14-16. (Chapter 1)

Communications Briefings. "37 Quick & Easy Tips You Can Use to Keep Your Customers" and "The Guide to Customer Service." Adapted in *AVA Update,* Sept./Oct. 1994. (Chapter 6)

Ellis, Susan J. *From the Top Down: The Executive Role in Volunteer Program Success,* rev. ed. Philadelphia: Energize, Inc. 1996. (Introduction)

Ellis, Susan J. "Special Considerations in thc Supervision of Volunteers," Workshop Handout, Philadelphia: Energize, Inc., 1985. (Chapter 1)

Ellis, Susan J. "Supervision Walk-Through Analysis," Workshop Handout, Philadelphia: Energize, Inc., 1990. (Chapter 9)

Fournies, Ferdinand. "Analyzing Performance Problems," in *Coaching for Improved Work Performance.* New York: McGraw-Hill Companies, 1988. (Chapter 6)

Gaston, Nancy A. "Easy Does it: Initiating a Performance Evaluation Process in an Existing Volunteer Program," *The Journal of Volunteer Administration,*** Vol. VII, No.1 (Fall 1989), pp. 27-30. (Chapter 7)

Hodgkins, Dick. "What is Supervision?" *Voluntary Action Leadership,** Spring, 1979, p. 24. (Chapter 2)

Isaksen, Scott G. "The Environment Conducive to Creativity." Buffalo, NY: The Creative Problem Solving Group, 1998. (Chapter 5) 1325 North Forest Road, Suite F-340, Williamsville, NY 14221

Labella, Arlene and Joy Dolores Leach. *Personal Power.* Boulder, CO: Career Track Publications, 1985. (Chapter 6)

MacKenzie, Marilyn. *Dealing with Difficult Volunteers.* Downers Grove, IL: VMSystems-Heritage Arts Publishing,*** 1988. (Chapters 5, 6)

McCurley, Steve and Rick Lynch. *Essential Volunteer Management.* Downers Grove, IL: Heritage Arts Publishing,*** 1989. (Chapters 1, 7) Revised and republished as:

McCurley, Steve and Rick Lynch. *Volunteer Management: Mobilizing all the Resources of the Community.* Downers Grove, IL: Heritage Arts Publishing,*** 1996. (Chapter 7)

McCurley, Steve and Sue Vineyard. *101 Ideas for Volunteer Programs.* Downers Grove, IL: Heritage Arts Publishing,*** 1986. (Chapter 6)

Meijs, Lucas. Working manuscript for "Management Is Not Always the Right Word!" *The Journal of Volunteer Administration,* Vol. XIV, No. 3 (Spring 1996), pp. 25-31. (Chapter 8)

---

* *Voluntary Action Leadership* is the former version of what is today *Volunteer Leadership,* published quarterly by the Points of Light Foundation, 1400 I Street, NW, Washington, DC 20005, 202-729-8000, www.pointsoflight.org

** All reprints from *The Journal of Volunteer Administration* are permission of the Association for Volunteer Administration, P.O. Box 32092, 3108 N. Parham Road, Richmond, VA 23294

***Heritage Arts Publishing, 1807 Prairie Avenue, Downers Grove, IL 60515

Contributor Credits

Metro Voluntary Action Center. *Get Organized! How to Set up a Volunteer Program.* Atlanta, GA: United Way, 1979. (Chapter 1)

Moses, Barbara S. *Volunteers in Zoos and Aquariums: A Resource Manual.* Wheeling, WV: American Association of Zoological Parks and Aquariums, 1981. (Chapter 8)

National Association of Partners in Education. *A Practical Guide to Creating and Managing Community Coalitions for Drug Abuse Prevention.* Alexandria, VA: NAPE , 1989. (Chapter 5)

Naylor, Harriet. *Leadership for Volunteering.* Dryden, NY: Dryden Associates, 1976. (Chapter 8)

Noyes (Campbell), Katherine H. *Opportunity or Dilemma: Court-Referred Community Service Workers.* Richmond, VA: Virginia Department of Volunteerism, 1985. (Chapter 8) 804-692-1950, e-mail: vol2@dss.state.va.us

Ohio Society of Directors of Volunteer Services. *Strategies for Success in Volunteer Services Administration.* Columbus, OH: Ohio Hospital Association, 1990. (Chapter 7)

Park, Jane Mallory. "Letting Go: Planning For Volunteer Release," Handout at Pennsylvania Association for Volunteerism Workshop, 1985. (Chapter 2)

Regan, Dennis. "Getting it Done with Volunteers: Recruiting, Training, Supervising and Evaluating," in the *Proceedings* of the Symposium on Volunteers and Communication in Natural Resource Education, 1990. (Chapter 3)

Scheier, Ivan H. *When Everyone's a Volunteer: The Effective Functioning of All-Volunteer Groups.* Philadelphia, PA: Energize, Inc., 1992. (Chapters 2, 8)

Schindler-Rainman, Eva. *Transitioning: Strategies for the Volunteer World.* Vancouver, Canada: Voluntary Action Resource Centre, 1981. (Chapter 8)

Sharratt, Gene. "Ensuring Volunteer Success Through Effective Delegation Techniques." *Voluntary Action Leadership,** Winter 1988-1989, p. 8. (Chapter 2)

Stallings, Betty B. *Resource Kit for Managers of Volunteers.* Pleasanton, CA: Building Better Skills, 1992. (Chapter 2)

Stallings, Betty Stallings, Betty B. *Training Busy Staff to Succeed with Volunteers.* Pleasanton, CA: Building Better Skills, 1996. (Chapter 9)

Vermont Department of Corrections. *Volunteer Services Manual.* 1996. (Chapters 3, 9)

The Volunteer Centre UK. *Managing Volunteers: A Handbook for Volunteer Organisers*, Mark Rankin, ed. London, UK: The Volunteer Centre, UK (now the National Centre on Volunteering), 1992. (Chapters 3, 5)

Walk, Marie-Francoise and Jerry Schoen. "Credibility with Volunteers: How to Establish and Maintain It." *Volunteer Monitor* (Volunteer Water Quality Monitoring), Fall 1992. (Chapters 1, 4)

Wilson, Marlene. *The Effective Management of Volunteer Programs.* Boulder, CO: Volunteer Management Associates, 1976. (Chapter 8)

Wroblewski, Celeste J. *The Seven R's of Volunteer Development.* Chicago, IL: YMCA of the USA, 1994. (Chapter 7)

Zoller, Mary B. "YMCA Teen Leadership Programs." 1992, in *The Seven Rs of Volunteer Development* by Celeste J. Wroblewski, Chicago, IL: YMCA of the USA, 1994. (Chapter 6)

"From The Field" Contributors

The people listed below submitted materials that appear either as quotations within the text of the book, as "From the Field" inserts, or on the Energize Web site. With our gratitude for the sharing of their collective wisdom:

Janice Allan
Director of Volunteers
Boulder County Justice System Volunteer Program
Boulder, CO

Marty Atherton
Coordinator of Volunteer Services
Families First
Atlanta, GA

Linda Bailey
Volunteer Coordinator
Mesa Police Department
Mesa, AZ

Judy Baillere
County 4-H Agent
Rutgers Cooperative Extension of Gloucester County
Clayton, NJ

Carol Baker
Audience Services Coordinator
Actors Theatre of Louisville
Louisville, KY

Susan Bartels
Case Manager
Big Brothers Big Sisters of Bucks County
Jamison, PA

John D. Bergeron
Volunteer Program Manager
Glaucoma Research Foundation
San Francisco, CA

Jeanne Bernard
Director, Volunteer and Community Resources
Montgomery County Department of Police
Gaithersburg, MD

Alison Bernstein
Director of Buddy Services
AIDS Coalition of Southern NJ
Audubon, NJ

Eve Breeden, CVA
Vice President
Barclay Woods Condo Association
Brielle, NJ

Rustie Brooke
Volunteer Coordinator
Wartburg Lutheran Home for the Aging
Brooklyn, NY

Contributor Credits

Susan Brown
Volunteer Coordinator
Elder Home Care Services of Worcester Area, Inc.
Worcester, MA

Ruth M. Buell
Manager of Volunteer Resources
Monterey Bay Aquarium
Monterey, CA

Susan Cairy
Volunteer Programs Coordinator
Spokane County Juvenile Court
Spokane, WA

Katherine Noyes Campbell, CVA
Executive Director
Association for Volunteer Administration
Richmond, VA

Mike Cataruzolo, CVA
Supervisor, Volunteer Services
Perkins School for the Blind
Watertown, MA

Dolores Cattiny, CVA
Coordinator of Volunteer Services
North Jersey Developmental Center
Totowa, NJ

Joel Cohen
Regional Director
Joint Action in Community Service
Philadelphia, PA

Alberta Conklin
Director of Volunteers
Good Samaritan Hospital
Suffern, NY

Patricia Connelly
South Florida Director
The Holiday Project
Bonaventure, FL

Sean Conyngham
Director of Shared Ministry
Church of the Presentation
Upper Saddle River, NJ

Jayne Cravens
Manager, Virtual Volunteering Project
ImpactONline in partnership with the
Charles A. Dana Center
University of Texas at Austin
Austin, TX

Maureen Crawford
Volunteer Programs and Internships
New England Aquarium
Boston, MA

Judy Cunningham
Volunteer Coordinator
City of Cottage Grove
Cottage Grove, OR

Donna Dandrilli
Volunteer Coordinator
Cabrini Hospice
New York, NY

Sue DeMartini
Chairperson, Shared Ministry Committee
Church of the Presentation
Upper Saddle River, NJ

Eileen A. Derr
Volunteer Coordinator
Palo Alto Police Department
Palo Alto, CA

Terry Dunn
Volunteer/Training Coordinator
Florida HIV/AIDS Hotline
Tallahassee, FL

Susan J. Ellis
President
Energize, Inc.
Philadelphia, PA

Sarah H. Elliston
Professional Development Associate
United Way Volunteer Resource Center
Cincinnati, OH

Jill Friedman Fixler
President
Training By Design
Denver, CO

Teresa Gardner-Williams, CVA
Volunteer Services Coordinator
Alexandria Division of Social Services
Alexandria, VA

Lisa M. Garey
Volunteer Coordinator
Chesterfield Fire Department
Chesterfield, VA

Nancy A. Gaston, CVA
Director of Christian Development
Moreland Presbyterian Church
Portland, OR

Linda L. Graff
Senior Associate
Graff and Associates
Dundas, ON

Mary Teresa Gray
Coordinator of Volunteers
Iona Senior Services
Washington, DC

Nan Hawthorne
Managing Director
Sound Volunteer Management
Seattle, WA

Amy Hohn
Director of Volunteer Resources
League for the Hard of Hearing
New York, NY

Contributor Credits

Stephen A. Horton
District Manager
Canadian Cancer Society
Prince George, BC

Linda Johnson
Director, Volunteer Services
Palo Pinto General Hospital
Mineral Wells, TX

Greg Kachejian
Manager, Patients Library
Memorial Sloan-Kettering Cancer Center
New York, NY

Kay Keenze
Director, Volunteer Services Program
The Free Library of Philadelphia
Philadelphia, PA

Rob Kerby
Public Information Officer
Northwest Arkansas Economic Development District
Green Forest, AR

Trish Kerlé
Director of Cultural Programs
Lesbian and Gay Community Services Center
New York, NY

Ann Wead Kimbrough
Financial Journalist
Atlanta Business Chronicle
Atlanta, GA

Laura J. King
Director of Volunteers
The Children's Inn at NIH
Bethesda, MD

Tom Konrad
President, Volunteer Council
Calvert Marine Museum
Solomons, MD

Wendy Lavine
Director, Volunteer Services
Triad Health Project
Greensboro, NC

Carla Lehn, CVA
Principal Consultant
The Lehn Group
Koloa, Kauai, HI

Joe Levandoski
Director, Southwark Branch
The Free Library of Philadelphia
Philadelphia, PA

Barbara Lightheart
Volunteer Manager
Travis County Jail
Austin, TX

Debra Lynne
Director of Volunteer Services and Events
The Children's Aid Society
New York, NY

Nancy Macduff
President
Macduff/Blunt Associates
Walla Walla, WA

Ruth McCreery
Board Member, Tokyo English Life Line
President, The Word Works, Ltd.
Yokohama, Japan

Lucy A. McGowan, CVA
Coordinator, Volunteer Services
Lake Oswego Public Library
Lake Oswego, OR

Paula Meadows
Manager of Volunteer Services
Denver Museum of Natural History
Denver, CO

Louise Menapace
Office Coordinator, Volunteer Services Department
The Medical Center at Princeton
Princeton, NJ

Vivian Nicholls
Volunteer Resources Coordinator
Calgary Police Service
Calgary, AL Canada

Keri Olson
Public Relations Director and Volunteer Coordinator
Circus World Museum
Baraboo, WI

Karen Paterson
Volunteer/Intern Coordinator
Mental Health Corporation of Denver
Denver, CO

Kim A. Payne
Director of Volunteer Resources
Victim Services, Inc
New York, NY

Lisa Perreault
Volunteer Program Assistant
Glaucoma Research Foundation
San Francisco, CA

Cindy Petty
Director of Planning and Marketing
Gibson General Hospital
Princeton, IN

Sarah Jane Rehnborg, PhD, CVA
Director, Volunteerism and Community Engagement
Charles A. Dana Center
University of Texas at Austin
Austin, TX

Jane Richardson
Volunteer Coordinator
Sunnyside Community Services
Sunnyside, NY

Kay Rittenhouse
Director of Volunteer Services
NAMI of St. Louis
St. Louis, MO

Contributor Credits

Carol Robins
Director of Volunteer Resources
The Lighthouse, Inc.
New York, NY

Beverly Robinson
Manager, Volunteer Services
Minnesota Masonic Home
Bloomington, MN

Jennifer Roe
Volunteer Projects Co-ordinator
Glasgow and West of Scotland Society for the Blind
Glasgow, UK

Brenda Roman/Jill Evertman
Volunteer Services
Children's Aid Society of Metropolitan Toronto
Toronto, ON

Nancy Roslund
Director of Lay Ministry
Los Altos United Methodist Church
Los Altos, CA

Lu Salisbury
Director of Volunteers
OMNI Youth Services
Buffalo Grove, IL

Jerome Scriptunas
Board President
Big Brothers Big Sisters of Monmouth County, Inc.
Eatontown, NJ

Bernice Skirboll, CVA
Executive Director and President
COMPEER, Inc.
Rochester, NY

Richard A. Smith
Assistant Director, Program Services
Department of Corrections
Waterburg, VT

Joseph H. Soncrant
Christian Service Coordinator
St. Andrew Catholic Church
Rochester, MI

Lin Spellman
Volunteer Services Manager
Pierce County Juvenile Court
Tacoma, WA

Ann Moore Stafford
Volunteer Services Coordinator
Austin Public Library
Austin, TX

Betty B. Stallings
President
Betty Stallings and Associates
Pleasanton, CA

Lisa Taylor
Director, Volunteer Services
Courage Center
Minneapolis, MN

Terrie Temkin, Ph.D.
President
NonProfit Management Solutions, Inc.
Hollywood, FL

Janet L. Unger
President
Unger Consulting Services
Philadelphia, PA

Peggy Wadsworth, CVA
Coordinator of Volunteer Services
Chester County Library
Exton, PA

Debbie W. Walker
*Foster Grandparent, Retired and
    Senior Volunteer Project Director*
Economic Opportunity Authority
Savannah, GA

Thomas Weber
Coordinator of Volunteers for Client Programs
Gay Men's Health Crisis
New York, NY

Jay N. Weinberg
President
Corporate Angel Network
White Plains, NY

Ann Weinwurn
Education and Training Associate
Hospice and Home Care by the Sea, Inc
Boca Raton, FL

Rhoda White
Director of Volunteer Services
Visiting Nurse Service of New York
New York, NY

Anne R. Wild
Supervisor of Volunteers for Help Line and Cheering
Help Line Telephone Services
New York, NY

Sheri Wilensky
Director, Volunteer Outreach
American Lung Association
New York, NY

Sheila Williams
Director of Volunteer Services & Membership
Girl Scouts of Southeastern Pennsylvania, Inc.
Ambler, PA

Elizabeth M. Wynn
Volunteer Coordinator
Orange County Community Corrections Department
Orlando, FL

Thank you to the people who submitted material and preferred to remain anonymous.

Contributor Credits

Volunteer Focus Group Participants

The following volunteer program leaders generously arranged for representative volunteers to participate in focus groups about supervision. Our thanks to them and to each of the volunteers whose names are below.

Brooklyn Botanic Garden
Brooklyn, NY

Lou Cesario
Director of Visitor Services and Volunteers
- Paul Howard
- Mary O'Connor
- Marie-Therese Smith
- Jo A. Windsor-Antrobus
- Helen Jacobs
- Pat Waisome

Eger Health Care and Rehabilitation Center
Staten Island, NY

Astrid Petersen
Volunteer Coordinator
- Caroline Emigholz
- Irene Maiurro
- Lillian McDonough
- Suzette Roberts
- Marilyn Romer
- Doris Tully

Hyacinth AIDS Foundation
New Brunswick, NJ

Paula Toynton
Director of Education and Volunteer Resources
- Chuck Holm
- Ken Howard
- Gloria Trumbo
- Barbara McQuaide
- Lydia Wells
- Scott Blankenship
- Lisa Brown
- Patricia Brown
- Barbara Duncan Carter
- Michelle Foster
- Andreanette Harris
- Clarence A. Mortoni
- Christine Perfinski

Passaic Valley Hospice
Totowa, NJ

Barbara Wiederecht
Director of Volunteers
- Aaron Pulhamus
- Doris Bauer
- Alice M. Brown
- Mary Garrity
- Rosemarie Harvey

Index

A

Accessibility of supervisor, 9, 11, 25, 58, 59
Aging in place, 84, 108
Agreements, written, *see* Contracts, written
All-volunteer organizations, 57, 79, 83, 118-9
Appreciation, *see* Recognition
Attitudes about volunteers, 2, 3, 5-6, 15-6, 17, 31, 34, 44, 61, 65, 81

B

Buddies as trainers, 31, 54, 108, 117
Bulletin boards, 11, 45, 47,
Bulletin boards, electronic, 53
Burnout, 19, 34, 68, 77, 79, 116

C

Captain Kirk model of supervision, 60
Career exploration, 112, 113
Coaching vs. supervising, 2, 10, 57-8, 74
Community building, 44
Community service, 109-12
Complainers, chronic, 76
Computer technology, 45, 49, 52-4, 120-2
Confidentiality, 45, 111, 136
Conflict management, 8, 80, 82
Continuing education, *see* Training volunteers, in-service
Contracts, written, 18, 20-3, 122
Corporate/business volunteers, 113
Court-ordered service, 110-11
Criticism, 43, 71, 74, 80

D

Delegation, 25, 26, 122
Designated supervisor, 54-5, 73
Disabilities, developmental, 114, 115

Disabilities, physical, 45, 114, 117, 118
Distance learning, 53
Documenting performance problems, 77, 85, 130
Donors as volunteers, 85

E

E-mail, use of, 49, 53-4, 121
Employees as volunteers, 117
Environment, work, 64, 65-6, 83, 124, 125-6
Evaluation forms, samples, 95-6, 98-9, 100-1, 102, 105
Evaluation of new volunteers, 94-6
Evaluation of volunteer satisfaction, 100-3
Evaluation, organizational, 85-6
Evaluation, performance, 60, 84-5, 94-100
Evaluation, self, 95, 96-8
Exit interviews/surveys, 67, 103, 105
Expectations, 6, 7, 15-27, 42, 44, 60, 67, 74

F

Families as volunteers, 112
Feedback, 10, 25, 48-9, 57, 58, 60, 65, 101, 111
Field, volunteers in the, *see* Off-site volunteers
Firing a volunteer, 22, 83-6, 130

G

Goals, focusing on, 7, 17, 29, 40-1, 44, 59, 113, 119
Grievance procedure, 79, 100
Group supervision, 36-8, 66
Groups, organized, 117-8

I

Instructions, good, 32-3, 73
Interviewing, 18, 132

J

Job descriptions, volunteer, 10, 16-18, 67, 74, 83, 85, 95, 96
Job design, volunteer, 8, 9, 15, 94, 115, 118

Index

L

Language, 1, 2, 46, 58, 74-6, 125
Leave of absence, 77, 79, 82-3, 85
Liability issues, 65, 71, 84
Liaison supervision, 53, 127-32
Listening, 42-3, 46, 58
Listservs, 52, 54
Logs, service, 47

M

Mandated volunteering, 109-12
Manuals/handbooks, 17, 31, 82, 83, 128, 134
Measuring results, 94
Meetings, 8, 34, 36-9, 49-50, 51, 52
Mental health issues, 77, 80, 114, 115, 116
Message forms, 47, 51, 54-5
Middle managers, 134
Minutes, 50-1
Motivation of volunteers, 40, 44, 54, 58, 60

N

National/local relationships, 122-4
Newsletters, electronic, 49, 52
Newsletters, paper, 48-9, 50

O

Off-site volunteers, 10, 39, 53, 54, 120, 122, 123
Older volunteers, 29, 82, 84, 108
One-time volunteers, 119
Orientation, 10, 18-19, 24, 125

P

Participant-volunteers, 117
Performance assessment, see Evaluation
Performance problems, analyzing, 63, 71-2, 85-6
Performance problems, discussion starters, 86-90
Performance problems, resolving, 8, 36, 74, 75, 77, 84, 130
Performance problems, types of, 73
Personal style, 80, 82-3
Policies, 17, 18, 30, 77, 79, 81, 83, 108, 123
Praise, 41, 58, 60, 62, 63
Principles of volunteer supervision, 1-2

R

Reassignment, 31-2, 36, 75-6, 77, 78, 79, 84-5, 94, 100
Recognition, 8, 11-12, 38, 39, 44, 47, 60-1, 62, 63, 64, 65, 66, 69-70, 82, 100, 112

Relationships between employees and volunteers, 61, 63, 123-4
Reporting, 36, 38, 47, 50-1, 52, 53, 59, 66, 104, 121
Retention, 40, 66-8, 101
Risk management, 30, 65, 71, 80, 83-4
Rotation policy, 17, 79, 84, 108

S

Secretary of the volunteer office, 134, 136
Self-assessment survey for supervisors, 141-2
Senior volunteers, see Older volunteers
Service-learning, 109, 111-2
Standard operating procedures, 32-3
Standards, 20, 22, 74
Students as volunteers, 109, 111-2
Success factors, 34-5
Suggestion boxes, 47-8
Support groups, 34-8, 39, 125

T

Teams, 8, 61, 63, 65
Technical assistance volunteers, 112-3
Telephone, use of, 51-2, 121
Termination, see Firing a volunteer
Time constraints, 6, 24-5, 58, 113
Training employees to supervise, 66, 128, 131, 133
Training volunteers, initial, 10, 19, 29, 30-2, 132
Training volunteers, in-service, 10, 29, 32-6, 42-3, 53, 61, 66
Transitional volunteers, 113-4

V

Virtual volunteering, 45, 53, 54, 120-2
Volunteer, definition of, 1-2, 109-10
Volunteer emeritus status, 82, 84
Volunteers as supervisors, 36, 51, 53, 61, 109, 119-20, 130

W

Warnings, 77, 83
Web sites, use of, 52-3
Welfare reform participants, 110, 111
Why involve volunteers, 3

Y

Young volunteers, 29, 108-9, 112

About the Authors

Jarene Frances Lee

Jarene Frances Lee is a trainer, consultant and writer in the field of volunteer program management. She was the director of the Department of Volunteer Resources at Memorial Sloan-Kettering Cancer Center in New York City from 1977 to 1994 and the director of volunteer services at Trenton (NJ) Psychiatric Hospital from 1968 to 1977.

Ms. Lee is the author of eight articles which were published in Voluntary Action Leadership and The Volunteer Leader. She teaches two courses in the Certification Program in Volunteer Management at Rutgers University and has conducted workshops in Arkansas, Massachusetts, New Jersey, New York and Pennsylvania. She has served on the board of the Association for Volunteer Administration (AVA) and numerous local and national committees.

Ms. Lee has an undergraduate degree in psychology from Chatham College, Pittsburgh, and a master's degree in journalism from Syracuse University.

Her volunteer activities have included church trustee, firefighter, Girl Scout leader, tutor and newsletter editor. She lives on Staten Island, New York with her husband, Rev. Adolf A. Pagliarulo, and their two teenage daughters.

Julia M. Catagnus

Julia M. Catagnus is Publications Director at Energize, Inc., in which capacity she interacts daily with publishers, distributors and authors of volunteerism literature. She has owned and managed an independent specialty book store and worked as a social worker in a variety of human service organizations.

Her volunteer experience includes counseling sexual assault survivors and serving on the boards of the Delaware Valley (PA) Task Force on Women and Addiction and the Committee Against Sexual Harassment in Columbus, OH. Ms. Catagnus has both a bachelor's and master's degree in social work, one from the University of Dayton (OH) and the other from the University of Minnesota.

She lives in Drexel Hill, PA with her husband, Richard Sauls, her step-daughter, and their two cats.

Energize Web site
keeps you on the cutting edge!

Already a favorite site among Internet users interested in volunteer issues, the Energize Web site is continually updated to be useful to you. You'll find:

- A monthly "hot topic" essay by Susan Ellis on an issue of timely interest to leaders of volunteers. And you can join in the dialogue by posting your response and opinion.

- An entire library of articles on volunteer program management.

- An Online Bookstore, with the chance to sample excerpts from more than 65 books on volunteer management.

- Professional education information.

- An up-to-the-minute calendar of conferences and training workshops.

- A DOVIA Directory — at last!

- Quotes and parables celebrating volunteering.

- A volunteer management job bank.

Bookmark it!

Mark the Energize Web site as a "favorite place" and come back often.

http://www.energizeinc.com

". . . your site has been the best and most comprehensive I've found so far. You have saved me literally DAYS of work on the new project our church is undertaking."

Ingrid Skantz, Collegedale Seventh-Day Adventist Church, TN

Receive free e-mail updates about our Web site and publications! Easy on-line sign-up at: www.energizeinc.com/fillin/mail.html